healthy
slow cooker
cookbook

200 Low-Fuss, Good-for-You Recipes

Clarkson Potter/Publishers
New York

acknowledgments

American Heart Association Consumer Publications
DIRECTOR: Linda S. Ball
MANAGING EDITOR: Deborah A. Renza
SENIOR EDITOR: Janice Roth Moss
SCIENCE EDITOR/WRITER: Jacqueline Fornerod Haigney
ASSISTANT EDITOR: Roberta Westcott Sullivan

Recipe Developers

Ellen Boeke
Janice Cole
Constance Hay
Nancy S. Hughes
Annie King
Jackie Mills, M.S., R.D.

Kathryn Moore
Julie Shapero, R.D., L.D.
Roxanne Wyss

Nutrition Analyst

Tammi Hancock, R.D.

Your contributions to the American Heart Association support research that helps make publications
like this possible. For more information, call 1–800-AHA-USA1 (1–800–242–8721) or contact us online
at www.heart.org.

Library of Congress Cataloging-in-Publication Data
American Heart Association healthy slow cooker cookbook.
Includes index.
1. Low-fat diet—Recipes. 2. Low-cholesterol diet—Recipes. 3. Salt-free diet—Recipes. 4. Electric cooking,
Slow. I. American Heart Association. II. Title: Healthy slow cooker cookbook. III. Title: Slow cooker cookbook.
RM237.7.A47 2012
641.5'6384—dc23 2012004813
ISBN 978-0-307-88802-0
eISBN 978-0-307-88803-7

Printed in the United States of America

Design by Ashley Tucker
Photographs by Ben Fink

10 9 8 7 6 5 4 3 2

First Edition

contents

preface

As part of our ongoing mission to build healthier lives through healthy diet and lifestyle, we are always looking for new and innovative ways to help you eat wisely and live well. For decades, we have published a variety of best-selling cookbooks that show you how to prepare delicious food that is good for you, too. This latest addition to our library, *American Heart Association Healthy Slow Cooker Cookbook*, demonstrates how you can use your slow cooker to serve healthy, sophisticated dishes that go far beyond the "dump-and-go" stereotype without spending hours in the kitchen.

We know it can be a challenge to create appealing and wholesome meals every night. The busier life gets, the more tempting it is to turn to convenience foods or to call for take-out. Yet studies show that preparing home-cooked meals is the best way to be sure you and your family are getting the nutrients you need. Cooking at home puts you in control of the foods you eat, so you can avoid the extra calories, sodium, added sugar, saturated fat, trans fat, and cholesterol that come with a regular diet of highly processed foods. You can rely on the American Heart Association to take the guesswork out of your meal planning so you can follow a balanced heart-healthy diet. The recipes and dietary information you'll find in this book are based on practical and scientifically sound recommendations that come from our leading experts on good nutrition.

We're also excited to show you how recipes for an old favorite—the dependable slow cooker—can be revitalized and renewed to provide exceptionally healthy and tasty results. This cookbook offers updated takes on classic family favorites such as Chicken Tortilla Soup (page 51) and Beef Goulash with Lemon (page 138), easy-to-fix potluck suppers such as Chunky Chili con Carne (page 136), and party favorites such as Smoked Turkey Meatballs (page 22). You'll also find surprising dishes that showcase how versatile slow cooking can be, such as Mojito Salmon (page 74).

So go ahead and browse through the wide range of recipes in this brand-new cookbook from the American Heart Association. Once you've seen all the intriguing possibilities you can enjoy, we know you'll want to go right to the cupboard, get out that slow cooker, and begin cooking.

Rose Marie Robertson, M.D.
Chief Science Officer, American Heart Association/American Stroke Association

slow cooking
a healthy twist on an old favorite

Slow cookers have been standard equipment in many American kitchens since the original avocado green and harvest gold models were introduced in the 1970s. For decades, cooks turned to their trusty slow cookers when preparing chilis, stews, soups, and hot dips, and the recipes they used usually included the canned soups, fatty meats, and melted cheeses that were so typical of those dishes. These same ingredients, however, are also chock full of harmful sodium, saturated fats, cholesterol, and calories. Today we are looking for a fresh, healthier approach to slow cooking—one that offers new options to create a full range of creative, delicious, *and* nutritious dishes that make it easy to follow a healthy diet.

In *American Heart Association Healthy Slow Cooker Cookbook,* you'll find modern, health-savvy ways to use this popular culinary device. The long, slow simmering of slow cooking is ideal for transforming the leanest meats into tender bites, and it allows the savory flavors in vegetable-rich stews to blend and mellow. Your slow cooker is also capable of gently cooking fish and seafood, steaming breads and desserts, and simmering complex sauces that can make a simple dish outstanding *and* heart healthy.

We understand that there are times when it makes sense to dump everything in the crock and leave it alone for hours—and other times when it's important to take time to attend to a few details. Prepping ingredients, browning meats, layering foods appropriately, preparing pasta or rice separately—these small steps may take a little extra time or effort, but they can make a big difference in your final product, yielding richer flavor and better texture. With this cookbook's wide assortment of recipes from appetizers to desserts and everything in between, you'll discover just how much your slow cooker can do.

In the pages that follow, "Enjoying the Benefits of Slow Cooking" discusses the advantages of using a slow cooker for your health, your budget, and your convenience. "Understanding How Slow Cookers Work" explains the technical aspects of slow cooking and how the differences in sizes and shapes can affect the process. "Getting the Best from Your Slow Cooker" covers the basics of effective slow cookery. These tricks of the trade will help you deliver the best results for your culinary efforts. In this section, you'll also find general slow cooker guidelines and information on flavor development and food safety. "Making Healthy Choices" outlines how to eat wisely and how a slow cooker can help.

And, finally, the 200 recipes starting on page 14 demonstrate the wide variety of dishes you can cook in a slow cooker. The best way to ensure that healthy, mouthwatering food comes *out* of your cooker is to pay attention to the ingredients you put *in* it. When you start with lean proteins, wholesome grains, and vegetables and fruits—without adding a lot of sodium, unhealthy fats, or sugar—you will enjoy both the health benefits and good flavor of the foods you prepare. We invite you to try any of the delicious *and* nutritious recipes in the pages that follow and let the tantalizing aromas from your slow cooker welcome you home tonight.

enjoying the benefits of slow cooking

Slow cooking offers several significant advantages: It's a great way to turn healthy ingredients into satisfying meals, it's economical, and, of course, it's convenient.

The slow process of cooking with moist heat at low temperatures produces succulent lean meats and poultry of falling-apart tenderness with little or no added fat—a great health bonus. Nutrition-rich vegetables often cook right in the crock with the protein source, so they're more likely to be part of your regular meal planning instead of being overlooked or a last-minute afterthought. Slow cookers are excellent for cooking legumes such as lentils and dried beans, those heart-healthy essentials that are full of fiber and protein but often are underused in the typical American diet. A slow cooker also makes easy work of preparing homemade stocks and long-simmered sauces to use in other recipes, such as soups and pasta dishes. Making your own soups and sauces allows you to control the amount of sodium and other additives in those foods.

By using your slow cooker, you can also save money on both food and energy costs. Because slow cooking breaks down the connective tissue in less-expensive cuts of meat, you won't need to spend an arm and a leg to enjoy a savory stew or roast. Slow cookers also can help you go green, since they require less energy than a traditional stove or oven. You can further reduce your kitchen "footprint" by cooking once and eating twice: Make large quantities of your favorite dishes, eat some now, and refrigerate or freeze the rest for a quick meal at another time.

Slow cookers also let you enjoy the many benefits of home-cooked meals with a minimum of hands-on attention. Because the heating elements are encased in a protective housing, the slow cooker doesn't need tending. Except in certain cases, you shouldn't stir the food, and you don't need to watch it or worry about it burning. You can simply leave the kitchen—and even the house—while your dinner is cooking. Slow cooking is also great for warmer months when you don't want to turn on the stove and heat up your kitchen.

understanding how slow cookers work

Slow cookers surround food with low, steady heat, resulting in long, slow cooking without burning. The outside metal housing contains low-wattage electric coils that heat to a designated temperature. As the coils heat, they transmit indirect heat to the inner crock (usually stoneware). Covering the crock with the lid creates a moisture-proof seal that ensures that the heat and steam released by the contents remain in the crock. This seal is important to maintain a steady temperature inside, and it also helps distribute and blend flavors as vapor condenses on the lid and returns to the food in the pot.

Temperature Modern cookers have low, high, and warm heat settings. Most cookers set to low heat reach temperatures ranging from 185°F to 200°F, depending on the individual cooker; on high, they reach temperatures between 250°F and 300°F. In actual practice, the internal temperature of different cookers can vary quite a lot from brand to brand; the age of the cooker also can make a significant difference because new models are made to reach higher temperatures than most older ones. (See page 7 for information on how to test the cooking temperature of your slow cooker so you'll know how to best estimate accurate cooking times.) For most recipes in this book, we've provided you the option of cooking on either low or high. Since the low setting can often take up to double the time to cook as the high setting, these options give you choices that work with your schedule. When the recipe calls for only one setting, then the alternate temperature is not recommended for that particular recipe.

Size Today's slow cookers come in several different sizes, each of which has its advantages. It's important to use the right cooker for the recipe you are preparing; the size of the cooker affects not only how much food you can cook but also the timing of your recipe. For effective cooking, the food should fill the crock enough to adequately cover the heating coils embedded in the sides of the cooker. If the cooker is too large, with a lot of empty space left, the food will cook too fast. If the cooker is too small for the total ingredients of your recipe, the crock will be too full and the food will not cook properly. If a recipe in this book requires a specific size for best results, that is noted. Most recipes, however, offer a range of recommended cooker sizes.

Shape The shape of your cooker affects how the heat is distributed, as well as what will fit comfortably in the crock itself. Round cookers are perfect for casseroles, stews, and soups and for recipes cooked in round baking pans. If you want to serve a whole fish, a large chicken or roast, or a recipe that cooks in a longer pan, such as meat loaf or bread, you need an oval cooker long enough to accommodate the food or the pan. When it is important to use a particular shape, it will be indicated in the recipe.

getting the best from your slow cooker

When slow cookers were first introduced, most recipes instructed the cook to open a few cans, dump their contents into the crock, and leave the food to cook for about 8 hours. Quick assembly and hands-off cooking still will be your top priority sometimes, but when you put in a little extra effort, your slow cooker will amply reward you.

following a few basic slow cooker guidelines

The best ways to escalate your slow cooking from so-so to super are to learn a few basic slow cooker do's and don'ts, know how your own cooker works, and observe basic food safety rules.

- Make the cooker work with your schedule. Try prepping a recipe the night before you plan to cook the food. Cover and refrigerate the prepped food in separate airtight containers overnight, fill the crock in the morning, and turn on the heat and, if your cooker has one, the timer.

- Prep foods so they will cook the most efficiently and evenly. For example, take care to cut carrots into pieces of the same approximate size so all the carrots in the dish will be done at the same time.

- Choose the correct size of cooker for the recipe you are preparing, and don't be tempted to substitute sizes. Different sizes make big differences in timing. Ideally, the cooker will be between one-half and two-thirds full of ingredients when you start the cooking process. For best results, use the size guidelines provided in the recipe.

- Resist the urge to stir or sneak a peek. Open the lid only when the recipe directs you to, complete the necessary actions, such as adding ingredients, and re-cover the cooker quickly. Every time you break the seal between the cover and the crock, you lose a lot of heat.

- Follow the recipe directions for how to arrange ingredients in the crock. Placement order and layering can make a big difference in timing and outcome. In general, for recipes that combine meat and vegetables, you'll place fibrous root vegetables at the bottom of the crock and then layer on the meat or poultry; if using tender vegetables as well, you often will be directed to add them on top toward the end of cooking.

- Trim the visible fat from poultry and meats, and in most cases discard the skin before cooking the poultry, both to cut down on unhealthy fats in the finished dish and for more even cooking. (Because fat holds more heat than water does, the more fat a food contains, the faster it will cook.) Some recipes may direct you to leave the skin on a whole chicken while cooking. If so, be sure to discard the skin before serving the chicken.

maximizing flavor with minimum effort

As you prepare meals in your slow cooker, take the time to get the best flavor results. As the recipes developed for this book demonstrate, incorporating a few simple prep steps and knowing when to add ingredients can make the difference between ho-hum and extraordinary. Here are a few flavor tips to keep in mind when using a slow cooker.

- Brown poultry and meats in a skillet before you add them to the cooker when the recipes call for it. (If your slow cooker has the option, brown the food in the crock.) Browning caramelizes the natural sugars, greatly improving the overall flavor and texture of a dish, as well as making it look more inviting.

- For most recipes, add ground herbs at the beginning of cooking, but add fresh herbs at the end to preserve their taste and appearance.

- Taste your dish before serving because the flavors of spices can mellow and dissipate during slow cooking more so than with other cooking methods.

- Perk up flavors by adding fresh ingredients just after you finish cooking the dish. Citrus juice or zest, fresh herbs, vinegars, or spicy peppers will brighten the blended taste of a long-simmered dish.

- Dry-roast nuts, such as walnuts, almonds, and pecans, in batches ahead of time to keep on hand for the recipes that call for them throughout this book, especially those with the Quick Prep icon (for more information on this, see page 12). See the Cook's Tips on pages 207 and 236 for how to dry-roast nuts in the oven or on the stovetop. Freeze them in an airtight container to use as needed. You don't even have to thaw them first!

keeping food safe

Slow cooking is safe and effective as long as you observe the safety guidelines that are specific to the slow cooker.

- Become familiar with your cooker's temperature range so you can gauge cooking times accurately. Cooking temperatures of units from different manufacturers vary in intensity, and today's cookers tend to cook hotter than the older models; your machine may cook a little hotter or cooler than the norm. If that's the case, the difference may affect not only the success of a recipe but also the safety of the food.

- To test the cooking temperature of your cooker, try this: Fill the crock one-half to two-thirds full of room-temperature water and heat the water, covered, on low for 8 hours. Uncover and immediately test the water temperature with an instant-read thermometer. (Act quickly because the temperature will drop when the lid is raised.) If the temperature is higher than 185°F, your cooker runs hot, and you should cook foods for slightly less time than recommended. If it is lower, foods may not reach an adequate cooking temperature quickly enough for safety. (If your cooker is not heating to a safe temperature, you should consider replacing it.) Altitude also will affect your cooker's performance, so modify your timing according to the manufacturer's instructions.

- Thaw any frozen foods, especially meat and poultry, in the refrigerator or microwave—but not at room temperature—before you put them in the cooker. Frozen ingredients will keep the internal temperature lower than it should be, and the contents of the crock may not reach high-enough temperatures to cook properly.

- Don't leave food on the warm or off setting in your slow cooker for more than 2 hours, to prevent harmful bacteria from multiplying.

- If you suspect that your cooker has been off for more than 2 hours because of a power outage, it's safest to discard the food in the cooker.

- Do not reheat slow cooker leftovers in the crock because bacteria can grow in the time it takes for the food to reach a safe temperature. Instead, reheat food in a microwave or on the stove.

- Let your slow cooker favorites cool before you put them in the freezer; you don't want the warm food to thaw surrounding frozen foods.

making healthy choices

As part of our commitment to help you improve your heart health, the American Heart Association has developed recommendations for how to enjoy a heart-healthy diet and lifestyle. The effects of small daily decisions add up over time, so it's important to focus on the ways you can make better choices, more often.

No matter what your eating habits are, every day presents you with new opportunities to choose foods that will nourish your body and foster better health. To be sure you include enough nutrient-rich foods and limit foods that are low in health benefits, keep in mind the following guidelines and number of servings (based on a daily 2,000-calorie diet) as you plan your meals. And, to help you focus on healthy foods in your slow cooker, we've offered some solutions below.

focus on nutrient-rich foods

Include a wide variety of VEGETABLES and FRUITS, especially those that are deeply colored—they have the highest concentrations of nutrients. *Aim for 4 to 5 servings of vegetables and 4 to 5 servings of fruit per day.*

SLOW COOKER SOLUTION: Slow cooking is a great way to enjoy root vegetables, such as beets, carrots, potatoes, parsnips, and turnips. To get started, try Balsamic-Glazed Beets with Toasted Walnuts (page 194) and Crock-Roasted Carrots and Parsnips with Cumin-Yogurt Sauce (page 199). The slow cooker is a perfect place to cook hearty fruits for nutritious and delicious side dishes such as Autumn Apple-Pear Sauce (page 211), breakfasts such as Apple-Maple Oatmeal (page 230), and desserts such as Sugar Plum Pears (page 241).

Eat high-fiber WHOLE GRAINS rather than refined grain products as often as possible. Serve whole-grain breads, pastas, cereals, and side dishes for the benefits of fiber and other important nutrients. Try to be sure at least half the grains you eat are whole grains (check that the labels on grain products list a whole grain as the first ingredient). *Aim for 6 to 8 servings per day.*

SLOW COOKER SOLUTION: Use your slow cooker to experiment with barley, farro, millet, quinoa, wild rice, and other less common varieties of whole grains. Try Double-Mushroom and Barley Soup (page 40), Cinnamon Quinoa with Peaches (page 229), and Wild Rice with Harvest Vegetables (page 207).

Include FAT-FREE, 1%, and LOW-FAT DAIRY products daily. Milk, cheeses, and yogurt are some examples. Limit whole-fat dairy products, such as whole milk and full-fat cheese, and compare labels for sodium levels. *Aim for 2 to 3 servings per day.*

SLOW COOKER SOLUTION: Even dairy products can be included in slow cooker meals. Recipes such as Rustic Two-Cheese Ratatouille (page 166), White and Greens Lasagna (page 168), and Tapioca Pudding with Blueberries (page 244) are easy ways to incorporate low-fat dairy products into your diet.

Eat FISH, especially fish high in omega-3 fatty acids. Seafood is a good source of protein and is low in saturated fat. Try different types of seafood and preparation techniques for variety. (Children, pregnant women, and those concerned about mercury should avoid fish with the highest mercury contamination—for example, shark, swordfish, tilefish, or mackerel. Remember, however, that for most people, the benefits of eating fish outweigh the risk.) *Aim for at least 2 servings each week.*

SLOW COOKER SOLUTION: Since many varieties of fish are delicate, they don't need much time in the slow cooker. In fact, often within as little as an hour or two a fish dish can be complete; it's the perfect choice when your time is limited. Salmon fillets are high in omega-3s and make excellent choices for slow cooking, so consider trying Salmon with Cucumber-Dill Aïoli (page 72) or Salmon Fillets with Pineapple-Melon Relish (page 73).

Choose LEAN POULTRY and MEAT. For poultry, choose white meat most often, discard all visible fat, and don't eat the skin. Lean cuts of beef (sirloin, round steak, and extra-lean ground beef) and pork (tenderloin and loin chops) are also heart-healthy if you discard all visible fat before cooking them. *Aim for no more than 2 servings per day.*

SLOW COOKER SOLUTION: Browning poultry and meats before adding them to the slow cooker will deepen their color and enrich the finished dish by intensifying the flavor. Try this flavorful cooking technique with recipes such as Chicken and Bean Soup with Lemon and Basil (page 47) and Brisket with Exotic-Mushroom and Onion Gravy (page 124).

Add LEGUMES, NUTS, and SEEDS to your diet. Legumes, such as dried beans and peas, lentils, and unsalted peanuts and low-sodium peanut butter, are a great source of fiber and meatless protein. Nuts and seeds are rich in monounsaturated fats, which may help keep blood cholesterol levels low when these fats are part of a diet that also is low in saturated fat and cholesterol. *Aim for 4 to 5 servings each week.*

SLOW COOKER SOLUTION: Nutritional powerhouses, legumes are a natural for the low, steady heat of slow cooking, which renders them tender but not mushy. Try Greek Lentils (page 173), Smoky Split Pea Soup (page 64), and Pistachio and Pumpkin Seed Snack Mix (page 25) for just a few among many of the fiber-filled, delicious recipes offered.

Use liquid vegetable OILS and spray or light tub MARGARINES. Vegetable oils such as olive and canola provide heart-healthy unsaturated fats. When you can't use an oil, use fat-free spray margarines or light tub spreads that are lowest in saturated fat, trans fat, and sodium. Avoid butter and stick margarines, and limit cakes, cookies, crackers, and other commercial products made with partially hydrogenated trans fat or saturated fat. *Aim for 2 to 3 servings per day.*

SLOW COOKER SOLUTION: Slow cooking can intensify the flavor of fats, so use good-quality heart-healthy oils, such as canola or corn oil in Shrimp-and-Fish Bayou Gumbo (page 85) or olive oil in Artichoke-Lemon Chicken (page 99), for prep steps such as browning foods before putting them in the cooker.

minimize the effects of nutrient-poor foods

Cut back on SODIUM. Most of the sodium you eat comes from packaged and pro-cessed foods. Compare the food labels of similar products to find the ones with less sodium, choose low-sodium or no-salt-added products, and beware of high-sodium restaurant meals. Limit condiments that are high in sodium. When cooking, use little or no salt. *Aim to eat no more than 1,500 milligrams of sodium per day.*

SLOW COOKER SOLUTION: Look for "hidden" sources of sodium in soups, beverages, sauces, breads, and other packaged foods and find lower sodium substitutes. Use your slow cooker to create healthier options such as Thai Coconut-Chicken Soup (page 45) and Warm and Spicy Tomato Punch (page 28).

Limit ADDED SUGAR. Keep your intake of sugar-sweetened beverages to no more than 450 calories or 36 ounces per week. (If you need fewer than 2,000 calories per day, avoid these beverages altogether.) Also, avoid sugary foods that are low in nutrients but high in calories. *Most women should aim to eat no more than 100 calories a day (about 6 teaspoons or 25 grams) from added sugars and most men, no more than 150 calories (about 9 teaspoons or 38 grams).*

SLOW COOKER SOLUTION: Read ingredient lists and choose products that don't list sugars in the first four ingredients. Common sugars include corn syrup, concen-trated fruit juice, honey, sucrose, or fructose. Try Chai Tea (page 29) and Decadent Chocolate Pudding Cake (page 234).

Cut back on SATURATED FAT, TRANS FAT, and dietary CHOLESTEROL. A diet high in these fats increases your risk of heart disease. Saturated fat is found primarily in foods from animals, such as meats, poultry, and whole-fat dairy products, or in tropical oils. Trans fat is present in manufactured foods that include partially hydro-genated oil. Cut back on trans fat by reading labels when choosing snacks, sweet treats, and fried foods. Common high-cholesterol foods include whole milk, full-fat cheese, egg yolks, and shellfish. *Limit your intake of saturated and trans fats; aim for no more than 300 milligrams of cholesterol per day.*

SLOW COOKER SOLUTION: Cut down on saturated fat and cholesterol by using more vegetables and healthy oils, using less poultry or meat, and choosing vegetarian entrées, such as Spicy Vegetable Curry (page 184), once or twice a week.

recipes

understanding the recipe icons

We know there are days when you won't have time to do much more than put some ingredients into your slow cooker and let it do its magic. For those hectic times, you'll like that nearly half the recipes in this book require you to do only the usual prep (chopping onions, trimming the fat from the meat) before the slow cooking begins, and maybe do something simple during cooking or at the end, such as stirring the food once while it cooks or sprinkling the finished dish with lemon zest. That's all—no browning onions, preparing dried beans, or boiling water for rice—to complete the dish. Look for recipes identified with this Quick Prep icon ✳ when you want to put in minimal effort and get maximum results.

In some recipes, you'll also notice the icon ■ ■ ■ in the ingredients list. You'll need the ingredients above the symbol right away, but you'll know not to set out the others—especially perishable items—yet. You won't need those for hours.

using the nutritional analyses

To help you plan meals and determine how a certain recipe fits into your overall diet, we have provided a nutrition analysis for each recipe in this book. The following guidelines give details about how the analyses were calculated and products that were used in the recipes. We have made every effort to provide accurate information. Because of the variables involved in analyzing foods, however, the serving sizes and nutritional values given should be considered approximate.

- Each analysis is for a single serving.

- Garnishes or optional ingredients are not included unless they significantly increase fat, sodium, cholesterol, or sugar content.

- Serving sizes are approximate.

- When more than one ingredient option is listed, the first one is analyzed. When a range of ingredients is given, the average is analyzed.

- Values other than fats are rounded to the nearest whole number. Fat values are rounded to the nearest half gram. Because of the rounding, values for saturated, trans, monounsaturated, and polyunsaturated fats may not add up to the amount shown for total fat value.

- We specify canola, corn, and olive oils in these recipes, but you can also use other heart-healthy unsaturated oils, such as safflower, soybean, and sunflower.

- Meats are analyzed as lean, with all visible fat discarded. Values for ground beef are based on extra-lean meat that is 95 percent fat free.

- If meat, poultry, or seafood is marinated and the marinade is discarded, we calculate only the amount of marinade absorbed.

- If alcohol is used in a cooked dish, we estimate that most of the alcohol calories evaporate as the food cooks.

- If a recipe in this book calls for commercial products, wherever possible we use and analyze the ones without added salt (for example, no-salt-added canned beans) or with the least sodium available (for example, soy sauce). (In some cases, we call for no-salt-added and low-sodium products and add table salt sparingly for flavor. The result still has far less sodium than the full-sodium product would.) If only a regular commercial product is available, we use the one with the lowest sodium available.

- If this book includes a recipe that can be used in another recipe, for example, Chicken Broth on page 31 that can be used in Shrimp and Chicken Paella (page 84), we use the data for our own version of broth, rather than a store-bought product, in the analysis and cross-reference the recipe.

- Because product labeling in the marketplace can vary and change quickly, we use the generic terms "fat-free" and "low-fat" throughout to avoid confusion.

- We use the abbreviations "g" for gram and "mg" for milligram throughout.

appetizers, snacks, and beverages

sun-dried tomato, kalamata, and tuna tapenade 15

baba ghanoush 16

curried garlic-bean spread 17

smoky red bell pepper hummus 18

gingered pear and apricot dip 20

artichoke-spinach "mini wraps" 21

smoked turkey meatballs 22

pork and water chestnut mini phyllo tarts 23

open-face empanadas 24

pistachio and pumpkin seed snack mix 25

hot pomegranate-cherry cider 26

mulled pineapple-citrus punch 27

warm and spicy tomato punch 28

chai tea 29

sun-dried tomato, kalamata, and tuna tapenade

serves 12
3 tablespoons per serving

slow cooker size/shape
3- to 4½-quart round or oval

slow cooking time
3½ to 4 hours on low, **OR**
1 hour 45 minutes to 2 hours
on high

Cooking spray

8 sun-dried tomato halves (about
1 ounce), cut into thin strips

1 cup grape tomatoes, halved

¼ cup finely chopped onion
(yellow preferred)

2 tablespoons water

2 medium garlic cloves, minced

■ ■ ■

1 cup grape tomatoes, halved

¼ cup chopped fresh basil

12 kalamata olives, finely chopped

2 tablespoons olive oil (extra
virgin preferred)

1 tablespoon red wine vinegar

3 ounces canned very low sodium
albacore tuna, packed in water,
rinsed in cold water, drained,
and coarsely flaked

"Colorful," "chunky," and "pungent" describe this mightily flavored tapenade. Spread it on whole-grain Melba toast, thin slices of toasted whole-grain bread, or even slices of chilled boiled red potatoes. *(See photo insert.)*

Lightly spray a 2-cup heatproof glass measuring cup with cooking spray. Put the sun-dried tomatoes, 1 cup grape tomatoes, the onion, water, and garlic in the measuring cup. Place the measuring cup in the slow cooker. Cook, covered, on low for 3½ to 4 hours or on high for 1 hour 45 minutes to 2 hours, or until the sun-dried tomatoes are very soft.

Carefully remove the measuring cup from the slow cooker. Pour the mixture into a shallow dish, such as a pie pan. To serve at room temperature, let stand for about 1 hour. To serve chilled, cover and refrigerate for 1 to 2 hours. The tapenade will thicken as it cools.

Just before serving, stir in the remaining ingredients except the tuna. Gently fold in the tuna.

per serving

Calories 65	Cholesterol 4 mg	Dietary Exchanges
Total Fat 4.5 g	Sodium 84 mg	1 vegetable, 1 fat
Saturated Fat 0.5 g	Carbohydrates 5 g	
Trans Fat 0.0 g	Fiber 1 g	
Polyunsaturated Fat 0.5 g	Sugars 2 g	
Monounsaturated Fat 3.0 g	Protein 3 g	

baba ghanoush

serves 10
¼ cup per serving

slow cooker size/shape
3- to 4½-quart round or oval

slow cooking time
3 to 3½ hours on low plus
3 to 3½ hours on low

Cooking spray

2 pounds eggplant (Japanese preferred), peeled, seeded if using large varieties, and cut into 1-inch cubes

½ cup water

■ ■ ■

¼ cup fresh mint

2 tablespoons tahini

2 tablespoons fresh lime juice

1 medium garlic clove, chopped

½ teaspoon smoked paprika (optional)

¼ teaspoon salt

Pomegranate seeds (optional)

1 tablespoon olive oil (extra virgin preferred) (optional)

When slow cooked, baba ghanoush (bah-bah gah-NOOSH) has a very mild flavor. If you want a hint of the smokiness of grilled or roasted eggplant, simply add a touch of smoked paprika to this Middle Eastern favorite. Serve it with toasted whole-grain pita wedges or crudités.

Lightly spray the slow cooker with cooking spray. Put the eggplant and water in the slow cooker. Cook, covered, on low for 3 to 3½ hours. Quickly stir once and re-cover the slow cooker. Cook for 3 to 3½ hours. Using a slotted spoon, transfer the eggplant to a food processor or blender. Discard the cooking liquid.

Add the mint, tahini, lime juice, garlic, paprika, and salt to the eggplant. Process until smooth and creamy. Transfer to a serving bowl. Serve garnished with the pomegranate seeds and/or drizzled with the oil. Refrigerate any leftovers in an airtight container for up to two days.

cook's tip on tahini: Tahini is a paste made from sesame seeds. Look for it in the condiment or ethnic-food sections in the grocery store.

per serving

Calories 38	Cholesterol 0 mg	Dietary Exchanges
Total Fat 1.5 g	Sodium 62 mg	1 vegetable, ½ fat
Saturated Fat 0.0 g	Carbohydrates 5 g	
Trans Fat 0.0 g	Fiber 3 g	
Polyunsaturated Fat 1.0 g	Sugars 2 g	
Monounsaturated Fat 0.5 g	Protein 1 g	

per serving (with optional ingredients)

Calories 50	Cholesterol 0 mg	Dietary Exchanges
Total Fat 3.0 g	Sodium 62 mg	1 vegetable, ½ fat
Saturated Fat 0.5 g	Carbohydrates 5 g	
Trans Fat 0.0 g	Fiber 3 g	
Polyunsaturated Fat 1.0 g	Sugars 2 g	
Monounsaturated Fat 1.5 g	Protein 1 g	

curried garlic-bean spread

serves 12
¼ cup per serving

slow cooker size/shape
1½- to 2½-quart round or oval

slow cooking time
4 to 6 hours on low, **OR**
2 to 3 hours on high

1 cup dried Great Northern
  beans (about 8 ounces), sorted
  for stones and shriveled beans,
  rinsed, and drained

3 cups water

1 large onion, coarsely chopped

4 large garlic cloves, minced

1½ teaspoons curry powder

1 teaspoon paprika

1 teaspoon ground turmeric

½ teaspoon ground cinnamon

¼ teaspoon pepper

Curry and garlic flavor this versatile bean mixture, which can be served warm or at room temperature as a spread on whole-grain crackers or as a dip with fresh vegetables. It's also a great sandwich spread or filling for whole-grain pita pockets.

Fill a small saucepan three-fourths full of water (not the 3 cups in the ingredients list). Bring to a boil over high heat. Stir in the beans. Return to a boil. Reduce the heat and simmer for 15 minutes. Pour the beans into a colander and rinse.

Pour the beans into the slow cooker. Add the remaining ingredients, stirring to combine. Cook, covered, on low for 4 to 6 hours or on high for 2 to 3 hours, or until the beans are tender.

Using a slotted spoon, transfer the mixture to a food processor or blender. Process until almost smooth but retaining some texture. Transfer to a medium bowl. If serving at room temperature, let stand for 1 hour. To serve chilled, cover and refrigerate for at least 30 minutes. The spread will keep well for up to three days in the refrigerator.

per serving

Calories 54	Cholesterol 0 mg	Dietary Exchanges
Total Fat 0.5 g	Sodium 4 mg	½ starch
Saturated Fat 0.0 g	Carbohydrates 10 g	
Trans Fat 0.0 g	Fiber 3 g	
Polyunsaturated Fat 0.0 g	Sugars 1 g	
Monounsaturated Fat 0.0 g	Protein 3 g	

smoky red bell pepper hummus

serves 8
¼ cup per serving (plus 4½
cups chickpeas remaining)

slow cooker size/shape
3- to 4½-quart round or oval

slow cooking time
10 hours on low

1 pound dried chickpeas, sorted
  for stones and shriveled
  chickpeas, rinsed, and drained

6 cups water

■ ■ ■

3 tablespoons sesame seeds, dry
  roasted

3 tablespoons fresh lemon juice

2 tablespoons fat-free plain
  Greek yogurt

3 tablespoons water

1 teaspoon olive oil and
  1 teaspoon olive oil (extra
  virgin preferred), divided use

2 medium garlic cloves, minced

2 medium strips of lemon peel
  (each about 3 inches by ½ inch)

¼ to ½ teaspoon smoked paprika

¼ teaspoon salt

1 medium roasted red bell
  pepper, quartered, drained if
  bottled

Slow cooking the chickpeas results in extra creaminess, so we went ahead and called for cooking a pound of them, even though you need about a third of that for this Middle Eastern spread. Serve the hummus on whole-grain pita wedges or with crudités, then enjoy the bonus chickpeas in soups, stews, and green salads.

Fill a large saucepan three-fourths full of water (not the 6 cups in the ingredients list). Bring to a boil over high heat. Stir in the chickpeas. Return to a boil. Reduce the heat and simmer for 15 minutes. Pour the chickpeas into a colander and rinse.

Pour the chickpeas into the slow cooker. Pour in the 6 cups water. Cook, covered, on low for 10 hours, adding more water if needed to keep the chickpeas covered. Be sure to quickly add the water and re-cover the slow cooker each time.

Measure out 2 cups of the cooked chickpeas for the hummus. Transfer the remaining 4½ cups to an airtight container and refrigerate for up to three days or freeze for up to six months for other uses.

To prepare the hummus, process the sesame seeds in a food processor or blender for 30 seconds. Add, in order, the lemon juice, yogurt, remaining 3 tablespoons water, 1 teaspoon oil, garlic, lemon peel, paprika, salt, 2 cups cooked chickpeas, and roasted pepper. Process until smooth.

Serve warm or transfer to an airtight container and cover and refrigerate until serving time. Just before serving, drizzle the hummus with the remaining 1 teaspoon oil.

cook's tip on roasted bell peppers: To prepare roasted bell peppers, preheat the broiler. Spray a broiler pan and rack with cooking spray. Broil the bell pepper on the broiler pan about 4 inches from the heat, turning until the pepper is charred all over. Put the pepper in a small bowl and let stand, covered, for at least 5 minutes. (It won't hurt the pepper to stand for as long as 20 minutes.) Rinse the pepper with cold water, removing and discarding the blackened skin, ribs, seeds, and stem. Blot the pepper dry.

cook's tip on dry-roasting seeds: To dry-roast seeds, such as the sesame seeds here, put them in a single layer in a small skillet. Cook over medium heat for about 4 minutes, or until the seeds darken and begin to pop, stirring frequently. Remove them from the skillet so they don't burn.

per serving

Calories 109	Cholesterol 0 mg	Dietary Exchanges
Total Fat 4.5 g	Sodium 80 mg	1 starch, ½ very lean
Saturated Fat 0.5 g	Carbohydrates 13 g	meat, ½ fat
Trans Fat 0.0 g	Fiber 4 g	
Polyunsaturated Fat 1.5 g	Sugars 3 g	
Monounsaturated Fat 2.0 g	Protein 5 g	

gingered pear and apricot dip

serves 8
¼ cup per serving

slow cooker size/shape
3- to 4½-quart round or oval

slow cooking time
3 to 3½ hours on low

    Cooking spray

2 medium, very firm (unripe) pears, peeled and diced

½ cup all-fruit apricot spread

■ ■ ■

1 teaspoon grated peeled gingerroot

You're in for a real treat with this dip made of bits of pears swimming in a sweet apricot and fresh ginger sauce. Use banana or pear slices for dipping, or spoon the mixture onto baked sweet potatoes or winter squash.

Lightly spray a 2-cup heatproof glass measuring cup with cooking spray. Put the pears in the measuring cup. Spoon the fruit spread on top. Cook, covered, on low for 3 to 3½ hours, or until the pears are just tender.

Carefully remove the measuring cup from the slow cooker. Pour the dip into a shallow bowl. Let stand for 1 hour, or until room temperature. Stir in the gingerroot.

cook's tip: If you use ripe pears, the dip will be mushy rather than slightly chunky.

per serving

Calories 66	Cholesterol 0 mg	Dietary Exchanges
Total Fat 0.0 g	Sodium 1 mg	1 fruit
Saturated Fat 0.0 g	Carbohydrates 17 g	
Trans Fat 0.0 g	Fiber 1 g	
Polyunsaturated Fat 0.0 g	Sugars 12 g	
Monounsaturated Fat 0.0 g	Protein 0 g	

artichoke-spinach "mini wraps"

serves 10
5 mini wraps per serving

slow cooker size/shape
3- to 4½-quart round or oval

slow cooking time
3½ to 4 hours on low
plus 5 minutes on high, **OR**
1 hour 45 minutes to 2 hours
on high plus 5 minutes on high

Cooking spray

1 teaspoon olive oil

1 medium onion, chopped

2 medium garlic cloves, minced

1 14-ounce can artichoke hearts,
drained and chopped

1 teaspoon dried oregano,
crumbled

■ ■ ■

4 ounces spinach (about 4 cups),
coarsely chopped

2 tablespoons light mayonnaise

1 tablespoon plus 2 teaspoons
olive oil (extra virgin preferred)

¼ cup shredded or grated
Parmesan cheese

50 medium to large spinach leaves,
stems discarded

Whether you're having guests over or simply feel like making a little something special, try these creamy mini wraps. Slow cook the artichoke-spinach mixture, spoon a small amount onto spinach leaves, fold the sides over, and enjoy.

Lightly spray the slow cooker and a 2-cup heatproof glass measuring cup with cooking spray. Set aside.

In a medium nonstick skillet, heat 1 teaspoon oil over medium-high heat, swirling to coat the bottom. Cook the onion for 3 minutes, or until soft, stirring frequently. Stir in the garlic and cook for 15 seconds, stirring constantly. Remove from the heat.

Stir in the artichokes and oregano. Spoon into the measuring cup. Place in the slow cooker. Cook, covered, on low for 3½ to 4 hours or on high for 1 hour 45 minutes to 2 hours, or until the onion is very soft.

Quickly and carefully spoon the artichoke mixture into the center of the slow cooker. Stir in the spinach and mayonnaise and re-cover the slow cooker. If using the low setting, change it to high. Cook for 5 minutes. Stir in the remaining 1 tablespoon plus 2 teaspoons oil. Transfer the mixture to a shallow serving dish. Sprinkle with the Parmesan.

Spoon 1 teaspoon of the artichoke mixture onto each spinach leaf. Fold the sides toward the center so they overlap slightly and form mini wraps.

per serving

Calories 68	Cholesterol 2 mg	Dietary Exchanges
Total Fat 4.0 g	Sodium 180 mg	1 vegetable, 1 fat
Saturated Fat 1.0 g	Carbohydrates 6 g	
Trans Fat 0.0 g	Fiber 2 g	
Polyunsaturated Fat 1.0 g	Sugars 2 g	
Monounsaturated Fat 2.5 g	Protein 3 g	

smoked turkey meatballs

serves 12
3 meatballs per serving

slow cooker size/shape
1½- to 2½-quart round or oval

slow cooking time
4 to 6 hours on low, **OR**
2 to 3 hours on high

meatballs

1 **pound ground skinless turkey breast**

½ **cup shredded carrot**

½ **cup shredded zucchini**

2 **large shallots or ½ medium onion, minced**

¼ **cup plain panko (Japanese bread crumbs)**

1 **tablespoon smoked paprika**

2 **large garlic cloves, minced**

¼ **teaspoon salt**

¼ **teaspoon pepper**

1 **large egg white, lightly beaten with a fork**

sauce

1 **8-ounce can no-salt-added tomato sauce**

1½ **tablespoons pure maple syrup**

1 **tablespoon smoked paprika**

■ ■ ■

1 **teaspoon canola or corn oil and 1 teaspoon canola or corn oil, divided use**

Shredded vegetables help moisten the lean ground turkey in these baby meatballs, which are cooked in a maple-sweetened barbecue-like sauce.

In a large bowl, using your hands or a spoon, gently combine all the meatball ingredients except the egg white. Don't overwork the mixture or it will become too compact and the meatballs will be heavy. Gently work in the egg white. Shape into 36 1-inch balls (about 1 tablespoon each). Place on a large baking sheet so they don't touch. Refrigerate for 15 to 30 minutes, or until chilled.

Meanwhile, in a small bowl, whisk together the sauce ingredients. Set aside.

When the meatballs have chilled, heat 1 teaspoon oil in a large nonstick skillet over medium heat, swirling to coat the bottom. Cook half the meatballs for 3 to 4 minutes, or until browned on all sides, adjusting the heat as necessary. Transfer to the slow cooker. Repeat with the remaining 1 teaspoon oil and remaining meatballs.

Pour the tomato sauce mixture into the skillet. Bring to a boil on high, scraping to dislodge any browned bits. Pour over the meatballs. Cook, covered, on low for 4 to 6 hours or on high for 2 to 3 hours, or until the meatballs are no longer pink in the center.

cook's tip on making meatballs: To save time and keep meatballs uniform in size, use a spring-loaded ice cream scoop to form them. For this recipe, try a #60 scoop; it holds about 1 tablespoon.

per serving

Calories 78	Cholesterol 23 mg	Dietary Exchanges
Total Fat 1.0 g	Sodium 81 mg	½ other carbohydrate,
Saturated Fat 0.0 g	Carbohydrates 6 g	1½ lean meat
Trans Fat 0.0 g	Fiber 1 g	
Polyunsaturated Fat 0.5 g	Sugars 3 g	
Monounsaturated Fat 0.5 g	Protein 10 g	

pork and water chestnut mini phyllo tarts

serves 15
3 mini tarts per serving

slow cooker size/shape
3- to 4½-quart round or oval

slow cooking time
3 hours on low
plus 1 minute on low, **OR**
1½ hours on high
plus 1 minute on high

Cooking spray

1 teaspoon canola or corn oil

8 ounces lean ground pork

1 small onion (yellow preferred), finely chopped

■ ■ ■

4 cups finely shredded cabbage

4 ounces canned water chestnuts, drained and diced

½ cup matchstick-size carrot strips, chopped

½ cup snipped fresh cilantro (optional)

2 tablespoons sugar

2 tablespoons soy sauce (lowest sodium available)

1½ to 2 tablespoons grated peeled gingerroot

¼ teaspoon crushed red pepper flakes, or to taste

45 frozen mini phyllo shells (3 1.90-ounce boxes), thawed

Do you sometimes wonder what you could do with those petite phyllo shells in the frozen food section of your supermarket? Put an Asian spin on them with this sweet-and-spicy filling of ground pork, cabbage, and fresh ginger.

Lightly spray the slow cooker and a 2-cup heatproof glass measuring cup with cooking spray. Set aside.

In a large nonstick skillet, heat the oil over medium-high heat, swirling to coat the bottom. Cook the pork and onion for 3 minutes, or until the pork is browned on the outside and no longer pink in the center, stirring frequently to turn and break up the pork. Transfer to the measuring cup. Place in the slow cooker. Cook, covered, on low for 3 hours or on high for 1½ hours, or until the onion is very soft.

Carefully remove the cup. Quickly pour the pork mixture into the slow cooker. Stir in the remaining ingredients except the phyllo shells. Cook for 1 minute, or until the cabbage is slightly wilted, stirring frequently. If serving immediately, spoon the filling into the phyllo shells. To serve while the filling is still hot but not immediately, spoon the hot filling into a serving bowl, surround the bowl with the shells, and let your guests fill the shells. (If you fill the shells too soon, they will become soggy.)

cook's tip: To save prep time, purchase packages of already cut matchstick-size carrots and shredded cabbage.

per serving

Calories 110	Cholesterol 10 mg	Dietary Exchanges
Total Fat 5.5 g	Sodium 107 mg	½ starch, 1 vegetable,
Saturated Fat 1.0 g	Carbohydrates 11 g	1 fat
Trans Fat 0.0 g	Fiber 1 g	
Polyunsaturated Fat 1.5 g	Sugars 3 g	
Monounsaturated Fat 2.5 g	Protein 3 g	

open-face empanadas

serves 12
2 wraps per serving

slow cooker size/shape
1½- to 2½-quart round or oval

slow cooking time
6 to 8 hours on low, **OR**
2½ to 4 hours on high

1 pound extra-lean ground beef

1 large onion, chopped

1 medium green bell pepper, chopped

3 large garlic cloves, minced

1 14.5-ounce can no-salt-added diced tomatoes, undrained

⅓ cup dark raisins

1 tablespoon no-salt-added tomato paste

2 teaspoons ground cumin

½ teaspoon ground cinnamon

¼ teaspoon salt

⅛ teaspoon pepper

■ ■ ■

⅓ cup slivered almonds

12 leaves of leaf lettuce, halved lengthwise

Like traditional empanadas, these are filled with ground beef seasoned with cumin and cinnamon and accented with raisins and almonds. Instead of fatty pastry dough, though, healthy lettuce leaves keep all the goodness inside. For a fun, do-it-yourself appetizer, serve the empanada filling in a festive bowl surrounded by the lettuce leaves, and let everyone fill and wrap their own empanadas. *(See photo insert.)*

Heat a large nonstick skillet over medium-high heat. Cook the beef for 3 minutes, or until no longer pink on the outside, stirring occasionally to turn and break up the beef. Drain if necessary.

Stir in the onion, bell pepper, and garlic. Cook for 2 minutes, or until the beef is browned and the onion and bell pepper are beginning to soften, stirring occasionally. Transfer to the slow cooker.

Stir in the tomatoes with liquid, raisins, tomato paste, cumin, cinnamon, salt, and pepper. Cook, covered, on low for 6 to 8 hours or on high for 2½ to 4 hours, or until the beef is no longer pink in the center and the mixture is bubbling.

Stir in the almonds. Spoon about 3 tablespoons empanada mixture down the center of each lettuce leaf half and roll up jelly-roll style.

per serving

Calories 103	Cholesterol 21 mg	Dietary Exchanges
Total Fat 3.5 g	Sodium 91 mg	½ other carbohydrate,
Saturated Fat 1.0 g	Carbohydrates 9 g	1 lean meat
Trans Fat 0.0 g	Fiber 2 g	
Polyunsaturated Fat 0.5 g	Sugars 5 g	
Monounsaturated Fat 1.5 g	Protein 10 g	

pistachio and pumpkin seed snack mix

QUICK PREP

serves 12
1/3 cup per serving

slow cooker size/shape
3- to 4½-quart round or oval

slow cooking time
2 hours on low, **OR**
1 hour on high

Cooking spray

2 tablespoons canola or corn oil

2 teaspoons smoked paprika

2 teaspoons yellow or Dijon mustard

2 teaspoons Worcestershire sauce (lowest sodium available)

½ teaspoon ground cumin

½ teaspoon garlic powder

⅛ teaspoon ground chipotle powder or cayenne

3 cups wheat snack-mix-type cereal squares

½ cup unsalted shelled pistachios or slivered almonds

⅓ cup unsalted pumpkin seeds with shells

■ ■ ■

⅛ teaspoon salt

Who doesn't like a little something crunchy in the middle of the day? Keep a few single-serving bags of this snack mix in your desk drawer or pack some for a treat in a brown-bag lunch.

Lightly spray the slow cooker with cooking spray. Set aside.

In a small bowl, whisk together the oil, paprika, mustard, Worcestershire sauce, cumin, garlic powder, and chipotle powder.

Put the cereal, pistachios, and pumpkin seeds in a large bowl. Add the oil mixture, stirring until well blended. Transfer to the slow cooker.

Cook, covered, on low for 2 hours, stirring every 40 minutes, or on high for 1 hour, stirring every 20 minutes, or just until the cereal is beginning to lightly brown.

Spread the mix in a single layer on a baking sheet. Sprinkle with the salt. Let stand for 2 hours (this is very important) so the flavors blend and the mix cools completely and "crisps up." Store the cooled mix in an airtight container for up to two weeks.

per serving

Calories 127	Cholesterol 0 mg	Dietary Exchanges
Total Fat 6.5 g	Sodium 135 mg	1 starch, 1 fat
Saturated Fat 1.0 g	Carbohydrates 15 g	
Trans Fat 0.0 g	Fiber 3 g	
Polyunsaturated Fat 2.0 g	Sugars 2 g	
Monounsaturated Fat 3.5 g	Protein 4 g	

hot pomegranate-cherry cider

serves 8
1 cup per serving

slow cooker size/shape
3- to 4½-quart round or oval

slow cooking time
4 hours 45 minutes to 5 hours
45 minutes on low plus
15 minutes on low, **OR**
2 hours 15 minutes to 2 hours
45 minutes on high plus
15 minutes on high

6 cups unsweetened apple cider
  or apple juice

2 cups pomegranate-cherry juice
  or other pomegranate juice
  blend

2 tablespoons sugar (optional)

3 cinnamon sticks (each about 3
  inches long)

8 whole cloves

⅛ to ¼ teaspoon anise seed

■ ■ ■

1 medium lemon, cut crosswise
  into ⅛-inch slices

Serve this delicious autumn treat in clear glass mugs so the light ruby color will shine through.

In the slow cooker, stir together the cider, pomegranate-cherry juice, sugar, and cinnamon sticks.

Put the cloves and anise seed in the center of a 4-inch-square piece of cheesecloth. Bring the ends together to make a bag. Tie it securely with kitchen twine. Add to the slow cooker. Cook, covered, on low for 4 hours 45 minutes to 5 hours 45 minutes, or on high for 2 hours 15 minutes to 2 hours 45 minutes.

Quickly stir in the lemon slices and re-cover the slow cooker. Cook for 15 minutes. Discard the cinnamon sticks and cheesecloth bag before serving the cider.

cook's tip: No cheesecloth? You can use the "bag" part of a teabag to hold the spices for this recipe. Simply open the teabag and discard the tea leaves. Fill the bag with the cloves and anise seed and tie securely with the teabag string.

per serving

Calories 121	Cholesterol 0 mg	Dietary Exchanges
Total Fat 0.0 g	Sodium 16 mg	2 fruit
Saturated Fat 0.0 g	Carbohydrates 29 g	
Trans Fat 0.0 g	Fiber 0 g	
Polyunsaturated Fat 0.0 g	Sugars 25 g	
Monounsaturated Fat 0.0 g	Protein 0 g	

per serving (with optional sugar)

Calories 133	Cholesterol 0 mg	Dietary Exchanges
Total Fat 0.0 g	Sodium 16 mg	2 fruit
Saturated Fat 0.0 g	Carbohydrates 32 g	
Trans Fat 0.0 g	Fiber 0 g	
Polyunsaturated Fat 0.0 g	Sugars 28 g	
Monounsaturated Fat 0.0 g	Protein 0 g	

mulled pineapple-citrus punch

QUICK PREP

serves 8
¾ cup per serving

slow cooker size/shape
3- to 4½-quart round or oval

slow cooking time
4 to 5 hours on low, **OR**
2 to 2½ hours on high

46 ounces canned pineapple juice

2 medium oranges, cut crosswise
into ⅛-inch slices

1 medium lemon, cut crosswise
into ⅛-inch slices

¼ cup firmly packed dark brown
sugar

▪ ▪ ▪

½ medium orange or ½ medium
lemon, cut crosswise into 4
slices, then halved (optional)

There's nothing complex about this four-ingredient punch except its flavor. The slow-simmered orange and lemon slices create a pleasantly potent undercurrent of citrus.

In the slow cooker, stir together the pineapple juice, orange and lemon slices, and brown sugar. Cook, covered, on low for 4 to 5 hours or on high for 2 to 2½ hours. Discard the orange and lemon slices (they may have lost their bright color).

Ladle the punch into cups. Garnish each cup with a half slice of the remaining orange or lemon.

cook's tip: Stir 1 tablespoon of rum or bourbon into each punch cup just before serving, if desired.

per serving

Calories 120
Total Fat 0.0 g
  Saturated Fat 0.0 g
  Trans Fat 0.0 g
  Polyunsaturated Fat 0.0 g
  Monounsaturated Fat 0.0 g

Cholesterol 0 mg
Sodium 9 mg
Carbohydrates 28 g
  Fiber 0 g
  Sugars 24 g
Protein 0 g

Dietary Exchanges
2 fruit

warm and spicy tomato punch

serves 12
½ cup per serving

slow cooker size/shape
3- or 3½-quart round or oval

slow cooking time
6 to 8 hours on low, **OR**
3 to 4 hours on high

3 14.5-ounce cans no-salt-added diced tomatoes, undrained

1 cup fresh orange juice

2 tablespoons chopped onion

½ to 1 medium fresh jalapeño, seeds and ribs discarded, chopped

1 teaspoon sugar

1 teaspoon Worcestershire sauce (lowest sodium available)

¼ teaspoon salt

¼ to ¾ teaspoon red hot-pepper sauce, or to taste

■ ■ ■

2 tablespoons fresh lime juice

1 medium lime, thinly sliced (optional)

This warm punch, with kicks of jalapeño and hot-pepper sauce, will add spice to a winter gathering.

In a food processor or blender, process the tomatoes with liquid, orange juice, onion, jalapeño, sugar, Worcestershire sauce, salt, and hot-pepper sauce until smooth except for the tomato seeds. If you wish, strain the ingredients as you pour them into the slow cooker. Cook, covered, on low for 6 to 8 hours or on high for 3 to 4 hours.

Just before serving, stir the lime juice into the punch. Float the lime slices on top.

cook's tip: To make this punch for a larger crowd, double the amounts and use a 4- or 4½-quart round or oval slow cooker; the cooking time remains the same. If you wish, add some vodka, tequila, or lemon rum to the punch before serving.

cook's tip on hot chiles: Hot chiles such as jalapeño, poblano, Anaheim, or serrano contain oils that can burn your skin, lips, and eyes. Remember to wear plastic gloves or wash your hands thoroughly with warm, soapy water immediately after handling hot chiles.

per serving

Calories 36	Cholesterol 0 mg	Dietary Exchanges
Total Fat 0.0 g	Sodium 63 mg	1 vegetable
Saturated Fat 0.0 g	Carbohydrates 8 g	
Trans Fat 0.0 g	Fiber 1 g	
Polyunsaturated Fat 0.0 g	Sugars 5 g	
Monounsaturated Fat 0.0 g	Protein 1 g	

chai tea

serves 8
1 cup per serving

slow cooker size/shape
3- to 4½-quart round or oval

slow cooking time
3 to 3½ hours on high

4 cups water

2 cups fat-free milk

2 cups fat-free half-and-half

¼ cup sugar (optional)

1½ teaspoons ground cinnamon

¾ teaspoon ground cardamom

½ teaspoon ground ginger

½ teaspoon ground nutmeg

¼ teaspoon ground cloves

8 single-serving bags of black tea
  (with tags preferred)

There's no need to run to the local coffee shop for a cup of chai tea when you can easily brew it at home in the slow cooker—and enjoy the enticing aroma of the Indian spices as they fill the air. The tea is equally good served hot or cold.

In the slow cooker, stir together all the ingredients except the tea bags. Add the tea bags, letting the tags hang over the side of the slow cooker. Cook, covered, on high for 3 to 3½ hours. Discard the tea bags. For hot tea, serve immediately. For cold tea, ladle the tea into a pitcher and refrigerate, covered, for up to three days. Serve the tea over ice.

cook's tip: If the tiny grains of spice in the tea bother you, you can strain the tea through a fine-mesh sieve to remove most of them or through a coffee filter to remove all of them.

per serving

Calories 64	Cholesterol 1 mg	Dietary Exchanges
Total Fat 0.0 g	Sodium 90 mg	1 fat-free milk
Saturated Fat 0.0 g	Carbohydrates 12 g	
Trans Fat 0.0 g	Fiber 0 g	
Polyunsaturated Fat 0.0 g	Sugars 7 g	
Monounsaturated Fat 0.0 g	Protein 6 g	

per serving (with optional sugar)

Calories 88	Cholesterol 1 mg	Dietary Exchanges
Total Fat 0.0 g	Sodium 90 mg	1 fat-free milk, ½ other
Saturated Fat 0.0 g	Carbohydrates 18 g	carbohydrate
Trans Fat 0.0 g	Fiber 0 g	
Polyunsaturated Fat 0.0 g	Sugars 13 g	
Monounsaturated Fat 0.0 g	Protein 6 g	

soups

chicken broth 31

dark-roasted beef broth 32

harvest vegetable broth 33

sweet and spicy pumpkin soup 34

butternut squash bisque 35

fresh tomato soup with goat cheese and basil 36

cream of cauliflower soup 37

creamy potato-broccoli soup 38

italian vegetable and pasta soup 39

double-mushroom and barley soup 40

corn and wild rice soup 41

bean florentine soup 42

cod and clam chowder 43

crab and red bell pepper soup 44

thai coconut-chicken soup 45

chicken and brown rice soup with blue cheese crumbles 46

chicken and bean soup with lemon and basil 47

herbed chicken soup with arugula 48

country chicken noodle soup 49

spicy chicken and corn soup 50

chicken tortilla soup 51

smoked turkey and rice soup with fresh sage 52

turkey sausage and lentil soup 53

ribollita 54

korean beef soup 55

countryside beef and garden vegetable soup 56

beef barley soup with vegetables 58

balsamic beef borscht 59

sherried steak-and-mushroom soup 60

black-eyed pea soup with soy crumbles 61

black bean and jalapeño soup 62

jamaican bean and vegetable soup 63

smoky split pea soup 64

curried lentil and vegetable soup 65

persian red lentil soup 66

moroccan lentil soup 67

chicken broth

makes 10 cups
1 cup per serving

slow cooker size/shape
5- to 7-quart round or oval

slow cooking time
10 to 12 hours on low
(preferred), **OR**
5 to 6 hours on high

1½ **pounds chicken wings or legs
with skin or 1 chicken carcass,
broken to fit cooker**

1 **large leek (white and light
green parts) or onion, coarsely
chopped**

1 **medium rib of celery, coarsely
chopped**

1 **medium carrot, coarsely
chopped**

1 **small parsnip or turnip,
peeled and coarsely chopped
(optional)**

½ **cup fresh parsley leaves, stems
discarded**

1 **medium garlic clove, crushed**

½ **teaspoon whole peppercorns**

1 **medium dried bay leaf**

1 **sprig of fresh thyme or
1 teaspoon dried, crumbled
(fresh preferred)**

⅛ **teaspoon salt**

12 **cups water (plus more as
needed)**

Making so-low-sodium chicken broth is so easy with a slow cooker. Just load the cooker and let the ingredients simmer. In addition to the cooking time, be sure to allow for at least eight hours of chilling time so you can easily remove the fat, which rises to the top. Keep a regular supply in the freezer so you'll have plenty on hand whenever you make a dish that calls for broth, such as Cream of Cauliflower Soup (page 37), Chicken and Dumplings (page 94), and Tuscan Pork and Beans (page 149).

In the slow cooker, stir together all the ingredients except the water. Pour in the water, adding more if needed to cover all. Cook, covered, on low for 10 to 12 hours or on high for 5 to 6 hours.

Using a colander, strain the broth into a large bowl, being careful to avoid steam burns. Discard the solids. Cover and refrigerate the broth for at least 8 hours so the flavors blend and the fat rises to the surface. Discard the fat before reheating the broth.

cook's tip on storing broth: If you are not using the broth right away, store it in an airtight container in the refrigerator for up to two days. For storage up to three months, we suggest separating the desired amounts into resealable plastic freezer bags and laying them flat to freeze; they take up very little space that way. If you would rather use airtight freezer containers, those, of course, work well, too.

per serving

Calories 10	Cholesterol 0 mg	Dietary Exchanges
Total Fat 0.0 g	Sodium 54 mg	Free
Saturated Fat 0.0 g	Carbohydrates 1 g	
Trans Fat 0.0 g	Fiber 0 g	
Polyunsaturated Fat 0.0 g	Sugars 0 g	
Monounsaturated Fat 0.0 g	Protein 2 g	

dark-roasted beef broth

makes 8 cups
1 cup per serving

slow cooker size/shape
5- to 7-quart round or oval

slow cooking time
8 to 10 hours on low, **OR**
4 to 6 hours on high

Cooking spray

3 pounds beef bones

2 medium onions, each cut into 8 wedges

2 medium carrots, each cut into 4 pieces

1 medium rib of celery, cut into 4 pieces

8 whole garlic cloves

2½ quarts water

1½ tablespoons instant coffee granules

2 medium dried bay leaves

1 teaspoon pepper (coarsely ground preferred)

1 teaspoon dried thyme, crumbled

2 whole cloves

⅛ teaspoon salt

This basic broth gets maximum flavor intensity by including instant coffee granules and roasted bones and veggies. After the broth slow cooks, you'll need to chill it for at least eight hours so the flavors can continue to mingle and the fat will solidify and be easy to remove. (See Cook's Tip on page 31 for storing broth.)

Preheat the oven to 475°F. Lightly spray the slow cooker and a broiler pan with cooking spray. Set the slow cooker aside.

Put the bones, onions, carrots, celery, and garlic in the pan. Lightly spray all with cooking spray. Roast for 40 minutes, or until richly browned, turning once halfway through. Transfer the bones, vegetables, garlic, and pan drippings to the slow cooker.

Stir in the remaining ingredients. Cook, covered, on low for 8 to 10 hours or on high for 4 to 6 hours.

Using a colander, strain the broth into a large bowl, being careful to avoid steam burns. Discard the solids. Cover and refrigerate the broth for at least 8 hours so the flavors blend and the fat rises to the surface. Discard the fat before reheating the broth.

per serving

Calories 10	Cholesterol 0 mg	Dietary Exchanges
Total Fat 0.0 g	Sodium 66 mg	Free
Saturated Fat 0.0 g	Carbohydrates 1 g	
Trans Fat 0.0 g	Fiber 0 g	
Polyunsaturated Fat 0.0 g	Sugars 0 g	
Monounsaturated Fat 0.0 g	Protein 2 g	

harvest vegetable broth

makes 7 cups
1 cup per serving

slow cooker size
3- to 4½-quart round or oval

slow cooking time
8 to 9 hours on low, **OR**
4 to 5 hours on high

Cooking spray

1 teaspoon canola or corn oil

1 medium green bell pepper, coarsely chopped

4 medium garlic cloves, minced

2 quarts water

3 medium carrots, halved crosswise

2 medium leeks (white part only), halved

2 medium parsnips or turnips, halved crosswise

1 large tomato, halved

1 cup tightly packed fresh parsley leaves, stems discarded

1 tablespoon dried thyme, crumbled

4 medium dried bay leaves

1 teaspoon pepper (coarsely ground preferred)

3 whole cloves

⅛ teaspoon salt

Just three cloves provide the subtle zing that makes this vegetable broth so good. Like the chicken and beef broths on the preceding pages, it is very handy for use in recipes in this cookbook, to replace water when you are cooking vegetables and grains for dinner, and to drop into other soups, stews, and casseroles to intensify their flavor. (See Cook's Tip on page 31 for storing broth.)

Lightly spray the slow cooker with cooking spray. Set aside.

In a large nonstick skillet, heat the oil over medium-high heat, swirling to coat the bottom. Cook the bell pepper for 7 minutes, or until the edges are richly browned, stirring occasionally.

Stir in the garlic. Cook for 30 seconds, stirring constantly. Transfer to the slow cooker.

Stir in the remaining ingredients. Cook, covered, on low for 8 to 9 hours or on high for 4 to 5 hours.

Using a colander, strain the broth into an airtight container, being careful to avoid steam burns. Discard the solids. Serve or cover and refrigerate the broth.

per serving

Calories 5	Cholesterol 0 mg	Dietary Exchanges
Total Fat 0.0 g	Sodium 52 mg	Free
Saturated Fat 0.0 g	Carbohydrates 1 g	
Trans Fat 0.0 g	Fiber 0 g	
Polyunsaturated Fat 0.0 g	Sugars 0 g	
Monounsaturated Fat 0.0 g	Protein 0 g	

sweet and spicy pumpkin soup

serves 4
1 cup per serving

slow cooker size/shape
3- to 4½-quart round or oval

slow cooking time
5 to 7 hours on low, **OR**
2 to 2½ hours on high

2½ cups fat-free, low-sodium vegetable broth, such as on page 33

1 15-ounce can solid-pack pumpkin (not pie filling)

1 medium potato, peeled and chopped

½ medium onion, chopped

2 teaspoons dried minced garlic

1 teaspoon light or dark brown sugar

1 teaspoon minced chipotle pepper canned in adobo sauce

½ teaspoon ground cinnamon

½ teaspoon ground ginger

■ ■ ■

¼ cup raw unsalted shelled pumpkin seeds

Cooking spray

½ teaspoon salt-free all-purpose seasoning blend

⅛ teaspoon salt

Pumpkin scores high in nutrition, and this soup—with its flair from chipotle pepper and seasoned roasted pumpkin seeds—scores high in flavor, too!

In the slow cooker, stir together the vegetable broth, pumpkin, potato, onion, garlic, brown sugar, chipotle pepper, cinnamon, and ginger. Cook, covered, on low for 5 to 7 hours or on high for 2 to 2½ hours.

While the soup is cooking, preheat the oven to 350°F.

Spread the pumpkin seeds in a single layer on a baking sheet. Lightly spray the seeds with cooking spray. Roast for 8 to 10 minutes, or until golden, stirring once halfway through. Transfer the baking sheet to a cooling rack. Immediately sprinkle the seeds with the seasoning blend and salt, stirring to coat. Let cool for 15 to 20 minutes. Set aside.

In a food processor or blender (vent the blender lid), process the soup in batches until smooth. Serve the soup sprinkled with the pumpkin seeds.

cook's tip on chipotle peppers in adobo sauce: Look in the Mexican food section of grocery stores for chipotle peppers (dried jalapeños that have a smoky flavor) canned in adobo sauce, also known as adobo paste, a moderately spicy mixture of chiles, vinegar, garlic, and herbs. You probably won't use an entire can for any single recipe, but the leftovers freeze nicely. Spread the peppers with sauce in a thin layer on a medium plate covered with cooking parchment or wax paper, then freeze them, uncovered, for about 2 hours, or just until firm. (This step will keep the peppers from sticking together later.) Transfer the peppers to an airtight freezer bag and freeze. Remove just the amount you need for your next recipe.

per serving

Calories 140	Cholesterol 0 mg	Dietary Exchanges
Total Fat 4.0 g	Sodium 124 mg	1½ starch, ½ fat
Saturated Fat 0.5 g	Carbohydrates 23 g	
Trans Fat 0.0 g	Fiber 6 g	
Polyunsaturated Fat 1.5 g	Sugars 6 g	
Monounsaturated Fat 1.0 g	Protein 6 g	

butternut squash bisque

serves 8
scant 1 cup per serving

slow cooker size/shape
3- to 4½-quart round or oval

slow cooking time
7½ to 8 hours on low
plus 15 minutes on low, **OR**
3 hours 45 minutes to 4 hours
on high plus 15 minutes on low

Cooking spray

36 ounces frozen butternut
squash, thawed

3 cups fat-free, low-sodium
chicken broth, such as on
page 31

3 medium carrots, chopped into
½-inch pieces

1 medium red onion, chopped

¼ cup sugar

1 teaspoon ground coriander

½ teaspoon ground cumin

⅛ teaspoon salt

■ ■ ■

½ cup fat-free half-and-half

⅛ teaspoon salt

You can enjoy this creamy soup alone or topped
with a dollop of fat-free sour cream, chopped
fresh pineapple, and snipped cilantro. It's a winner
either way!

Lightly spray the slow cooker with cooking spray. Put the
squash, broth, carrots, onion, sugar, coriander, cumin, and
⅛ teaspoon salt in the slow cooker, stirring to combine.
Cook, covered, on low for 7½ to 8 hours or on high for
3 hours 45 minutes to 4 hours, or until the squash is very
tender.

In a food processor or blender (vent the blender lid), process
the soup in batches until smooth. Return the soup to the
slow cooker.

If using the high setting, change it to low. Stir the
half-and-half and remaining ⅛ teaspoon salt into the soup.
Cook, covered, for 15 minutes, or until heated through.

cook's tip on fresh butternut squash: If you want to use fresh butternut squash and convenience is important, look in the refrigerated section
of the produce area for packages of already peeled chunks of squash. You'll
need about 4 cups for this recipe. If you're more interested in saving money,
prepare the squash yourself. For this recipe, buy a squash of about 2 pounds
and pierce it with a fork in several places. Put the squash in a microwaveable pie pan or on a large rimmed plate, and microwave on 100 percent
power (high) for 2 minutes, turning over halfway through. Using a vegetable
peeler, remove the skin. Discard the seeds and strings. Cut the flesh into
1-inch cubes, transfer them to the slow cooker, and proceed as directed.

per serving ⎯⎯⎯⎯⎯⎯⎯⎯⎯⎯⎯⎯⎯⎯⎯⎯⎯⎯⎯⎯⎯⎯⎯⎯⎯⎯⎯⎯⎯⎯⎯⎯⎯⎯

Calories 129	Cholesterol 0 mg	Dietary Exchanges
Total Fat 0.5 g	Sodium 132 mg	2 starch
Saturated Fat 0.0 g	Carbohydrates 31 g	
Trans Fat 0.0 g	Fiber 3 g	
Polyunsaturated Fat 0.0 g	Sugars 13 g	
Monounsaturated Fat 0.0 g	Protein 4 g	

fresh tomato soup with goat cheese and basil

serves 6
1 heaping cup per serving

slow cooker size/shape
5- to 7-quart round or oval

slow cooking time
3 to 4 hours on low, **OR**
2 hours on high

■ ■ ■

**3 pounds very ripe tomatoes,
each tomato cut into 8 wedges**

1 cup water

1 medium onion, minced

1 teaspoon dried minced garlic

¼ teaspoon salt

¼ teaspoon pepper

■ ■ ■

**⅓ cup fresh basil, rolled and cut
into thin strips**

**3 tablespoons goat cheese
crumbles**

This soup brings the flavors of southern Italy to your table. It is especially delicious when tomatoes are at the height of their season, but you might need to substitute no-salt-added canned tomatoes when fresh are not available. *(See photo insert.)*

In the slow cooker, stir together the tomatoes, water, onion, garlic, salt, and pepper. Cook, covered, on low for 3 to 4 hours or on high for 2 hours.

In a food processor or blender (vent the blender lid), process the soup in batches until smooth. Serve sprinkled with the basil and goat cheese.

cook's tip: Toast whole-wheat bread cubes and sprinkle just a few on the soup right before serving.

cook's tip on cutting fresh basil: To make thin strips of fresh basil (or chiffonade) for an attractive garnish, stack several leaves with the stem end pointing toward you. Roll tightly from bottom to top, making a cylinder. Cut it crosswise into thin ribbons.

per serving

Calories 71	Cholesterol 5 mg	Dietary Exchanges
Total Fat 2.0 g	Sodium 127 mg	2 vegetable, ½ fat
Saturated Fat 1.0 g	Carbohydrates 11 g	
Trans Fat 0.0 g	Fiber 3 g	
Polyunsaturated Fat 0.0 g	Sugars 8 g	
Monounsaturated Fat 0.5 g	Protein 4 g	

cream of cauliflower soup

serves 6
scant 1 cup per serving

slow cooker size/shape
3- to 4½-quart round or oval

slow cooking time
5 to 7 hours on low, **OR**
3 to 5 hours on high

3 cups fat-free, low-sodium
   chicken broth, such as on
   page 31

1 medium head of cauliflower
   (about 1¾ pounds), florets
   cut into 1-inch pieces (about 4
   cups)

1 medium baking potato (about
   9 ounces), peeled and chopped

1 small onion, chopped

2 medium garlic cloves, chopped

⅛ teaspoon salt

■ ■ ■

2 teaspoons fresh lemon juice

   Pinch of pepper (white
   preferred)

¼ cup plus 2 tablespoons
   shredded low-fat Cheddar
   cheese (sharp preferred)

Forget the high-fat, high-calorie cream! Puréed vegetables give this soup its luxurious, velvety texture.

In the slow cooker, stir together the broth, cauliflower, potato, onion, garlic, and salt. Cook, covered, on low for 5 to 7 hours or on high for 3 to 5 hours, or until the vegetables are tender.

In a food processor or blender (vent the blender lid), process the soup in batches until smooth. For piping hot soup, return the soup to the slow cooker. If using the low setting, change it to high. Reheat, covered, for 10 minutes.

Stir in the lemon juice and pepper. Ladle the soup into bowls. Sprinkle with the Cheddar.

cook's tip on blending hot liquids: Any time you use a blender to purée a hot liquid, be sure to vent the cover so the steam can safely escape. If the blender you are using doesn't have a vented cover, allow the liquid to cool slightly, then blend and reheat.

per serving

Calories 85	Cholesterol 2 mg	Dietary Exchanges
Total Fat 1.0 g	Sodium 151 mg	½ starch, 2 vegetable
Saturated Fat 0.5 g	Carbohydrates 15 g	
Trans Fat 0.0 g	Fiber 3 g	
Polyunsaturated Fat 0.0 g	Sugars 3 g	
Monounsaturated Fat 0.0 g	Protein 6 g	

creamy potato-broccoli soup

serves 6
⅔ cup per serving

slow cooker size/shape
3- to 4-quart round or oval

slow cooking time
5 to 6 hours on low
plus 10 minutes on high, **OR**
3 to 4 hours on high
plus 10 minutes on high

1 teaspoon olive oil

1 cup coarsely chopped onion

½ cup sliced leek (white and light
green parts) or chopped onion

2 large garlic cloves, minced

2 cups fat-free, low-sodium
chicken broth, such as on
page 31

14 ounces russet potatoes, peeled
and chopped

¼ teaspoon dried thyme,
crumbled

¼ teaspoon salt

⅛ teaspoon pepper

▪ ▪ ▪

9 ounces frozen broccoli florets,
thawed

¼ cup fat-free half-and-half

Using russet potatoes, also known as baking potatoes, is key to getting the best results with this soup. Along with the half-and-half, they make it lusciously creamy. The leek adds a sweet, mild onion flavor.

In a large nonstick skillet, heat the oil over medium heat, swirling to coat the bottom. Cook the onion and leek for 3 minutes, or until beginning to soften, stirring frequently.

Stir in the garlic. Cook for 30 seconds, stirring constantly. Transfer to the slow cooker.

Stir in the broth, potatoes, thyme, salt, and pepper. Cook, covered, on low for 5 to 6 hours or on high for 3 to 4 hours, or until the vegetables are tender.

If using the low setting, change it to high. Quickly add the broccoli and re-cover the slow cooker. Cook for 10 minutes, or until the broccoli is tender. For the best results, let the soup cool for about 15 minutes.

In a food processor or blender (vent the blender lid), process the soup in small batches until slightly smooth but with some texture, or to the desired consistency.

Just before serving, stir in the half-and-half.

per serving

Calories 96	Cholesterol 0 mg	Dietary Exchanges
Total Fat 1.0 g	Sodium 142 mg	1 starch, 1 vegetable
Saturated Fat 0.0 g	Carbohydrates 19 g	
Trans Fat 0.0 g	Fiber 3 g	
Polyunsaturated Fat 0.0 g	Sugars 3 g	
Monounsaturated Fat 0.5 g	Protein 4 g	

italian vegetable and pasta soup

serves 8
¾ cup per serving

slow cooker size/shape
3- to 4½-quart round or oval

slow cooking time
8 to 10 hours on low
plus 20 minutes on high, **OR**
5 to 6 hours on high
plus 20 minutes on high

4 cups fat-free, low-sodium
   vegetable broth, such as on
   page 33

1 14.5-ounce can no-salt-added
   diced tomatoes, undrained

2 medium carrots, chopped

2 medium ribs of celery, chopped

1 medium onion, chopped

2 medium garlic cloves, minced

½ teaspoon dried oregano,
   crumbled

½ teaspoon dried basil, crumbled

¼ teaspoon salt

⅛ teaspoon pepper

■ ■ ■

1 cup dried whole-grain elbow
   macaroni

3 tablespoons shredded or
   grated Parmesan cheese

Pasta in a slow cooker? It works perfectly in this veggie-packed soup. Any leftovers will make a satisfying lunch later in the week.

In the slow cooker, stir together the broth, tomatoes with liquid, carrots, celery, onion, garlic, oregano, basil, salt, and pepper. Cook, covered, on low for 8 to 10 hours or on high for 5 to 6 hours.

If using the low setting, change it to high. Quickly stir in the macaroni and re-cover the slow cooker. Cook for 20 minutes, or until the macaroni is tender. Serve sprinkled with the Parmesan.

per serving

Calories 85	Cholesterol 1 mg	Dietary Exchanges
Total Fat 1.0 g	Sodium 157 mg	½ starch, 1 vegetable
Saturated Fat 0.5 g	Carbohydrates 16 g	
Trans Fat 0.0 g	Fiber 3 g	
Polyunsaturated Fat 0.0 g	Sugars 4 g	
Monounsaturated Fat 0.5 g	Protein 3 g	

double-mushroom and barley soup

QUICK PREP

serves 4
1¼ cups per serving

slow cooker size/shape
3- to 4½-quart round or oval

slow cooking time
5 to 7 hours on low, **OR**
2 to 3 hours on high

2¼ **cups water**

1¾ **cups fat-free, low-sodium beef broth, such as on page 32**

½ **large Vidalia, Maui, Oso Sweet, or other sweet onion, chopped**

4 **ounces button mushrooms, sliced**

1 **medium carrot, chopped**

1 **medium rib of celery, chopped**

¼ **cup dried mushrooms, such as chanterelle or a mixture, chopped or broken up if large**

3 **tablespoons uncooked pearl barley (not quick-cooking or instant)**

1 **tablespoon dried minced garlic**

1 **teaspoon dried dillweed, crumbled**

¼ **teaspoon pepper**

⅛ **teaspoon salt**

■ ■ ■

1 **tablespoon snipped fresh dillweed**

Dried mushrooms add an earthiness and depth to this soup and are a delightful contrast to the fresh, bright flavor of the dill.

In the slow cooker, stir together all the ingredients except the fresh dillweed. Cook, covered, on low for 5 to 7 hours or on high for 2 to 3 hours. Just before serving, sprinkle the soup with the fresh dillweed.

cook's tip on barley: Pearl barley has had the outer bran layer removed and has been steamed and polished. Even after processing, however, barley is rich in fiber and other nutrients.

per serving

Calories 69
Total Fat 0.5 g
  Saturated Fat 0.0 g
  Trans Fat 0.0 g
  Polyunsaturated Fat 0.0 g
  Monounsaturated Fat 0.0 g

Cholesterol 0 mg
Sodium 131 mg
Carbohydrates 14 g
  Fiber 3 g
  Sugars 3 g
  Protein 4 g

Dietary Exchanges
  ½ starch, 1 vegetable

corn and wild rice soup

serves 10
¾ cup per serving

slow cooker size/shape
3- to 4½-quart round or oval

slow cooking time
5 to 7 hours on low
plus 1 hour on high, **OR**
2½ to 3 hours on high
plus 1 hour on high

4 cups fat-free, low-sodium
   vegetable broth, such as on
   page 33

3 medium carrots, chopped

1 cup water

1 medium rib of celery, chopped

½ medium onion, chopped

¼ medium red bell pepper,
   chopped

2 teaspoons dried minced garlic

2 teaspoons dried sage

¼ teaspoon salt

¼ teaspoon pepper

■ ■ ■

1 cup frozen whole-kernel corn,
   thawed

½ cup uncooked wild rice, rinsed
   and drained

All it takes is a small amount of wild rice to elevate
this soup, full of vividly colored vegetables, to
special status.

In the slow cooker, stir together the broth, carrots, water,
celery, onion, bell pepper, garlic, sage, salt, and pepper. Cook,
covered, on low for 5 to 7 hours or on high for 2½ to
3 hours.

If using the low setting, change it to high. Quickly stir in the
corn and rice and re-cover the slow cooker. Cook on high for
1 hour.

per serving

Calories 62	Cholesterol 0 mg	Dietary Exchanges
Total Fat 0.5 g	Sodium 100 mg	1 starch
Saturated Fat 0.0 g	Carbohydrates 14 g	
Trans Fat 0.0 g	Fiber 2 g	
Polyunsaturated Fat 0.0 g	Sugars 2 g	
Monounsaturated Fat 0.0 g	Protein 2 g	

bean florentine soup

serves 8
1 cup per serving

slow cooker size/shape
5- to 7-quart round or oval

slow cooking time
7 to 9 hours on low, **OR**
4 to 5 hours on high

1 pound dried navy or Great
   Northern beans, sorted for
   stones and shriveled beans,
   rinsed, and drained
8 cups fat-free, low-sodium
   vegetable broth, such as on
   page 33
1 large onion, diced
1 teaspoon dried minced garlic
1 teaspoon dried basil, crumbled
½ teaspoon salt
¼ teaspoon pepper

◼ ◼ ◼

6 ounces spinach (about 6 cups)

Fresh spinach added at the end of the cooking time gives this side soup a nutritional boost and a pop of color.

Fill a large saucepan three-fourths full of water. Bring to a boil over high heat. Stir in the beans. Return to a boil. Reduce the heat and simmer for 15 minutes. Pour the beans into a colander and rinse.

Pour the beans into the slow cooker. Stir in the remaining ingredients except the spinach. Cook, covered, on low for 7 to 9 hours or on high for 4 to 5 hours. Just before serving, stir the spinach into the soup.

cook's tip: Because of the protein and fiber in this soup, you can serve it as an easy main dish for four, if you prefer.

per serving

Calories 203	Cholesterol 0 mg	Dietary Exchanges
Total Fat 1.0 g	Sodium 215 mg	2½ starch, 1 very lean
Saturated Fat 0.0 g	Carbohydrates 38 g	meat
Trans Fat 0.0 g	Fiber 15 g	
Polyunsaturated Fat 0.5 g	Sugars 2 g	
Monounsaturated Fat 0.0 g	Protein 12 g	

cod and clam chowder

serves 4
1½ cups per serving

slow cooker size/shape
3- to 4½-quart round or oval

slow cooking time
7 hours 40 to 45 minutes on low plus 20 minutes on low, **OR** 3 hours 45 to 50 minutes on high plus 10 minutes on high

1 6.5-ounce can chopped clams in clam juice (lowest sodium available)

2 medium russet potatoes (about 10 ounces total), peeled and shredded

1 medium red bell pepper, diced

1 8-ounce bottle clam juice (lowest sodium available)

1 cup fat-free, low-sodium chicken broth, such as on page 31

1½ medium ribs of celery, cut crosswise into ¼-inch slices

1 medium dried bay leaf

1 tablespoon snipped fresh thyme or 1 teaspoon dried thyme, crumbled

⅛ teaspoon pepper

2 teaspoons olive oil

3 medium carrots, cut crosswise into ¼-inch slices

1 cup chopped onion

1 medium garlic clove, minced

■ ■ ■

12 ounces cod or other mild white fish fillets, about 1 inch thick, rinsed and patted dry, cut into 1-inch cubes

½ cup fat-free half-and-half

During the last 10 or 20 minutes of cooking the chowder, stir in the mild, flaky fish. That's all the cooking it needs.

Drain the clams, pouring the juice into the slow cooker. Put the clams in an airtight container and refrigerate until needed. Add the potatoes, bell pepper, bottled clam juice, broth, celery, bay leaf, snipped thyme, and pepper to the slow cooker, stirring to combine. Set aside.

In a medium nonstick skillet, heat the oil over medium-high heat, swirling to coat the bottom. Cook the carrots and onion for 5 minutes, or until the onion is soft, stirring frequently. Stir in the garlic. Cook for 30 seconds, stirring constantly. Stir into the potato mixture. Cook, covered, on low for 7 hours 40 to 45 minutes or on high for 3 hours 45 to 50 minutes.

About 20 minutes before the end of the cooking time if using the low setting, or 10 minutes if using the high setting, quickly stir in the fish and clams and re-cover the slow cooker. Cook on low for 20 minutes or on high for 10 minutes, or until the fish flakes easily when tested with a fork.

Pour in the half-and-half, gently stirring for 2 to 3 minutes, or until heated through. Discard the bay leaf.

cook's tip on potatoes as a soup thickener: The starch in potatoes is a natural thickening agent for long-cooking soups. Raw potatoes can be used to thicken slow cooker soups, but potatoes used to thicken soups cooked on the stovetop need to be cooked first.

per serving

Calories 236	Cholesterol 50 mg	Dietary Exchanges
Total Fat 3.0 g	Sodium 487 mg	1½ starch, 2 vegetable,
Saturated Fat 0.5 g	Carbohydrates 31 g	2½ lean meat
Trans Fat 0.0 g	Fiber 5 g	
Polyunsaturated Fat 0.5 g	Sugars 8 g	
Monounsaturated Fat 1.5 g	Protein 23 g	

crab and red bell pepper soup

serves 4
1 cup per serving

slow cooker size/shape
3- to 4½-quart round or oval

slow cooking time
3 to 3½ hours on low
plus 15 minutes on high, **OR**
1½ hours to 1 hour 45 minutes
on high plus 15 minutes
on high

Cooking spray

1 large red bell pepper, diced

2 medium carrots, halved
lengthwise, then thinly sliced
crosswise

2 medium green onions, chopped

2 tablespoons water

1 medium garlic clove, minced

⅛ teaspoon cayenne

⅛ teaspoon salt

■ ■ ■

1 13.5- to 13.75-ounce can lite
coconut milk

1 cup fat-free half-and-half

6 ounces canned crabmeat,
drained, cartilage discarded

½ cup snipped fresh cilantro

2 medium green onions, chopped

1 tablespoon fresh lime juice

2 teaspoons sugar

1 teaspoon grated peeled
gingerroot, or to taste

1 medium lime, cut into 4 wedges

Fresh ginger is the key ingredient in this slightly spicy, slightly sweet, creamy soup. For a higher level of heat and more pronounced kick, add extra gingerroot instead of more cayenne.

Lightly spray the slow cooker with cooking spray. Put the bell pepper, carrots, 2 green onions, water, garlic, cayenne, and salt in the slow cooker, stirring to combine. Cook, covered, on low for 3 to 3½ hours or on high for 1½ hours to 1 hour 45 minutes, or until the carrots are tender.

If using the low setting, change it to high. Quickly stir in the remaining ingredients except the lime and re-cover the slow cooker. Cook for 15 minutes, or until heated through. Serve with the lime wedges to squeeze over the soup.

cook's tip on lite coconut milk: Be sure to use only lite coconut milk; it has about 60 percent less fat than the regular version. Refrigerate leftover coconut milk in an airtight container for up to three days. You can use it in a smoothie by blending it with pineapple, banana, fat-free yogurt, and ice. Another use is drizzled over fresh mango and banana chunks for a light dessert.

per serving

Calories 181	Cholesterol 41 mg	Dietary Exchanges
Total Fat 5.5 g	Sodium 369 mg	2 vegetable, 1 other
Saturated Fat 3.5 g	Carbohydrates 22 g	carbohydrate, 1½ lean
Trans Fat 0.0 g	Fiber 3 g	meat
Polyunsaturated Fat 1.0 g	Sugars 12 g	
Monounsaturated Fat 0.5 g	Protein 13 g	

thai coconut-chicken soup

serves 4
1½ cups per serving

slow cooker size/shape
3- to 4½-quart round or oval

slow cooking time
5 to 6 hours on low plus
15 to 20 minutes on high, **OR**
2½ to 3 hours on high plus
15 to 20 minutes on high

1 pound boneless, skinless
  chicken breasts, all visible fat
  discarded, cut into ½-inch
  cubes

2 cups fat-free, no-salt-added
  chicken broth, such as on
  page 31

1 medium carrot, cut into
  matchstick-size strips

1 tablespoon minced peeled
  gingerroot

½ to 1 medium fresh serrano
  pepper, seeds and ribs
  discarded, chopped

2 medium garlic cloves, minced

½ teaspoon grated lime zest

■ ■ ■

1 cup lite coconut milk

½ medium red bell pepper, cut
  into matchstick-size strips

3 ounces shiitake mushrooms,
  stems discarded, sliced

¼ cup snipped fresh cilantro

¼ cup sliced green onions (green
  and white parts)

This soup is a feast for the eyes as well as the palate. Adding bright red bell pepper strips, dark brown mushrooms, and deep green cilantro for only a few minutes at the end of the cooking time maintains their color and texture.

In the slow cooker, stir together the chicken, broth, carrot, gingerroot, serrano pepper, garlic, and lime zest. Cook, covered, on low for 5 to 6 hours or on high for 2½ to 3 hours.

Using a slotted spoon, quickly skim off any solids and discard. Stir in the coconut milk, bell pepper, and mushrooms. Re-cover the slow cooker. If using the low setting, change it to high. Cook for 15 to 20 minutes, or until the vegetables are tender-crisp. Serve the soup sprinkled with the cilantro and green onions.

per serving

Calories 194	Cholesterol 73 mg	Dietary Exchanges
Total Fat 6.0 g	Sodium 198 mg	1 vegetable, 3 lean
Saturated Fat 2.5 g	Carbohydrates 7 g	meat
Trans Fat 0.0 g	Fiber 2 g	
Polyunsaturated Fat 0.5 g	Sugars 3 g	
Monounsaturated Fat 1.0 g	Protein 26 g	

chicken and brown rice soup with blue cheese crumbles

serves 6
1 cup soup, ⅓ cup rice, and 1 tablespoon cheese per serving

slow cooker size/shape
3- to 4½-quart round or oval

slow cooking time
5½ to 6 hours on low, **OR**
2 hours 45 minutes to 3 hours on high

Cooking spray

1 pound boneless, skinless chicken breasts, all visible fat discarded, cut into bite-size pieces

1 14.5-ounce can no-salt-added diced tomatoes, undrained

1¾ cups fat-free, low-sodium chicken broth, such as on page 31

1 large onion, diced

2 teaspoons sugar

2 teaspoons dried oregano, crumbled

1 teaspoon dried thyme, crumbled

½ teaspoon garlic powder

■ ■ ■

10 ounces frozen brown rice

2 tablespoons mild Louisiana-style hot-pepper sauce

1 tablespoon olive oil (extra virgin preferred)

¼ cup plus 2 tablespoons crumbled reduced-fat blue cheese

¼ cup snipped fresh parsley

No ordinary soup here! This unusual bowl of comfort features a good-size splash of mild Louisiana-style hot-pepper sauce and enough blue cheese to give it that wow factor. The flavorful chicken-vegetable soup tops microwaved brown rice.

Lightly spray the slow cooker with cooking spray. Put the chicken, tomatoes with liquid, broth, onion, sugar, oregano, thyme, and garlic powder in the slow cooker, stirring to combine. Cook, covered, on low for 5½ to 6 hours or on high for 2 hours 45 minutes to 3 hours, or until the onion is very soft.

About 10 minutes before serving the soup, prepare the rice using the package directions. Spoon into soup bowls.

Stir the hot sauce and oil into the soup. Ladle over the rice. Top with the blue cheese and parsley.

cook's tip on louisiana-style hot-pepper sauce: Louisiana-style hot-pepper sauce is mild rather than wild, and it puts more flavor than heat in your dishes.

per serving

Calories 217	Cholesterol 52 mg	Dietary Exchanges
Total Fat 6.0 g	Sodium 242 mg	1 starch, 1 vegetable,
Saturated Fat 1.5 g	Carbohydrates 19 g	2½ lean meat
Trans Fat 0.0 g	Fiber 2 g	
Polyunsaturated Fat 0.5 g	Sugars 5 g	
Monounsaturated Fat 2.5 g	Protein 21 g	

chicken and bean soup with lemon and basil

serves 5
1½ cups per serving

slow cooker size/shape
4- to 6-quart round or oval

slow cooking time
8 to 10 hours on low
plus 5 minutes on low, OR
5 to 6 hours on high
plus 5 minutes on high

1 cup dried cannellini beans, sorted for stones and shriveled beans, rinsed, and drained

5 cups fat-free, low-sodium chicken broth, such as on page 31

1 medium carrot, chopped

1 medium rib of celery, chopped

1 small onion, chopped

2 medium garlic cloves, minced

¼ teaspoon salt

⅛ teaspoon pepper

■ ■ ■

1 pound boneless, skinless chicken breasts, all visible fat discarded, cut into ½-inch cubes

¼ teaspoon salt

⅛ teaspoon pepper

2 teaspoons olive oil

1 large tomato, chopped

2 teaspoons grated lemon zest

¼ cup chopped fresh basil

It's the last-minute addition of lemon zest and a heap of fresh basil that make this soup stand out.

Fill a small saucepan three-fourths full of water. Bring to a boil over high heat. Stir in the beans. Return to a boil. Reduce the heat and simmer for 15 minutes. Pour the beans into a colander and rinse. Pour into the slow cooker.

Stir in the broth, carrot, celery, onion, garlic, ¼ teaspoon salt, and ⅛ teaspoon pepper. Cook, covered, on low for 8 to 10 hours or on high for 5 to 6 hours, or until the beans are tender.

Sprinkle the chicken with the remaining ¼ teaspoon salt and remaining ⅛ teaspoon pepper.

In a large nonstick skillet, heat the oil over medium-high heat, swirling to coat the bottom. Cook the chicken for 5 to 6 minutes, or until lightly browned on the outside and no longer pink in the center, stirring occasionally.

Quickly stir the chicken, tomato, and lemon zest into the soup and re-cover the slow cooker. Cook for 5 minutes, or until the tomato is heated through. Just before serving, stir in the basil.

per serving

Calories 291	Cholesterol 58 mg	Dietary Exchanges
Total Fat 4.5 g	Sodium 419 mg	1½ starch, 1 vegetable,
Saturated Fat 1.0 g	Carbohydrates 30 g	3½ lean meat
Trans Fat 0.0 g	Fiber 8 g	
Polyunsaturated Fat 0.5 g	Sugars 4 g	
Monounsaturated Fat 2.0 g	Protein 32 g	

herbed chicken soup with arugula

serves 4
1¼ cups per serving

slow cooker size/shape
3- to 4½-quart round or oval

slow cooking time
3½ to 4 hours on low, **OR**
1 hour 45 minutes to 2 hours
on high

Cooking spray

1 8-ounce boneless, skinless chicken breast, all visible fat discarded

3 cups fat-free, low-sodium chicken broth, such as on page 31

½ teaspoon dried rosemary, crushed

½ teaspoon dried oregano, crumbled

½ teaspoon garlic powder

■ ■ ■

2 ounces dried whole-grain vermicelli or spaghetti, broken into thirds

1 ounce arugula or mixed spring greens, coarsely chopped (about 1 cup)

1 cup grape tomatoes, quartered

4 medium green onions, finely chopped

1 tablespoon olive oil (extra virgin preferred)

¼ teaspoon salt

¼ teaspoon pepper, or to taste (coarsely ground preferred)

¼ cup shredded Asiago or Parmesan cheese

When it's almost serving time, turn off the slow cooker and let this herb soup barely "cook" the arugula, baby tomatoes, and green onions. You'll have soup and salad all in one bowl!

Lightly spray the slow cooker with cooking spray. Put the chicken, broth, rosemary, oregano, and garlic powder in the slow cooker, stirring to combine. Cook, covered, on low for 3½ to 4 hours or on high for 1 hour 45 minutes to 2 hours, or until the chicken is no longer pink in the center.

About 30 minutes before serving, prepare the pasta using the package directions, omitting the salt. Drain well in a colander. Set aside.

Using a slotted spoon, quickly transfer the chicken to a cutting board, leaving the liquid in the slow cooker. Re-cover the slow cooker. Cut the chicken into bite-size pieces.

Stir the chicken and remaining ingredients except the Asiago into the broth mixture. Turn off the slow cooker. Let stand, covered, for 5 minutes. Serve the soup sprinkled with the Asiago.

per serving

Calories 207	Cholesterol 43 mg	Dietary Exchanges
Total Fat 7.5 g	Sodium 332 mg	½ starch, 1 vegetable,
Saturated Fat 2.0 g	Carbohydrates 17 g	2 lean meat
Trans Fat 0.0 g	Fiber 4 g	
Polyunsaturated Fat 1.5 g	Sugars 3 g	
Monounsaturated Fat 3.5 g	Protein 18 g	

country chicken noodle soup

serves 4
1¼ cups per serving

slow cooker size/shape
3- to 4½-quart round or oval

slow cooking time
3½ to 4 hours on low
(preferred) plus 20 minutes
on high, **OR**
1 hour 45 minutes to 2 hours
on high plus 20 minutes
on high

1 teaspoon canola or corn oil

1 8-ounce boneless, skinless
chicken breast, all visible fat
discarded

1 large onion, diced

3 cups fat-free, low-sodium
chicken broth, such as on
page 31

3 medium dried bay leaves

1 teaspoon dried thyme,
crumbled

½ teaspoon garlic powder

½ teaspoon pepper (coarsely
ground preferred)

■ ■ ■

2 ounces dried whole-grain
no-yolk noodles

½ cup frozen green peas, thawed

1 4-ounce jar diced pimientos,
undrained

¼ cup snipped fresh parsley

2 tablespoons light tub
margarine

¼ teaspoon salt

¼ cup plus 2 tablespoons grated
low-fat sharp Cheddar cheese

A bowl of chicken noodle soup is always welcome, and with a few unexpected ingredients—green peas, pimientos, and Cheddar—our version will surely satisfy the soup lover in you.

In a large nonstick skillet, heat the oil over medium-high heat, swirling to coat the bottom. Cook the chicken for 3 to 5 minutes on each side, or until lightly browned. Transfer to the slow cooker.

In the same skillet, cook the onion for 3 minutes, or until beginning to lightly brown, stirring frequently. Transfer to the slow cooker.

Stir in the broth, bay leaves, thyme, garlic powder, and pepper. Cook, covered, on low for 3½ to 4 hours or on high for 1 hour 45 minutes to 2 hours, or until the chicken is no longer pink in the center.

Quickly transfer the chicken to a cutting board, stir the pasta into the broth mixture, and re-cover the slow cooker. If using the low setting, change it to high. Cook, covered, for 20 minutes, or until the pasta is tender.

Meanwhile, using one or two forks, shred the chicken. When the pasta is tender, stir the chicken and remaining ingredients except the Cheddar into the broth mixture. Let stand, covered, for 5 minutes.

Just before serving, discard the bay leaves. Sprinkle the soup with the Cheddar.

per serving

Calories 210	Cholesterol 39 mg	Dietary Exchanges
Total Fat 6.0 g	Sodium 388 mg	1 starch, 1 vegetable,
Saturated Fat 1.0 g	Carbohydrates 19 g	2 lean meat
Trans Fat 0.0 g	Fiber 4 g	
Polyunsaturated Fat 1.5 g	Sugars 4 g	
Monounsaturated Fat 3.0 g	Protein 20 g	

spicy chicken and corn soup

serves 4
1½ cups per serving

slow cooker size/shape
3- to 4-quart round or oval

slow cooking time
6 to 8 hours on low, **OR**
3 to 4 hours on high

1 pound boneless, skinless chicken breasts, all visible fat discarded, cut into ½-inch cubes

¼ teaspoon salt and ¼ teaspoon salt, divided use

⅛ teaspoon pepper

2 teaspoons olive oil

3½ cups fat-free, low-sodium chicken broth, such as on page 31

1 14.5-ounce can no-salt-added diced tomatoes, undrained

10 ounces frozen whole-kernel corn, thawed

1 medium onion, diced

2 tablespoons no-salt-added tomato paste

½ medium fresh jalapeño, seeds and ribs discarded, minced

2 medium garlic cloves, minced

1 tablespoon chili powder

2 teaspoons ground cumin

■ ■ ■

2 tablespoons fresh lime juice

¼ cup snipped fresh cilantro

¼ cup shredded low-fat Cheddar cheese (sharp preferred)

This light one-dish meal gets a colorful and flavorful boost from tomatoes and corn, a hint of heat from the jalapeño, and a touch of freshness from lime juice and cilantro added just before serving.

Sprinkle both sides of the chicken with ¼ teaspoon salt and the pepper. Using your fingertips, gently press the seasonings so they adhere to the chicken.

In a large nonstick skillet, heat the oil over medium-high heat, swirling to coat the bottom. Cook the chicken for 5 to 6 minutes, or until lightly browned, stirring occasionally. Transfer to the slow cooker.

Stir in the broth, tomatoes with liquid, corn, onion, tomato paste, jalapeño, garlic, chili powder, cumin, and remaining ¼ teaspoon salt. Cook, covered, on low for 6 to 8 hours or on high for 3 to 4 hours, or until the vegetables are tender.

Stir in the lime juice. Ladle into bowls. Sprinkle each serving with the cilantro and Cheddar.

cook's tip: To serve a crowd or just enjoy the soup for several meals, double the recipe and use a 4- or 5-quart slow cooker. Cover and refrigerate any leftover soup (without the lime juice, cilantro, and Cheddar) for up to four days, or freeze it for longer storage.

per serving

Calories 296	Cholesterol 74 mg	Dietary Exchanges
Total Fat 7.0 g	Sodium 573 mg	1½ starch, 2 vegetable,
Saturated Fat 1.5 g	Carbohydrates 29 g	3 lean meat
Trans Fat 0.0 g	Fiber 5 g	
Polyunsaturated Fat 1.0 g	Sugars 10 g	
Monounsaturated Fat 3.0 g	Protein 32 g	

chicken tortilla soup

serves 4
1½ cups per serving

slow cooker size/shape
3- to 4½-quart round or oval

slow cooking time
6 to 8 hours on low, **OR**
3 to 4 hours on high

1 pound boneless, skinless chicken breasts, all visible fat discarded, cut into ½-inch cubes

2 cups frozen whole-kernel corn, thawed

2 cups fat-free, no-salt-added chicken broth, such as on page 31

1 14.5-ounce can no-salt-added diced tomatoes, undrained

¼ cup finely chopped onion

1 teaspoon sugar

1 teaspoon ancho powder

2 medium garlic cloves, minced

¼ teaspoon salt

■ ■ ■

2 6-inch corn tortillas, cut into ¼-inch-wide strips, and 1 6-inch corn tortilla, torn into pieces, divided use

2 to 4 tablespoons snipped fresh cilantro

¼ cup finely chopped avocado

¼ medium red bell pepper, cut into matchstick-size strips

A garnish of avocado bits, thinly sliced red bell pepper, and crisp tortilla strips adds texture and color to this popular soup. *(See photo insert.)*

In the slow cooker, stir together the chicken, corn, broth, tomatoes with liquid, onion, sugar, ancho powder, garlic, and salt. Cook, covered, on low for 6 to 8 hours or on high for 3 to 4 hours.

Meanwhile, preheat the oven to 350°F.

Arrange the tortilla strips in a single layer on a baking sheet. Bake for 8 to 10 minutes, or until crisp. Transfer the baking sheet to a cooling rack. Let the strips stand for about 15 minutes, or until cool. Transfer to an airtight container and set aside.

When the soup is ready, transfer 1 cup to a food processor or blender. Stir in the tortilla pieces. Let the mixture stand for 1 minute so the tortilla pieces soften. Process until smooth. Stir the mixture into the soup. Stir in the cilantro.

Ladle the soup into bowls. Sprinkle with the avocado, bell pepper, and reserved baked tortilla strips.

cook's tip: Adding the processed soup and tortilla mixture to the rest of the soup gives the finished product more body and distributes the tortilla flavor.

per serving

Calories 292	Cholesterol 73 mg	Dietary Exchanges
Total Fat 5.5 g	Sodium 350 mg	1½ starch, 2 vegetable,
Saturated Fat 1.0 g	Carbohydrates 33 g	3 lean meat
Trans Fat 0.0 g	Fiber 5 g	
Polyunsaturated Fat 1.0 g	Sugars 8 g	
Monounsaturated Fat 2.0 g	Protein 30 g	

smoked turkey and rice soup with fresh sage

serves 4
1½ cups per serving

slow cooker size/shape
3- to 4½-quart round or oval

slow cooking time
5½ to 6 hours on low
plus 15 minutes on high, **OR**
2 hours 45 minutes to 3 hours
on high plus 15 minutes
on high

Cooking spray

1 8-ounce smoked turkey leg,
skin discarded

3 cups fat-free, low-sodium
chicken broth, such as on
page 31

1 medium zucchini, chopped

1 medium red bell pepper, diced

1 medium onion, diced

1 medium rib of celery, thinly
sliced

1 medium carrot, thinly sliced

2 tablespoons chopped fresh
sage

1 teaspoon dried thyme,
crumbled

▪ ▪ ▪

½ cup uncooked instant brown
rice

1 tablespoon olive oil (extra
virgin preferred)

¼ teaspoon salt

2 tablespoons chopped fresh
sage

Fresh sage sets this soup apart. Adding it at both the start and the end of the cooking time suffuses the soup with flavor.

Lightly spray the slow cooker with cooking spray. Place the turkey in the slow cooker. Stir in the broth, zucchini, bell pepper, onion, celery, carrot, 2 tablespoons sage, and the thyme. Cook, covered, on low for 5½ to 6 hours or on high for 2 hours 45 minutes to 3 hours, or until the onion is very soft.

Quickly transfer the turkey to a cutting board, leaving the broth mixture in the slow cooker. Set the turkey aside. Quickly stir the rice into the broth mixture and re-cover the slow cooker. If using the low setting, change it to high. Cook, covered, for 15 minutes, or until the rice is tender.

Meanwhile, bone the turkey leg. Cut the turkey into bite-size pieces. When the rice is cooked, stir the turkey, oil, salt, and remaining 2 tablespoons sage into the soup.

per serving

Calories 173	Cholesterol 27 mg	Dietary Exchanges
Total Fat 6.5 g	Sodium 452 mg	½ starch, 2 vegetable,
Saturated Fat 1.5 g	Carbohydrates 18 g	1 lean meat, ½ fat
Trans Fat 0.0 g	Fiber 3 g	
Polyunsaturated Fat 1.5 g	Sugars 6 g	
Monounsaturated Fat 3.5 g	Protein 12 g	

turkey sausage and lentil soup

serves 8
1½ cups per serving

slow cooker size/shape
4- to 6-quart round or oval

slow cooking time
8 to 10 hours on low, **OR**
5 to 6 hours on high

2 teaspoons olive oil

8 ounces mild or spicy Italian
    turkey sausage, casings
    discarded and sausage
    crumbled

1 medium onion, chopped

4 cups fat-free, low-sodium
    chicken broth, such as on
    page 31

4 cups water

1 pound dried brown lentils
    (about 2¼ cups), sorted for
    stones and shriveled lentils,
    rinsed, and drained

1 14.5-ounce can no-salt-added
    diced tomatoes, undrained

2 medium carrots, chopped

1 medium rib of celery, chopped

¼ cup no-salt-added tomato
    paste

2 teaspoons dried oregano,
    crumbled

1 teaspoon dried basil, crumbled

2 medium garlic cloves, minced

½ teaspoon salt

¼ teaspoon pepper

This hearty soup is comforting to come home to on a winter evening. Serve it with warm crusty whole-grain bread and finish the meal with pear wedges for dessert.

In a large nonstick skillet, heat the oil over medium-high heat, swirling to coat the bottom. Cook the sausage and onion for 5 minutes, or until both are lightly browned, stirring occasionally. Transfer to the slow cooker.

Stir in the remaining ingredients. Cook, covered, on low for 8 to 10 hours or on high for 5 to 6 hours.

per serving

Calories 284	Cholesterol 21 mg	Dietary Exchanges
Total Fat 4.0 g	Sodium 379 mg	2 starch, 2 vegetable,
Saturated Fat 1.0 g	Carbohydrates 41 g	2 very lean meat
Trans Fat 0.0 g	Fiber 15 g	
Polyunsaturated Fat 1.0 g	Sugars 8 g	
Monounsaturated Fat 1.5 g	Protein 22 g	

ribollita

serves 8
1¼ cups per serving

slow cooker size/shape
5- to 7-quart round or oval

slow cooking time
8 to 10 hours on low, **OR**
4 to 5 hours on high

2 slices turkey bacon, chopped

2 cups chopped onions

3 large garlic cloves, minced

4 cups fat-free, low-sodium chicken broth, such as on page 31

1 28-ounce can or 2 14.5-ounce cans no-salt-added diced tomatoes, undrained

1 15.5-ounce can no-salt-added cannellini beans, rinsed and drained

8 ounces cabbage, cut into 1-inch chunks (about 3 cups)

2 large carrots, cut crosswise into ½-inch pieces

1 medium green bell pepper, cut into 1½-inch squares

1 tablespoon dried basil, crumbled

2 teaspoons dried oregano, crumbled

■ ■ ■

2 slices whole-wheat bread (lowest sodium available), cut into ½-inch cubes

Olive oil spray

¼ cup shredded or grated Parmesan cheese

Ribollita means "twice cooked"; traditionally this Italian soup was made with leftover minestrone or other vegetable soup. Usually, the soup is thickened with chunks of bread, but we substitute toasted bread cubes sprinkled on top.

Heat a medium nonstick skillet over medium heat. Cook the bacon for 5 minutes, or until browned, stirring frequently.

Stir in the onions. Cook for 3 minutes, or until soft, stirring frequently. Stir in the garlic. Cook for 30 seconds, stirring constantly. Transfer to the slow cooker.

Stir in the broth, tomatoes with liquid, beans, cabbage, carrots, bell pepper, basil, and oregano. Cook, covered, on low for 8 to 10 hours or on high for 4 to 5 hours, or until the vegetables are tender.

Meanwhile, preheat the oven to 400°F. Arrange the bread cubes in a single layer on a small rimmed baking sheet. Lightly spray the tops with olive oil spray.

Bake the bread cubes for 5 to 8 minutes, or until lightly browned. If baked more than 2 hours in advance, transfer the bread cubes to an airtight container until needed.

Serve the soup topped with the bread cubes and sprinkled with the Parmesan.

per serving

Calories 141	Cholesterol 4 mg	Dietary Exchanges
Total Fat 2.0 g	Sodium 185 mg	½ starch, 3 vegetable,
Saturated Fat 0.5 g	Carbohydrates 24 g	½ lean meat
Trans Fat 0.0 g	Fiber 6 g	
Polyunsaturated Fat 0.0 g	Sugars 8 g	
Monounsaturated Fat 0.5 g	Protein 8 g	

korean beef soup

serves 6
1½ cups per serving

slow cooker size/shape
3- to 4½-quart round or oval

slow cooking time
8 to 10 hours on low
plus 5 to 8 minutes on low, **OR**
4 to 5 hours on high
plus 5 to 8 minutes on low

5 cups fat-free, low-sodium beef broth, such as on page 32

2 cups chopped onions

1 large red bell pepper, cut into 1-inch squares

1 cup sliced carrots (¼-inch pieces)

2 tablespoons soy sauce (lowest sodium available)

1 tablespoon toasted sesame oil

3 large garlic cloves, minced

¼ to ½ teaspoon chili garlic sauce or paste

■ ■ ■

2 cups fresh bean sprouts

6 ounces dried linguine-style rice noodles

1 teaspoon canola or corn oil

1 pound boneless top sirloin steak, all visible fat discarded, cut into thin strips

¼ cup thinly sliced green onions

1 tablespoon sesame seeds, dry-roasted

A slow-cooked, veggie-rich beef broth makes the flavorful base for this soup, which is a simplified version of a Korean soup that usually calls for marrow bones and knuckle bones to be simmered in the stock.

In the slow cooker, stir together the broth, onions, bell pepper, carrots, soy sauce, sesame oil, garlic, and chili garlic sauce. Cook, covered, on low for 8 to 10 hours or on high for 4 to 5 hours, or until the vegetables are tender.

Quickly stir in the bean sprouts and rice noodles and re-cover the slow cooker. If using the high setting, change it to low. Cook for 5 to 8 minutes, or until the bean sprouts are steaming hot (this is very important for food safety) and the rice noodles are tender but with a slight bite.

Meanwhile, in a large nonstick skillet, heat the canola oil over medium-high heat, swirling to coat the bottom. Cook the beef for 3 to 5 minutes, or until browned on the outside but still pink in the center, stirring constantly. Don't overcook or the beef will become tough. Stir the beef into the soup. Ladle into bowls. Sprinkle with the green onions and sesame seeds.

cook's tip: If you can't find linguine-style rice noodles, you can substitute whole-grain linguine. Prepare the pasta using the package directions, omitting the salt, before adding it to the slow cooker.

per serving

Calories 306	Cholesterol 40 mg	Dietary Exchanges
Total Fat 7.5 g	Sodium 261 mg	1½ starch, 2 vegetable,
Saturated Fat 2.0 g	Carbohydrates 34 g	2½ lean meat
Trans Fat 0.0 g	Fiber 4 g	
Polyunsaturated Fat 2.0 g	Sugars 7 g	
Monounsaturated Fat 3.5 g	Protein 25 g	

countryside beef and garden vegetable soup

serves 6
1 cup per serving

slow cooker size/shape
3- to 4½-quart round or oval

slow cooking time
7½ to 8 hours on low plus
30 minutes on high, **OR**
3 hours 45 minutes to 4 hours
on high plus 30 minutes
on high

1 teaspoon canola or corn oil

12 ounces boneless chuck
shoulder pot roast, all visible
fat discarded

1 cup water and 1 cup water,
divided use

4 medium tomatoes, chopped

1 large red or yellow bell pepper,
chopped

1 cup fresh cauliflower florets
(about 1-inch pieces)

1 medium red potato (about 6
ounces), chopped

4 ounces fresh or frozen cut
green beans, cut into 1½-inch
pieces if fresh, thawed if frozen

1 medium rib of celery, thinly
sliced crosswise

2 tablespoons no-salt-added
tomato paste

1½ tablespoons sugar

1 tablespoon Worcestershire
sauce (lowest sodium available)

(continued)

The pot roast in this soup cooks to such sublime tenderness that you can easily shred it with a fork. *(See photo insert.)*

In a medium nonstick skillet, heat the oil over medium heat, swirling to coat the bottom. Cook the beef on one side for 3 minutes, or until browned. Transfer with the browned side up to the slow cooker.

Pour 1 cup water into the skillet, scraping the bottom and side to dislodge any browned bits. Pour into the slow cooker. Stir in the remaining ingredients including the additional 1 cup water but not the cabbage. Cook, covered, on low for 7½ to 8 hours or on high for 3 hours 45 minutes to 4 hours, or until the beef is very tender.

Quickly transfer the beef to a cutting board, leaving the liquid in the slow cooker. Quickly stir in the cabbage and re-cover the slow cooker. If using the low setting, change it to high. Cook for 30 minutes, or until the cabbage is tender.

Meanwhile, using one or two forks, shred the beef. Set aside until the cabbage is ready. Stir the beef into the soup.

cook's tip: Using precut veggies from the wide range in the produce area or salad bar of your grocery store will save you time. In addition, when you need only a small amount, you can actually save money with precut produce because you buy only what you need—no wasted veggies.

cook's tip on chuck shoulder: Chuck is a lean, flavorful, and inexpensive beef cut taken from between the neck and the shoulder blade. It's a great way to get beefy flavor without the fat that many other cuts contain. For maximum tenderness, chuck cuts need to be cooked slowly and in liquid, making them an excellent choice for the slow cooker.

1 tablespoon cider vinegar

2 teaspoons dried oregano, crumbled

1 packet (1 teaspoon) salt-free beef bouillon

½ teaspoon salt

■ ■ ■

1½ cups coarsely chopped cabbage

per serving

Calories 173
Total Fat 5.0 g
 Saturated Fat 1.5 g
 Trans Fat 0.0 g
 Polyunsaturated Fat 0.5 g
 Monounsaturated Fat 2.5 g

Cholesterol 30 mg
Sodium 252 mg
Carbohydrates 19 g
 Fiber 4 g
 Sugars 10 g
Protein 14 g

Dietary Exchanges
½ starch, 2 vegetable,
1½ lean meat

beef barley soup with vegetables

serves 4
1¾ cups per serving

slow cooker size/shape
4- to 6-quart round or oval

slow cooking time
5 hours 45 minutes to 7 hours
45 minutes on low plus
15 minutes on low, **OR**
2½ to 3½ hours on high
plus 15 minutes on low

---

1 pound lean stew meat, all visible fat discarded

3½ cups fat-free, low-sodium beef broth, such as on page 32

½ cup water

1 medium green bell pepper, diced

⅔ cup chopped onion

⅔ cup frozen whole-kernel corn, thawed

⅔ cup frozen cut (not chopped) broccoli

½ cup sliced carrot

1 packet (1 teaspoon) salt-free beef bouillon

1 teaspoon dried thyme, crumbled

1 teaspoon extra-spicy salt-free all-purpose seasoning blend (optional)

½ teaspoon pepper

¼ teaspoon salt

■ ■ ■

⅓ cup uncooked quick-cooking barley

Classic beef barley soup gets a tasty makeover courtesy of a wide array of colorful, healthy vegetables.

In the slow cooker, stir together all the ingredients except the barley. Cook, covered, on low for 5 hours 45 minutes to 7 hours 45 minutes or on high for 2½ to 3½ hours.

Quickly stir in the barley and re-cover the slow cooker. If using the high setting, change it to low. Cook for 15 minutes, or until the barley is tender.

per serving

Calories 271	Cholesterol 71 mg	Dietary Exchanges
Total Fat 8.5 g	Sodium 269 mg	1 starch, 1 vegetable,
Saturated Fat 3.0 g	Carbohydrates 23 g	3 lean meat
Trans Fat 0.0 g	Fiber 4 g	
Polyunsaturated Fat 0.5 g	Sugars 4 g	
Monounsaturated Fat 3.5 g	Protein 27 g	

balsamic beef borscht

serves 8
1½ cups per serving

slow cooker size/shape
3- to 4½-quart round or oval

slow cooking time
8 to 10 hours on low, **OR**
4 to 5 hours on high

1 teaspoon olive oil and 1 teaspoon olive oil, divided use

1½ pounds boneless top round steak, all visible fat discarded, diced and patted dry

2 medium ribs of celery, sliced crosswise into ¼-inch pieces

1 medium onion, chopped

4 medium garlic cloves, minced

4 cups finely sliced green or red cabbage (about 1 pound)

3 medium beets (about 1 pound total), peeled and diced

1 cup thinly sliced carrots

1 medium red, yellow, or green bell pepper, diced

1 medium dried bay leaf

2 cups fat-free, low-sodium beef broth, such as on page 32, or water

1 6-ounce can no-salt-added tomato paste

4 cups water

½ teaspoon salt

½ teaspoon pepper

■ ■ ■

2 tablespoons balsamic vinegar

2 tablespoons plus 2 teaspoons fat-free sour cream (optional)

Often made primarily of beets and served hot or cold as a side dish, borscht can also be a hearty meal when you add beef and lots of other vegetables to the mix. The sweetness of the balsamic vinegar brings out the flavor of the vegetables, and the bit of sour cream provides a nice color contrast to the soup.

In a large nonstick skillet, heat 1 teaspoon oil over medium-high heat, swirling to coat the bottom. Cook the beef for 5 minutes, or until browned on all sides, stirring occasionally. Transfer to the slow cooker. Set aside.

In the same skillet, heat the remaining 1 teaspoon oil, still over medium-high heat, swirling to coat the bottom. Cook the celery, onion, and garlic for 5 minutes, or until softened, stirring occasionally and reducing the heat to medium if necessary. Spread over the beef.

Making a layer of each, add the cabbage, beets, carrots, and bell pepper. Don't stir. Put the bay leaf on top. Set aside.

In a large bowl, whisk together the broth and tomato paste. Whisk in the water, salt, and pepper. Pour into the slow cooker. Don't stir. Cook, covered, on low for 8 to 10 hours or on high for 4 to 5 hours, or until the beef is tender. Discard the bay leaf.

Just before serving, stir in the vinegar. Top each serving with the sour cream.

per serving

Calories 178	Cholesterol 43 mg	Dietary Exchanges
Total Fat 3.5 g	Sodium 261 mg	3 vegetable, 2½ lean
Saturated Fat 1.0 g	Carbohydrates 15 g	meat
Trans Fat 0.0 g	Fiber 4 g	
Polyunsaturated Fat 0.5 g	Sugars 9 g	
Monounsaturated Fat 2.0 g	Protein 22 g	

black bean and jalapeño soup

serves 4
1 cup per serving

slow cooker size/shape
3- to 4½-quart round or oval

slow cooking time
9½ to 10 hours on low, **OR**
4 hours 45 minutes to 5 hours
on high

1 quart water

8 ounces dried black beans
   (about 1 cup), sorted for stones
   and shriveled beans, rinsed,
   and drained

   Cooking spray

3 cups fat-free, low-sodium
   vegetable broth, such as on
   page 33

1 medium onion, diced

1 4-ounce can chopped mild
   green chiles, undrained

3 medium fresh jalapeños, seeds
   and ribs discarded if desired,
   diced

2 medium dried bay leaves

½ teaspoon dried thyme,
   crumbled

½ teaspoon ground cumin

■ ■ ■

2 tablespoons olive oil (extra
   virgin preferred)

½ teaspoon salt

¼ cup snipped fresh cilantro

1 medium lime, cut into 4 wedges

You might think that three jalapeños would make this soup too hot to handle, but they don't. Cooking them over a long period of time lessens the heat, but not the flavor. Still concerned? Discard the seeds and ribs before dicing the peppers.

In a large saucepan, stir together the water and beans. Bring to a boil over high heat. Reduce the heat and simmer for 2 minutes. Remove from the heat. Let stand, covered, for 1 hour.

Lightly spray the slow cooker with cooking spray. Rinse and drain the beans in a colander. Transfer to the slow cooker. Stir in the broth, onion, green chiles, jalapeños, bay leaves, thyme, and cumin. Cook, covered, on low for 9½ to 10 hours or on high for 4 hours 45 minutes to 5 hours, or until the beans are soft.

Stir in the oil and salt. Discard the bay leaves. Just before serving, sprinkle with the cilantro. Serve with the lime wedges to squeeze over the soup.

cook's tip: If you have leftovers or make the soup in advance for more intense flavor, leave the bay leaves in until after you reheat the soup. Don't sprinkle with the cilantro or squeeze the lime wedges over the soup until serving time.

per serving

Calories 262	Cholesterol 0 mg	Dietary Exchanges
Total Fat 7.5 g	Sodium 437 mg	2 starch, 1 vegetable,
Saturated Fat 1.0 g	Carbohydrates 37 g	1 lean meat, 1 fat
Trans Fat 0.0 g	Fiber 13 g	
Polyunsaturated Fat 1.0 g	Sugars 3 g	
Monounsaturated Fat 5.0 g	Protein 13 g	

jamaican bean and vegetable soup

serves 4
1¾ cups per serving

slow cooker size/shape
3- to 4½-quart round or oval

slow cooking time
5 to 6 hours on low, **OR**
2½ to 3 hours on high

2½ cups fat-free, low-sodium
  vegetable broth, such as on
  page 33

1 15.5-ounce can no-salt-added
  red kidney or black beans,
  rinsed and drained

1 14.5-ounce can no-salt-added
  diced tomatoes, undrained

1 medium sweet potato, peeled
  and cut into 1-inch cubes

2 medium carrots, cut crosswise
  into ¼- to ½-inch pieces

½ medium red bell pepper,
  chopped

½ medium onion, chopped

2 medium garlic cloves, minced

1 teaspoon ground cumin

⅛ teaspoon salt

⅛ teaspoon crushed red pepper
  flakes

Experience the flavor of a different cuisine right in your own kitchen with this soup, which was inspired by a traditional Jamaican dish, red pea soup (red peas are kidney beans). The hot pepper, tomatoes, and sweet potato also are common in Jamaican cooking.

In the slow cooker, stir together all the ingredients. Cook, covered, on low for 5 to 6 hours or on high for 2½ to 3 hours.

per serving

Calories 184
Total Fat 0.5 g
  Saturated Fat 0.0 g
  Trans Fat 0.0 g
  Polyunsaturated Fat 0.0 g
  Monounsaturated Fat 0.0 g

Cholesterol 0 mg
Sodium 187 mg
Carbohydrates 37 g
  Fiber 13 g
  Sugars 11 g
  Protein 10 g

Dietary Exchanges
  2 starch, 2 vegetable

smoky split pea soup

serves 5
1½ cups per serving

slow cooker size/shape
4- to 6-quart round or oval

slow cooking time
8 to 10 hours on low, **OR**
5 to 6 hours on high

4 cups fat-free, low-sodium
   vegetable broth, such as on
   page 33

1 pound dried green split peas
   (about 2¼ cups), sorted for
   stones and shriveled peas,
   rinsed, and drained

2 cups water

2 medium carrots, chopped

2 medium ribs of celery, chopped

1 medium onion, diced

2 teaspoons ground cumin

2 teaspoons minced chipotle
   pepper canned in adobo sauce

2 medium garlic cloves, minced

½ teaspoon salt

¼ teaspoon pepper

■ ■ ■

1 tablespoon plus 1 teaspoon
   white wine vinegar

Canned chipotle pepper adds a smoky hint to this soup, which is not only delicious but also high fiber and low cost.

In the slow cooker, stir together all the ingredients except the vinegar. Cook, covered, on low for 8 to 10 hours or on high for 5 to 6 hours, or until the peas are tender. Stir in the vinegar.

cook's tip: The amount of chipotle in this recipe adds a mild smokiness and a bit of spice. If you're tempted to add more, wait until the soup is done and taste it first; although some seasonings lose their strength with the long cooking time, the chile flavor can intensify.

per serving

Calories 343	Cholesterol 0 mg	Dietary Exchanges
Total Fat 1.5 g	Sodium 326 mg	4 starch, 2 very lean
Saturated Fat 0.0 g	Carbohydrates 62 g	meat
Trans Fat 0.0 g	Fiber 25 g	
Polyunsaturated Fat 0.5 g	Sugars 11 g	
Monounsaturated Fat 0.0 g	Protein 23 g	

curried lentil and vegetable soup

serves 5
1⅔ cups per serving

slow cooker size/shape
3- to 4½-quart round or oval

slow cooking time
7 to 8 hours on low, **OR**
3 to 4 hours on high

A hefty dose of curry powder flavors the lentils and vegetables in this soup and transforms it from ordinary to exotic.

2 cups water

1 14.5-ounce can no-salt-added diced tomatoes, undrained

1¾ cups fat-free, low-sodium vegetable broth, such as on page 33

⅔ cup dried lentils, sorted for stones and shriveled lentils, rinsed, and drained

2 medium carrots, chopped

1 medium potato, chopped

1 medium rib of celery, chopped

½ medium onion, chopped

1 tablespoon plus 1 teaspoon curry powder

1 tablespoon dried minced garlic

1½ teaspoons ground cumin

½ teaspoon salt

½ teaspoon pepper

⅛ teaspoon crushed red pepper flakes

In the slow cooker, stir together all the ingredients. Cook, covered, on low for 7 to 8 hours or on high for 3 to 4 hours.

cook's tip on dried seasonings in slow cooking: Whenever you cook with dried herbs and spices, you want them to still be aromatic and not "over the hill." This is especially so in slow cooking because seasonings that are past their prime not only won't add full flavor but may even give your dish a bitter or stale taste. It's recommended that you use dried herbs and spices within six months of purchase or freeze them for longer storage.

per serving

Calories 169	Cholesterol 0 mg	Dietary Exchanges
Total Fat 0.5 g	Sodium 293 mg	1½ starch, 2 vegetable,
Saturated Fat 0.0 g	Carbohydrates 33 g	½ lean meat
Trans Fat 0.0 g	Fiber 7 g	
Polyunsaturated Fat 0.0 g	Sugars 7 g	
Monounsaturated Fat 0.0 g	Protein 10 g	

persian red lentil soup

serves 6
1½ cups per serving

slow cooker size/shape
4- to 6-quart round or oval

slow cooking time
6 to 8 hours on low, **OR**
3 to 4 hours on high

1 tablespoon olive oil

1½ cups chopped onions

4 large garlic cloves, minced

1 cup sliced carrots (1-inch pieces)

1 cup sliced celery (1-inch pieces)

4 cups fat-free, low-sodium vegetable broth, such as on page 33

1 pound dried red lentils (about 2 cups), sorted for stones and shriveled lentils, rinsed, and drained

2 cups cauliflower florets (about 1½-inch pieces) (about 1¼-pound head)

1 teaspoon ground allspice

1 teaspoon paprika

½ teaspoon ground cinnamon

¼ teaspoon salt

¼ teaspoon pepper

¼ teaspoon ground cardamom

■ ■ ■

¼ cup plus 2 tablespoons fat-free plain yogurt

The spice mix in this soup is based on *baharat*, a Persian spice blend now used in many North African countries and from Turkey to Syria and Iran. Its slightly sweet flavor hides a kick of spice.

In a large nonstick skillet, heat the oil over medium-high heat, swirling to coat the bottom. Cook the onions for 3 minutes, or until soft, stirring frequently.

Stir in the garlic. Cook for 30 seconds, stirring constantly.

Stir in the carrots and celery. Cook for 2 minutes, or until beginning to soften, stirring frequently. Transfer to the slow cooker.

Stir the remaining ingredients except the yogurt into the onion mixture. Cook, covered, on low for 6 to 8 hours or on high for 3 to 4 hours, or until the lentils and vegetables are very tender.

Serve with a dollop of yogurt spooned onto each serving.

cook's tip on red lentils: Red lentils are smaller and rounder than the more common brown lentils. The red will cook to a softer, creamier consistency because they are skinless. If you can't find red lentils, you can use brown in this recipe.

cook's tip on baharat: Like many other traditional blends, *baharat* varies from cook to cook, but it often contains about nine spices. Black pepper, cinnamon, and allspice are quite common in *baharat,* which often includes cumin as well. Try using it to season meats, vegetables, and rice dishes.

per serving

Calories 330	Cholesterol 0 mg	Dietary Exchanges
Total Fat 3.5 g	Sodium 190 mg	3 starch, 2 vegetable,
Saturated Fat 0.5 g	Carbohydrates 55 g	2 lean meat
Trans Fat 0.0 g	Fiber 20 g	
Polyunsaturated Fat 0.5 g	Sugars 9 g	
Monounsaturated Fat 2.0 g	Protein 24 g	

moroccan lentil soup

serves 8
1½ cups per serving

slow cooker size/shape
5- to 7-quart round or oval

slow cooking time
8 to 10 hours on low, **OR**
5 to 6 hours on high

4 cups fat-free, low-sodium
   vegetable broth, such as on
   page 33

4 cups water

1 pound dried brown lentils
   (about 2¼ cups), sorted for
   stones and shriveled lentils,
   rinsed, and drained

1 14.5-ounce can no-salt-added
   diced tomatoes, undrained

1 medium onion, chopped

1 medium red bell pepper,
   chopped

½ cup no-salt-added tomato
   paste

2 medium garlic cloves, minced

2 teaspoons grated peeled
   gingerroot

1 teaspoon ground cumin

1 teaspoon ground turmeric

½ teaspoon salt

⅛ teaspoon ground cinnamon

■ ■ ■

1 tablespoon fresh lime juice

½ cup snipped fresh mint, parsley,
   or cilantro or finely chopped
   green onions

Filled with spices popular in Moroccan cuisine,
this budget-minded soup has international flavor
befitting a gourmet meal.

In the slow cooker, stir together the broth, water, lentils,
tomatoes with liquid, onion, bell pepper, tomato paste, garlic, gingerroot, cumin, turmeric, salt, and cinnamon. Cook,
covered, on low for 8 to 10 hours or on high for 5 to 6 hours.

Just before serving, stir in the lime juice. Sprinkle each serving with the mint.

per serving

Calories 233	Cholesterol 0 mg	Dietary Exchanges
Total Fat 1.0 g	Sodium 204 mg	2 starch, 2 vegetable,
Saturated Fat 0.0 g	Carbohydrates 42 g	1 lean meat
Trans Fat 0.0 g	Fiber 15 g	
Polyunsaturated Fat 0.5 g	Sugars 9 g	
Monounsaturated Fat 0.0 g	Protein 17 g	

seafood

lemony fish and vegetable stew

serves 5
1½ cups per serving

slow cooker size/shape
4- to 6-quart round or oval

slow cooking time
8 to 10 hours on low
plus 20 minutes on high, **OR**
5 to 6 hours on high
plus 20 minutes on high

2 14.5-ounce cans no-salt-added diced tomatoes, undrained

2 cups fat-free, low-sodium chicken broth, such as on page 31

2 medium carrots, chopped

2 medium ribs of celery, chopped

1 medium onion, chopped

¼ cup no-salt-added tomato paste

2 medium garlic cloves, minced

½ teaspoon dried basil, crumbled

½ teaspoon dried oregano, crumbled

⅛ teaspoon pepper

■ ■ ■

1 pound thin mild white fish fillets, such as tilapia or cod, rinsed and patted dry, cut into ½-inch squares

2 tablespoons snipped fresh parsley

2 teaspoons grated lemon zest

1 tablespoon fresh lemon juice

This easy Italian recipe turns simple ingredients into a satisfying fish stew. Stir in fresh parsley and lemon just before serving for a bit of panache.

In the slow cooker, stir together the tomatoes with liquid, broth, carrots, celery, onion, tomato paste, garlic, basil, oregano, and pepper. Cook, covered, on low for 8 to 10 hours or on high for 5 to 6 hours, or until the vegetables are tender.

If using the low setting, change it to high. Quickly stir in the fish and re-cover the slow cooker. Cook for 20 minutes, or until the fish flakes easily when tested with a fork. Just before serving, stir in the parsley, lemon zest, and lemon juice.

cook's tip on testing fish for doneness: When you check the fish for doneness, work as quickly as you can and re-cover the slow cooker quickly as well so you don't lose a lot of heat (in case you need to continue cooking the fish).

per serving

Calories 168
Total Fat 1.5 g
  Saturated Fat 0.5 g
  Trans Fat 0.0 g
  Polyunsaturated Fat 0.5 g
  Monounsaturated Fat 0.5 g

Cholesterol 45 mg
Sodium 136 mg
Carbohydrates 17 g
  Fiber 4 g
  Sugars 10 g
Protein 22 g

Dietary Exchanges
  3 vegetable, 2½ lean meat

fish amandine in foil

serves 4
3 ounces fish per serving

slow cooker size/shape
3- to 4½-quart oval

slow cooking time
1½ to 2 hours on high

4 slices red onion

4 thin mild white fish fillets,
   such as tilapia, sole, or walleye
   (about 4 ounces each), rinsed
   and patted dry

¼ teaspoon pepper

¼ teaspoon paprika

⅛ teaspoon salt

1 tablespoon plus 1 teaspoon
   sliced almonds

■ ■ ■

2 tablespoons sliced green
   onions

1 medium lemon, cut into
   4 wedges

cook's tip: An oval slow cooker works
best for this recipe because you want to
lay the foil packet as flat as possible in
the cooker.

This take on fish amandine, which calls for all the
fillets to be enclosed in one aluminum foil packet,
would be delicious with a crisp salad, steamed
carrots seasoned with your favorite herb, and a
whole-grain roll.

Cut an 18 x 12-inch sheet of aluminum foil. Put the foil on a
flat surface so that a long end faces you. Place the onion slices
in the middle of the foil, making two rows of two slices each.
Space the slices somewhat apart—they will form a "rack" for
the fish. Center a fillet on each onion slice so that the fillets are
parallel to the short ends of the foil and the thin ends of the
fish overlap in the middle. Sprinkle the fish with the pepper,
paprika, and salt. Using your fingertips, gently press the seasonings so they adhere to the fish. Sprinkle with the almonds.

Bring the short ends of the foil together and crimp to seal.
Leaving a small amount of air space in the packet, crimp the
long ends (don't bring them to the center). Place the packet
in the slow cooker. Cook, covered, on high for 1½ to 2 hours,
or until the fish flakes easily when tested with a fork. (Use
the tines of a fork to carefully open the packet away from
you to avoid steam burns.)

When the fish is done, carefully remove the packet from the
slow cooker. Again using the tines of a fork, carefully open
it away from you. Sprinkle the fish with the green onions.
Serve the lemon wedges on the side to squeeze over the fish.

per serving

Calories 126
Total Fat 3.0 g
   Saturated Fat 0.5 g
   Trans Fat 0.0 g
   Polyunsaturated Fat 0.5 g
   Monounsaturated Fat 1.0 g

Cholesterol 57 mg
Sodium 133 mg
Carbohydrates 2 g
   Fiber 1 g
   Sugars 1 g
Protein 23 g

Dietary Exchanges
   3 lean meat

citrus cod

serves 4
3 ounces fish per serving

slow cooker size/shape
3- to 4½-quart round or oval

slow cooking time
1½ to 2 hours on high

4 cod or other mild white fish fillets (about 4 ounces each), about ½ inch thick, rinsed and patted dry

1 tablespoon grated orange zest

½ cup fresh orange juice

2 tablespoons snipped fresh parsley

1 teaspoon fresh lemon juice

1 medium garlic clove, minced

■ ■ ■

1 tablespoon plus 1 teaspoon chopped green onions (green part only)

Fresh orange juice and zest, with a bit of lemon juice added for good measure, are the major flavor components of this easy fish dish.

Place the fish in the slow cooker.

In a small bowl, stir together the remaining ingredients except the green onions. Pour over the fish, gently turning to coat. Cook, covered, on high for 1½ to 2 hours, or until the fish flakes easily when tested with a fork. Serve sprinkled with the green onions.

cook's tip on mild white fish: Any number of factors may affect your choice of fish for this and other recipes that call for mild white fish. Let your taste preferences and the availability, freshness, price, and current recommendations for seafood sustainability guide your selections.

per serving

Calories 101
Total Fat 1.0 g
  Saturated Fat 0.0 g
  Trans Fat 0.0 g
  Polyunsaturated Fat 0.0 g
  Monounsaturated Fat 0.0 g

Cholesterol 43 mg
Sodium 63 mg
Carbohydrates 4 g
  Fiber 0 g
  Sugars 3 g
  Protein 18 g

Dietary Exchanges
3 lean meat

salmon with cucumber-dill aïoli

serves 6
3 ounces fish and 1 heaping tablespoon aïoli per serving

slow cooker size/shape
3-quart round or oval (preferred)

slow cooking time
1½ to 2½ hours on low, **OR** 1 hour to 1 hour 15 minutes on high

---

1½ large onions, coarsely chopped

4 to 5 large garlic cloves, coarsely chopped

3 cups water

3 slices lemon

1½ pounds salmon fillet, about 1 inch thick, skin discarded, rinsed and patted dry

■ ■ ■

3 tablespoons finely chopped peeled and seeded cucumber

¼ cup plus 2 tablespoons light mayonnaise

1½ teaspoons snipped fresh dillweed

¾ teaspoon fresh lemon juice

¾ to 1½ medium garlic cloves, minced

Dash of pepper

Using a slow cooker is the ultimate way to poach salmon because the fish will cook slowly and evenly. This poached salmon is served with a garlicky mayonnaise known as aïoli (ay-OH-lee or i-OH-lee), given a twist here with the addition of cucumber and fresh dillweed.

Put the onions and garlic in the slow cooker. Pour in the water. Add the lemon slices. Place the fish on top. Cook, covered, on low for 1½ to 2½ hours or on high for 1 hour to 1 hour 15 minutes, or until the fish is the desired doneness. Watch the fish carefully to make sure it doesn't overcook.

Just before serving, place the chopped cucumber on a cutting board. Using the side of a chef's knife or the tines of a fork, crush the cucumber. Transfer it and any liquid to a small bowl. Stir in the remaining ingredients to make the aïoli.

When the fish is ready, using a slotted spatula, carefully transfer it to a platter. Discard the cooking liquid, onion, garlic, and lemon. Serve with the aïoli to spoon on top or use as a dipping sauce.

cook's tip: Using crushed cucumber will yield a smoother sauce that still has some texture.

per serving

Calories 135	Cholesterol 40 mg	Dietary Exchanges
Total Fat 7.0 g	Sodium 188 mg	2½ lean meat
Saturated Fat 1.0 g	Carbohydrates 1 g	
Trans Fat 0.0 g	Fiber 0 g	
Polyunsaturated Fat 3.0 g	Sugars 0 g	
Monounsaturated Fat 2.0 g	Protein 16 g	

salmon fillets with pineapple-melon relish

serves 4
3 ounces fish and ⅓ cup relish per serving

slow cooker size/shape
3- to 4½-quart round or oval

slow cooking time
3 hours on low, **OR**
1½ hours on high

Cooking spray

1 large lemon, cut crosswise into 6 slices

4 salmon fillets with skin (about 5 ounces each), rinsed and patted dry

¼ cup water

1 teaspoon salt-free steak seasoning blend

½ teaspoon dried thyme, crumbled

¼ teaspoon garlic powder

¼ teaspoon salt

▪ ▪ ▪

½ cup diced fresh pineapple

½ cup diced cantaloupe

3 tablespoons to ¼ cup chopped fresh mint

1 medium fresh jalapeño, seeds and ribs discarded, minced

2 tablespoons finely chopped red onion

1 teaspoon grated lemon zest

1 tablespoon fresh lemon juice

2 teaspoons sugar

Steak seasoning blend is an unexpected but surprisingly effective flavoring for moist salmon fillets, made even more delicious with a minty, zesty fruit relish. *(See photo insert.)*

Lightly spray the slow cooker with cooking spray. Arrange the lemon slices in a single layer in the slow cooker. Place the fish with the skin side down on the lemon. Pour the water over the fish.

In a small bowl, stir together the seasoning blend, thyme, garlic powder, and salt. Sprinkle over the fish. Using your fingertips, gently press the seasonings so they adhere to the fish. Cook, covered, on low for 3 hours or on high for 1½ hours, or to the desired doneness.

About 15 minutes before serving time, in a small bowl, stir together the remaining ingredients. Set the relish aside.

Using a slotted spatula, transfer the fish to a serving platter, discarding the cooking liquid and lemon. Serve the fish with the relish spooned on top or at the side.

per serving

Calories 183	Cholesterol 53 mg	Dietary Exchanges
Total Fat 5.0 g	Sodium 241 mg	½ fruit, 3 lean meat
Saturated Fat 1.0 g	Carbohydrates 9 g	
Trans Fat 0.0 g	Fiber 1 g	
Polyunsaturated Fat 1.0 g	Sugars 6 g	
Monounsaturated Fat 1.5 g	Protein 25 g	

mojito salmon

QUICK
PREP

serves 6
3 ounces fish per serving

slow cooker size/shape
3-quart round or oval
(preferred)

slow cooking time
1½ to 2½ hours on low, **OR**
1 hour to 1 hour 15 minutes
on high

1½ **large onions, coarsely chopped**

2¼ **cups water**

¾ **cup dry white wine (regular or nonalcoholic) or water**

½ **medium lime, cut into 3 slices**

1½ **pounds salmon fillet, about 1 inch thick, skin discarded, rinsed and patted dry**

▪ ▪ ▪

3 **tablespoons snipped fresh Italian (flat-leaf) parsley**

3 **tablespoons thinly sliced green onions**

1½ **tablespoons chopped fresh mint**

1 **tablespoon grated lime zest**

▪ ▪ ▪

1½ **medium limes, cut into 6 wedges**

A topping with fresh mint and lime mimics a refreshing mojito and pairs perfectly with the silky consistency of slow-cooked salmon.

Put the onion in the slow cooker. Pour in the water and wine. Add the lime slices. Place the fish on top. Cook, covered, on low for 1½ to 2½ hours or on high for 1 hour to 1 hour 15 minutes, or until the desired doneness. Check the fish at the minimum cooking time to make sure it doesn't overcook.

Just before serving, in a small bowl, stir together the remaining ingredients except the lime wedges.

When the fish is ready, using a slotted spatula, carefully transfer it to a platter. Discard the cooking liquid, onion, and lime. Sprinkle the fish with the parsley mixture. Serve with the lime wedges to squeeze on top.

per serving

Calories 151
Total Fat 5.0 g
  Saturated Fat 1.0 g
  Trans Fat 0.0 g
  Polyunsaturated Fat 1.0 g
  Monounsaturated Fat 1.5 g

Cholesterol 53 mg
Sodium 90 mg
Carbohydrates 1 g
  Fiber 0 g
  Sugars 0 g
  Protein 24 g

Dietary Exchanges
  3 lean meat

asparagus-and-sole rolls

serves 4
1 roll per serving

slow cooker size/shape
3- to 4½-quart round or oval

slow cooking time
1 to 1½ hours on high

1 medium shallot, sliced

½ medium lemon, cut crosswise
into 4 slices

¼ cup water

4 sole or other thin mild fish
fillets (about 4 ounces each),
rinsed and patted dry

20 pencil-thin asparagus spears
(each about 6 inches long),
trimmed

¼ teaspoon pepper

⅛ teaspoon salt

■ ■ ■

1 tablespoon plus 1 teaspoon
snipped fresh parsley

1 medium lemon, cut into
4 wedges

Spring has sprung and the really thin spears of asparagus have arrived. Wrap some in mild fish fillets, turn on the slow cooker, and in an hour or so, enjoy your dinner.

Put the shallot, lemon slices, and water in the slow cooker. Set aside.

Wrap a fish fillet around a bundle of 5 asparagus spears. Transfer the roll with the smooth side up to the slow cooker. Repeat with the remaining fish and asparagus. Sprinkle with the pepper and salt. Cook, covered, on high for 1 to 1½ hours, or until the fish flakes easily when tested with a fork. Transfer to plates.

Sprinkle the rolls with the parsley. Serve the lemon wedges on the side for squeezing over all.

cook's tip: If you can't find pencil-thin asparagus spears, cut thicker spears lengthwise to the proper thickness, or use three slightly larger spears instead of the five thin ones for each roll.

per serving

Calories 100	Cholesterol 51 mg	Dietary Exchanges
Total Fat 2.0 g	Sodium 409 mg	1 vegetable, 3 lean
Saturated Fat 0.5 g	Carbohydrates 4 g	meat
Trans Fat 0.0 g	Fiber 2 g	
Polyunsaturated Fat 0.5 g	Sugars 2 g	
Monounsaturated Fat 0.5 g	Protein 16 g	

lime-infused tilapia with salsa

serves 4
3 ounces fish and ¼ cup salsa
per serving

slow cooker size/shape
1½- to 2½-quart round or oval
(preferred)

slow cooking time
2 to 2½ hours on low, **OR**
1 hour to 1 hour 15 minutes
on high

1 medium and 1 large lime

1 teaspoon olive oil

1 cup chopped onion

2 medium garlic cloves, minced

1 pound tilapia or other thin
   mild white fish fillets, such
   as catfish, sole, striped bass,
   or red snapper, rinsed and
   patted dry

¼ teaspoon salt

⅛ teaspoon pepper

2 cups water (plus more as
   needed)

■ ■ ■

8 ounces tomatillos, papery
   husks discarded, rinsed well
   and coarsely chopped (about
   1¾ cups)

½ small serrano pepper, seeds and
   ribs discarded, minced (about
   1 teaspoon)

⅓ cup coarsely chopped onion

3 tablespoons snipped fresh
   cilantro

Here, tilapia is seasoned with fresh lime zest, cooked in a broth infused with lime, and served with a tomatillo salsa with a hint of lime.

Zest the limes, reserving 1½ teaspoons for the fish and ¾ teaspoon for the salsa. Cut 3 thin slices from one of the limes. Set aside the 1½ teaspoons zest and the lime slices. Save the remaining limes and zest for another use.

In a medium nonstick skillet, heat the oil over medium heat, swirling to coat the bottom. Cook 1 cup onion for 3 minutes, or until beginning to soften, stirring occasionally. Stir in the garlic. Cook for 30 seconds, stirring constantly. Transfer to the slow cooker. Top with the lime slices.

Sprinkle both sides of the fish with the salt, pepper, and 1½ teaspoons of the reserved lime zest. Using your finger-tips, gently press the seasonings so they adhere to the fish. Place the fish in the slow cooker; you may need to make two layers. Pour in the water, adding more if needed to barely cover the fish. Cook, covered, on low for 2 to 2½ hours or on high for 1 hour to 1 hour 15 minutes, or until the fish just begins to flake when tested with a fork. Using a slotted spatula, carefully transfer the fish to plates. Discard the cooking liquid, onion, and lime.

Meanwhile, in a food processor or blender, process the tomatillos, serrano pepper, remaining ⅓ cup onion, and remaining ¾ teaspoon reserved lime zest until almost smooth. Stir in the cilantro. At serving time, spoon the salsa over the fish.

per serving

Calories 145
Total Fat 3.5 g
   Saturated Fat 1.0 g
   Trans Fat 0.0 g
   Polyunsaturated Fat 1.0 g
   Monounsaturated Fat 1.5 g

Cholesterol 57 mg
Sodium 206 mg
Carbohydrates 5 g
   Fiber 2 g
   Sugars 3 g
Protein 24 g

Dietary Exchanges
   1 vegetable, 3 lean
   meat

tilapia with lemon potatoes

serves 4
3 ounces fish, ¾ cup potatoes, and ⅓ cup broth per serving

slow cooker size/shape
5- to 7-quart oval

slow cooking time
5 hours on high
plus 30 minutes on high

2½ **cups fat-free, low-sodium chicken broth, such as on page 31**

1 **pound medium red potatoes (about 3), halved and thinly sliced**

1 **small onion, thinly sliced**

1 **medium garlic clove**

2 **teaspoons grated lemon zest**

1 **tablespoon fresh lemon juice**

⅛ **teaspoon salt**

⅛ **teaspoon pepper**

■ ■ ■

4 **tilapia or other thin mild fish fillets (about 4 ounces each), rinsed and patted dry**

2 **teaspoons grated lemon zest**

⅛ **teaspoon salt**

⅛ **teaspoon pepper**

2 **tablespoons snipped fresh parsley**

The slow cooker makes this elegant dish easy enough for a weeknight. Let the potatoes simmer in the cooker while you go about your day, then add the fish and cook for 30 minutes. All that's left to do is cook your favorite green vegetable to serve alongside.

In the slow cooker, stir together the broth, potatoes, onion, garlic, 2 teaspoons lemon zest, the lemon juice, ⅛ teaspoon salt, and ⅛ teaspoon pepper. If the potatoes aren't submerged in the broth, add enough water to cover. Cook, covered, on high for 5 hours.

Sprinkle the fish on both sides with the remaining 2 teaspoons lemon zest, remaining ⅛ teaspoon salt, and remaining ⅛ teaspoon pepper. Using your fingertips, gently press the seasonings so they adhere to the fish. Transfer to the slow cooker, quickly arranging the fish in a single layer on the potatoes. Re-cover the slow cooker. Cook for 30 minutes, or until the fish flakes easily when tested with a fork.

At serving time, transfer the fish to soup bowls (large shallow bowls preferred). Stir the parsley into the potato mixture. Spoon the potatoes around the fish. Spoon the broth over all.

cook's tip: Although you can cook this dish on low (for 8 hours, plus 30 minutes on high after the fish is added), the potatoes turn an unappealing shade of brown.

per serving

Calories 210	Cholesterol 57 mg	Dietary Exchanges
Total Fat 2.0 g	Sodium 261 mg	1½ starch, 3 lean meat
Saturated Fat 0.5 g	Carbohydrates 22 g	
Trans Fat 0.0 g	Fiber 3 g	
Polyunsaturated Fat 0.5 g	Sugars 3 g	
Monounsaturated Fat 0.5 g	Protein 27 g	

whole rosemary trout

serves 4
3 ounces fish per serving

slow cooker size/shape
5- to 7-quart oval

slow cooking time
1½ to 2 hours on high

Cooking spray

1 medium shallot, sliced

4 whole trout (about 8 ounces each), rinsed and patted dry, heads discarded if desired

¼ teaspoon pepper

4 sprigs of fresh rosemary

¼ cup water

The slow cooker produces an extremely moist trout, this one suffused with savory rosemary. Add mixed-fruit salad and sautéed spinach for colorful, nutritious sides.

Lightly spray the slow cooker with cooking spray.

Spread the shallot slices in the slow cooker.

Sprinkle the cavity of each trout with pepper. Place a sprig of rosemary in each trout. Place the trout in the slow cooker (there may be some overlap). Cook, covered, on high for 1½ to 2 hours, or until the fish flakes easily when tested with a fork.

per serving

Calories 124
Total Fat 4.5 g
  Saturated Fat 1.0 g
  Trans Fat 0.0 g
  Polyunsaturated Fat 1.0 g
  Monounsaturated Fat 1.0 g

Cholesterol 98 mg
Sodium 69 mg
Carbohydrates 0 g
  Fiber 0 g
  Sugars 0 g
Protein 20 g

Dietary Exchanges
3 lean meat

super-simple asian tuna

serves 4
3 ounces fish per serving

slow cooker size/shape
3- to 4½-quart round or oval

slow cooking time
1 to 1½ hours on high

4 **medium green onions**

1 **1-pound tuna steak, about 1
inch thick, rinsed and patted
dry, cut into 4 pieces**

2 **teaspoons soy sauce (lowest
sodium available)**

1 **teaspoon minced peeled
gingerroot**

1 **medium garlic clove, minced**

¼ **to ½ teaspoon chili sauce, such
as sriracha**

Stir-fry or steam a colorful combination of vegetables to serve with this spicy tuna steak, which cooks on a "rack" of green onions. Adjust the amount of chili sauce to suit your love of spice.

Arrange the green onions in a single row in the slow cooker. Place the fish crosswise on the green onions.

In a small bowl, whisk together the remaining ingredients. Spread over the fish. Cook, covered, on high for 1 to 1½ hours, or until the fish is the desired doneness. Serve with the cooking liquid spooned on top.

cook's tip on chili sauces: When shopping for chili sauce for this recipe, be sure to buy the kind made primarily of hot peppers and garlic, not the mild tomato-based product that is often used as the sauce for shrimp cocktail.

per serving

Calories 137
Total Fat 0.5 g
  Saturated Fat 0.0 g
  Trans Fat 0.0 g
  Polyunsaturated Fat 0.0 g
  Monounsaturated Fat 0.0 g

Cholesterol 44 mg
Sodium 131 mg
Carbohydrates 3 g
  Fiber 1 g
  Sugars 1 g
Protein 28 g

Dietary Exchanges
3 lean meat

spanish-style tuna

serves 4
3 ounces fish and ¾ cup
vegetables per serving

slow cooker size/shape
3- to 4½-quart round or oval

slow cooking time
4 to 6 hours on low plus
5 to 20 minutes on high, **OR**
2 to 3 hours on high plus
5 to 20 minutes on high

Cooking spray

1 pound small red potatoes, 1½-
to 2 inch-diameter, quartered

1 medium green bell pepper,
diced

1 medium red bell pepper, diced

2 teaspoons olive oil

1 cup finely chopped onion

2 medium garlic cloves, minced

2 tablespoons all-purpose flour

1 cup fat-free, low-sodium
chicken broth, such as on
page 31

8 ounces Italian plum (Roma)
tomatoes, seeded and chopped

1 small fresh jalapeño, seeds and
ribs discarded, minced

1 medium dried bay leaf

½ teaspoon smoked paprika

¼ teaspoon salt

⅛ teaspoon pepper

■ ■ ■

1 pound tuna steaks, about 1
inch thick, rinsed and patted
dry, cut into 1-inch cubes

Fishermen in northern Spain are said to make a similar stew using ingredients they commonly carry aboard ship, such as the potatoes, bell peppers, onion, olive oil, garlic, and paprika used here, to complement their tuna catch.

Lightly spray the slow cooker with cooking spray. Put the potatoes and bell peppers in the slow cooker. Set aside.

In a large skillet, heat the oil over medium-high heat, swirling to coat the bottom. Cook the onion for 3 minutes, or until tender, stirring frequently. Stir in the garlic. Cook for 30 seconds, stirring constantly. Stir in the flour. Cook for 2 to 3 minutes, stirring constantly.

Pour in the broth, stirring to combine. Bring to a boil, still over medium-high heat. Boil for 1 minute, or until thickened, stirring constantly. Stir in the remaining ingredients except the fish. Pour into the slow cooker. Cook, covered, on low for 4 to 6 hours or on high for 2 to 3 hours, or until the potatoes are tender when pierced with a fork.

Quickly stir in the fish and re-cover the slow cooker. If using the low setting, change it to high. Cook for 5 to 20 minutes, or until the fish reaches the desired doneness. Discard the bay leaf before serving the fish.

per serving

Calories 281	Cholesterol 44 mg	Dietary Exchanges
Total Fat 3.5 g	Sodium 237 mg	1½ starch, 2 vegetable,
Saturated Fat 0.5 g	Carbohydrates 30 g	3 lean meat
Trans Fat 0.0 g	Fiber 5 g	
Polyunsaturated Fat 0.5 g	Sugars 7 g	
Monounsaturated Fat 2.0 g	Protein 32 g	

sicilian tuna farfalle

serves 4
scant 1½ cups per serving

slow cooker size/shape
2- to 3-quart round or oval

slow cooking time
8 to 10 hours on low
plus 15 minutes on low, **OR**
3½ to 4½ hours on high
plus 15 minutes on low

1 tablespoon olive oil

1½ cups chopped onions

2 medium ribs of celery,
including leaves, cut crosswise
into ½-inch pieces

3 large garlic cloves, minced

2 pounds 4 ounces Italian plum
(Roma) tomatoes, chopped
(about 6 cups)

1 tablespoon no-salt-added
tomato paste

¼ teaspoon salt

¼ teaspoon pepper

■ ■ ■

5 ounces canned very low sodium
white albacore tuna, packed in
water, drained and flaked

¼ cup halved kalamata olives

8 ounces dried whole-grain bow-
tie pasta (farfalle)

2 tablespoons snipped fresh basil

Slow cooking intensifies the sweetness of tomatoes, the staple ingredient for the simple, chunky sauce in this dish. Once the sauce is ready, add tuna and kalamata olives to warm up while you boil the pasta. A perfect weeknight entrée, this dish needs only a salad of mixed greens garnished with sweet onion and cucumber to round out the menu.

In a medium skillet, heat the oil over medium-high heat, swirling to coat the bottom. Cook the onions for 3 minutes or until soft, stirring frequently.

Stir in the celery and garlic. Cook for 30 seconds, stirring constantly. Transfer to the slow cooker.

Stir in the tomatoes, tomato paste, salt, and pepper. Cook, covered, on low for 8 to 10 hours or on high for 3½ to 4½ hours, or until the tomatoes are tender.

If using the high setting, change it to low. Quickly stir the tuna and olives into the sauce and re-cover the slow cooker. Cook for 15 minutes.

Meanwhile, prepare the pasta using the package directions, omitting the salt. Drain well in a colander. Serve the pasta topped with the sauce. Sprinkle with the basil.

cook's tip: Italian plum (Roma) tomatoes are the best tomatoes to use for this sauce because they have lots of thick pulp and less juice than other tomatoes.

per serving

Calories 383	Cholesterol 15 mg	Dietary Exchanges
Total Fat 9.0 g	Sodium 367 mg	3 starch, 3 vegetable,
Saturated Fat 1.0 g	Carbohydrates 61 g	1½ lean meat
Trans Fat 0.0 g	Fiber 11 g	
Polyunsaturated Fat 1.5 g	Sugars 13 g	
Monounsaturated Fat 5.0 g	Protein 20 g	

cioppino with white wine

serves 4
1¼ cups per serving

slow cooker size/shape
4- to 6-quart round or oval

slow cooking time
5 hours on low plus
20 minutes on high plus
15 minutes on high, **OR**
2½ hours on high
plus 20 minutes on high
plus 15 minutes on high

Cooking spray

1 14.5-ounce can no-salt-added diced tomatoes, undrained

1 medium onion, diced

½ cup dry white wine (regular or nonalcoholic)

2 medium garlic cloves, minced

⅛ to ¼ teaspoon crushed red pepper flakes

■ ■ ■

6 ounces bay or sea scallops, rinsed and patted dry, sea scallops quartered if large

12 fresh debearded and rinsed mussels in the shell

6 ounces tilapia fillets, rinsed and patted dry, cut into 1-inch pieces

¼ cup chopped fresh basil

2 tablespoons olive oil

⅛ teaspoon salt

Let this fish stew's saucy tomato base simmer on its own until almost mealtime, then add scallops, mussels, and finally bite-size pieces of mild fish. The result is perfection, since the slow cooker assures the gentle handling seafood needs.

Lightly spray the slow cooker with cooking spray. Put the tomatoes with liquid, onion, wine, garlic, and red pepper flakes in the slow cooker, stirring to combine. Cook, covered, on low for 5 hours or on high for 2½ hours, or until the onion is very soft.

If using the low setting, change it to high. Quickly stir in the scallops and mussels (don't add the fish here) and re-cover the slow cooker. Cook for 20 minutes.

Quickly and gently stir in the fish and the remaining ingredients. Re-cover the slow cooker. Cook for 15 minutes, or until the fish flakes easily when tested with a fork. Discard any unopened mussels. Ladle the cioppino into bowls.

cook's tip: Don't be tempted to add the fish with the scallops and mussels. It will overcook and break down, giving the dish an unappealing texture.

per serving

Calories 229	Cholesterol 45 mg	Dietary Exchanges
Total Fat 9.0 g	Sodium 414 mg	2 vegetable, 3 lean
Saturated Fat 1.5 g	Carbohydrates 12 g	meat
Trans Fat 0.0 g	Fiber 2 g	
Polyunsaturated Fat 1.0 g	Sugars 5 g	
Monounsaturated Fat 5.5 g	Protein 21 g	

shrimp jambalaya

QUICK PREP

serves 4
1½ cups per serving

slow cooker size/shape
3- to 4½-quart round or oval

slow cooking time
5 to 6 hours on low
plus 30 minutes on high, **OR**
2½ to 3 hours on high
plus 30 minutes on high

1 14.5-ounce can no-salt-added tomatoes, undrained

1 cup water (if cooking on low) or 1½ cups water (if cooking on high)

½ cup finely chopped onion

1 medium rib of celery, sliced crosswise

1 small green bell pepper, chopped

2 ounces lower-sodium, low-fat smoked ham, all visible fat discarded, finely chopped (about ⅓ cup)

2 teaspoons dried parsley, crumbled

1 teaspoon dried oregano, crumbled

2 medium garlic cloves, minced

½ teaspoon dried thyme, crumbled

⅛ to ¼ teaspoon cayenne

1 medium dried bay leaf

■ ■ ■

8 ounces raw medium shrimp, thawed if frozen, peeled, rinsed, and patted dry

1 cup frozen cut okra, thawed

1 cup uncooked instant brown rice

¼ cup snipped fresh parsley

The word "jambalaya" is thought to come from *jambon*, the French word for ham. It's a given, then, that ham is one of the primary ingredients of jambalaya; however, you don't need much when you use smoked ham and chop it finely to distribute its distinct flavor throughout the dish. *(See photo insert.)*

In the slow cooker, stir together the tomatoes with liquid, water, onion, celery, bell pepper, ham, parsley, oregano, garlic, thyme, cayenne, and bay leaf. Cook, covered, on low for 5 to 6 hours or on high for 2½ to 3 hours, or until the vegetables are tender.

If using the low setting, change it to high. Quickly stir in the shrimp, okra, and rice and re-cover the slow cooker. Cook for 30 minutes, or until the rice is tender. Discard the bay leaf. Serve the jambalaya sprinkled with the parsley.

per serving

Calories 196	Cholesterol 78 mg	Dietary Exchanges
Total Fat 2.0 g	Sodium 472 mg	1½ starch, 2 vegetable,
Saturated Fat 0.5 g	Carbohydrates 30 g	1½ lean meat
Trans Fat 0.0 g	Fiber 4 g	
Polyunsaturated Fat 0.5 g	Sugars 7 g	
Monounsaturated Fat 0.5 g	Protein 14 g	

shrimp and chicken paella

serves 4
1½ cups per serving

slow cooker size/shape
2½- to 3½-quart round or oval

slow cooking time
2 hours 15 minutes to
2½ hours on low plus
10 to 15 minutes on high
(preferred), **OR**
1 hour 15 minutes to
1½ hours on high plus 10 to
15 minutes on high

1 tablespoon paprika

1 teaspoon dried oregano,
  crumbled

½ teaspoon garlic powder

¼ teaspoon salt

¼ teaspoon pepper

2 boneless, skinless chicken
  breasts (about 4 ounces each),
  each cut crosswise into 4 pieces

1 teaspoon olive oil and ½
  teaspoon olive oil, divided use

1½ cups chopped onions

1 cup uncooked converted rice

1 large tomato, chopped

2 cups fat-free, low-sodium
  chicken broth, such as on
  page 31

■ ■ ■

8 ounces raw large shrimp,
  peeled, rinsed, and patted dry

½ cup frozen green peas, thawed

To preserve their bright colors and avoid overcooking, wait until the end before adding the shrimp and peas to the chicken, rice, and tomato foundation of this traditional dish from Spain.

In a medium bowl, stir together the paprika, oregano, garlic powder, salt, and pepper. Sprinkle all over the chicken. Using your fingertips, gently press the seasonings so they adhere to the chicken.

In a medium nonstick skillet, heat 1 teaspoon oil over medium-high heat, swirling to coat the bottom. Cook the chicken for 3 to 5 minutes on each side, or until lightly browned on both sides. Transfer to a medium plate.

Reduce the heat to medium. Add the remaining ½ teaspoon oil, swirling to coat the bottom. Cook the onions for 1½ minutes, stirring frequently.

Stir in the rice. Cook for 1 minute, stirring constantly. Transfer to the slow cooker.

Place the chicken on the onion mixture. Top with the tomato. Pour the broth over all. Don't stir. Cook, covered, on low for 2 hours 15 minutes to 2½ hours or on high for 1 hour 15 minutes to 1½ hours, or until the rice is tender, almost all the liquid is absorbed, and the chicken is no longer pink in the center.

If using the low setting, change it to high. Quickly stir in the shrimp and peas and re-cover the slow cooker. Cook for 10 to 15 minutes, or until the shrimp are pink on the outside and the peas are tender.

per serving

Calories 348	Cholesterol 108 mg	Dietary Exchanges
Total Fat 4.0 g	Sodium 583 mg	3 starch, 1 vegetable,
Saturated Fat 0.5 g	Carbohydrates 49 g	3 lean meat
Trans Fat 0.0 g	Fiber 3 g	
Polyunsaturated Fat 0.5 g	Sugars 5 g	
Monounsaturated Fat 2.0 g	Protein 27 g	

shrimp-and-fish bayou gumbo

serves 4
1¼ cups per serving

slow cooker size/shape
3- to 4½-quart round or oval

slow cooking time
5½ to 6 hours on low plus
15 minutes on high, **OR**
2 hours 45 minutes to 3 hours
on high plus 15 minutes on
high

2 tablespoons canola or corn oil

2 tablespoons all-purpose flour

1 large green bell pepper,
chopped

1 cup fresh or frozen chopped
okra, thawed if frozen

1 medium onion, chopped

1 medium rib of celery, sliced

1 14.5-ounce can no-salt-added
tomatoes, undrained

2 medium dried bay leaves

2 teaspoons salt-free seafood
seasoning blend

¾ teaspoon dried thyme,
crumbled

■ ■ ■

8 ounces raw or frozen medium
shrimp, thawed if frozen,
peeled, rinsed, and patted dry

8 ounces tilapia or other thin
mild white fish fillets, rinsed
and patted dry, cut into 1-inch
pieces

2 tablespoons mild Louisiana-
style hot-pepper sauce

2 teaspoons olive oil (extra virgin
preferred)

⅛ teaspoon salt

Making gumbo can require a lot of attention, and if you include crabmeat, the dish can be expensive. This recipe takes care of both! The slow cooker does much of the work for you, and after cooking briefly, the tilapia breaks down and acquires a crablike texture—but for a fraction of the cost. While the fish is cooking, prepare some instant brown rice on the stovetop to create the perfect bed for this delicious gumbo.

In a large nonstick skillet, heat the oil over medium heat, swirling to coat the bottom. Cook the flour for 5 minutes, or until caramel color, stirring constantly. Cook the bell pepper, okra, onion, and celery for 4 minutes, or until the onion is soft, stirring frequently. Transfer to the slow cooker.

Stir in the tomatoes with liquid, bay leaves, seasoning blend, and thyme. Cook, covered, on low for 5½ to 6 hours or on high for 2 hours 45 minutes to 3 hours.

If using the low setting, change it to high. Quickly stir in the remaining ingredients and re-cover the slow cooker. Cook for 15 minutes, or until the shrimp is pink on the outside. Discard the bay leaves before serving the gumbo.

cook's tip: If possible, refrigerate the gumbo overnight in an airtight container so the flavors blend.

per serving

Calories 214	Cholesterol 100 mg	Dietary Exchanges
Total Fat 7.5 g	Sodium 494 mg	3 vegetable, 3 lean
Saturated Fat 1.0 g	Carbohydrates 16 g	meat
Trans Fat 0.0 g	Fiber 3 g	
Polyunsaturated Fat 1.5 g	Sugars 7 g	
Monounsaturated Fat 4.5 g	Protein 22 g	

shrimp and grits

serves 5
½ cup shrimp mixture and heaping ½ cup grits per serving

slow cooker size/shape
1½- to 2½-quart round or oval

slow cooking time
3 to 4 hours on low plus 10 minutes on high, **OR**
1½ to 2 hours on high plus 10 minutes on high

3 cups water

¼ teaspoon salt

¼ teaspoon pepper

1 cup yellow or white grits (stone-ground preferred)

■ ■ ■

9 ounces frozen whole-kernel corn, thawed

1 teaspoon olive oil

¾ cup chopped onion

½ cup chopped green bell pepper

2 large garlic cloves, minced

1 pound raw medium shrimp, peeled, rinsed, and patted dry

1½ cups chopped tomatoes

¼ teaspoon red hot-pepper sauce, or to taste

Shrimp and grits is a southern specialty that has become a favorite in restaurants around the country. You can easily replicate the dish at home using a slow cooker. It generates the steady heat needed to yield perfect grits.

In the slow cooker, stir together the water, salt, and pepper. Slowly stir in the grits. Cook, covered, on low for 3 to 4 hours or on high for 1½ to 2 hours, or until the water is absorbed and the grits are tender.

If using the low setting, change it to high. Quickly stir in the corn and re-cover the slow cooker. Cook for 10 minutes, or until the corn is tender.

While the corn is cooking, in a large nonstick skillet, heat the oil over medium heat, swirling to coat the bottom. Cook the onion and bell pepper for 3 minutes, or until beginning to soften, stirring frequently.

Stir in the garlic. Cook for 30 seconds, stirring constantly.

Stir the shrimp, tomatoes, and hot-pepper sauce into the onion mixture. Cook for 2 to 3 minutes, or until the shrimp are pink on the outside and the tomatoes are hot. Serve over the grits.

per serving

Calories 250
Total Fat 2.5 g
  Saturated Fat 0.5 g
  Trans Fat 0.0 g
  Polyunsaturated Fat 0.5 g
  Monounsaturated Fat 1.0 g

Cholesterol 114 mg
Sodium 642 mg
Carbohydrates 42 g
  Fiber 4 g
  Sugars 5 g
Protein 17 g

Dietary Exchanges
  2½ starch, 1 vegetable, 2 lean meat

mediterranean fish stew with rouille

serves 4
1½ cups per serving

slow cooker size/shape
3- to 4½-quart round or oval

slow cooking time
4 hours on low plus 10 to 15 minutes on high, **OR**
2 hours on high plus 10 to 15 minutes on high

2 teaspoons olive oil

1¼ cups chopped onions

1 medium fennel bulb, chopped (about 1½ cups), stems discarded, fronds reserved

4 medium garlic cloves, minced

1 32-ounce can no-salt-added diced tomatoes, undrained

¾ cup water

⅛ teaspoon pepper

◼ ◼ ◼

8 ounces fresh debearded and rinsed mussels in the shell

5 ounces cod, rinsed and patted dry, cut into 1-inch pieces

5 ounces shucked clams

¼ cup chopped fresh Italian (flat-leaf) parsley

◼ ◼ ◼

3 tablespoons light mayonnaise

1 tablespoon minced roasted red bell pepper

½ medium garlic clove, minced

1 or 2 dashes of cayenne, or to taste

Similar to bouillabaisse, this hearty stew features an assortment of seafood in a tomato base with the addition of a rouille (ROO-ee), a spicy reddish sauce (*rouille* is French for "rust").

In a medium nonstick skillet, heat the oil over medium heat, swirling to coat the bottom. Cook the onions for 3 minutes, or until beginning to soften, stirring occasionally. Stir in the fennel. Cook for 3 minutes, or until slightly softened, stirring occasionally. Stir in the garlic. Cook for 30 seconds, stirring constantly. Transfer to the slow cooker.

Stir in the tomatoes with liquid, water, and pepper. Cook, covered, on low for 4 hours or on high for 2 hours, or until the onions and fennel are tender.

If using the low setting, change it to high. Quickly stir in the mussels and re-cover the slow cooker. Cook for 3 minutes. Quickly stir in the fish and clams and re-cover the slow cooker. Cook for 5 to 8 minutes, or until the mussels have opened. Discard any unopened mussels. Stir in the parsley.

While the seafood cooks, in a small bowl, stir together the mayonnaise, bell pepper, remaining garlic, and the cayenne for the rouille. Just before serving, stir 2 tablespoons of the rouille into the stew. Garnish each serving with 1½ teaspoons of the remaining rouille and the fennel fronds.

per serving

Calories 233	Cholesterol 40 mg	Dietary Exchanges
Total Fat 6.5 g	Sodium 496 mg	5 vegetable, 2 lean
Saturated Fat 1.0 g	Carbohydrates 24 g	meat
Trans Fat 0.0 g	Fiber 5 g	
Polyunsaturated Fat 2.5 g	Sugars 9 g	
Monounsaturated Fat 2.5 g	Protein 19 g	

poultry

chicken and fresh fennel cassoulet

QUICK PREP

serves 4
3 ounces chicken and
1 cup vegetables per serving

slow cooker size/shape
3- to 4½-quart round or oval

slow cooking time
4 to 5 hours on low plus
30 minutes to 1 hour on low
(preferred), **OR**
2½ to 3 hours on high plus
15 to 30 minutes on high

1 **medium fennel bulb, trimmed, thinly sliced, and quartered**

1 **medium Vidalia, Maui, Oso Sweet, or other sweet onion, thinly sliced and quartered**

¼ **cup matchstick-size dry-packed sun-dried tomatoes**

2 **medium garlic cloves, minced**

4 **boneless, skinless chicken breast halves (about 4 ounces each), all visible fat discarded**

½ **teaspoon dried oregano, crumbled**

¼ **teaspoon pepper**

⅛ **teaspoon salt**

½ **cup fat-free, low-sodium chicken broth, such as on page 31**

■ ■ ■

1 **15.5-ounce can no-salt-added Great Northern beans, rinsed and drained**

2 **tablespoons snipped fresh Italian (flat-leaf) parsley**

A combination of fennel, sun-dried tomatoes, and herbs richly flavors the beans and chicken in this casserole.

In the slow cooker, make one layer each of the fennel, onion, and tomatoes. Sprinkle with the garlic. Place the chicken on top. Sprinkle the mixture with the oregano, pepper, and salt. Pour the broth over all. Don't stir. Cook, covered, on low for 4 to 5 hours or on high for 2½ to 3 hours.

Pour the beans over the chicken. Sprinkle with the parsley. Don't stir. Cook, covered, on low for 30 minutes to 1 hour or on high for 15 to 30 minutes, or until the chicken is no longer pink in the center.

cook's tip on fennel: Although most recipes calling for fennel use only the bulb, there are uses for all parts of the plant. First, cut the fernlike fronds, or leaves, from the stems and the stems from the bulb. After discarding the tips of any fronds that seem coarse, use the fronds as a garnish or snip them to use as a seasoning (add just before serving the dish). The stems can be thinly sliced to use in salads, but many people find them too tough and use them primarily to season broths.

To prepare the bulb, which is used as a vegetable, trim the bottom, halve and core the bulb, then thinly slice it. Use sliced fennel raw in a tossed salad or slaw or with fruits, such as oranges and apples. Fennel also is tasty when you simmer or braise it, such as in soups, stews, pot roasts, or vegetable dishes. The aniselike, but milder and sweeter, flavor of fennel becomes more delicate with cooking.

per serving

Calories 268	Cholesterol 73 mg	Dietary Exchanges
Total Fat 4.0 g	Sodium 283 mg	1 starch, 2 vegetable,
Saturated Fat 0.5 g	Carbohydrates 27 g	3 very lean meat
Trans Fat 0.0 g	Fiber 10 g	
Polyunsaturated Fat 0.5 g	Sugars 4 g	
Monounsaturated Fat 1.0 g	Protein 30 g	

chicken with autumn vegetables

1 teaspoon ground cumin

½ teaspoon pepper

½ teaspoon salt

¾ **pound butternut squash,
peeled, seeds and strings
discarded, cut into 1-inch
pieces (about 2 cups)**

1 **medium red potato, halved,
then each half quartered**

1 **medium carrot, halved
lengthwise and cut crosswise
into 1-inch pieces**

1 **small onion, cut into thin
wedges**

½ **medium fresh jalapeño, seeds
and ribs discarded, minced**

2 **medium garlic cloves, chopped**

2 **cups fat-free, low-sodium
chicken broth, such as on
page 31**

1 **medium lime, quartered**

6 **sprigs of fresh cilantro**

1 **3-pound chicken, skin,
all visible fat, and giblets
discarded**

Based on *sancocho*, a spicy stew native to the Canary Islands, Puerto Rico, and some Latin American countries, our version features a whole chicken and hardy vegetables simmered in a jalapeño-spiked broth. It's just soupy enough to require a bowl rather than a plate.

In a small dish, stir together the cumin, pepper, and salt. Set aside.

In a large bowl, stir together the squash, potato, carrot, onion, jalapeño, and garlic. Add ¾ teaspoon of the cumin mixture, stirring to coat. Set the remaining cumin mixture aside. Transfer the squash mixture to the slow cooker. Pour in the broth.

Place the lime quarters and sprigs of cilantro in the cavity of the chicken. Sprinkle the remaining cumin mixture all over the chicken. Using your fingertips, gently press the mixture so it adheres to the chicken. Place the chicken on the squash mixture. Cook, covered, on low for 8 to 10 hours or on high for 5 to 6 hours, or until the thickest part of a breast registers 165°F on an instant-read thermometer.

(continued)

Transfer the chicken to a cutting board, leaving the squash mixture and liquid in the crock. Let the chicken stand for 15 minutes so the juices can redistribute. (The chicken will cook a little more during the standing time.)

Add the lime juice and snipped cilantro to the slow cooker, stirring to combine.

Carve the chicken into slices. Transfer to soup bowls. Spoon the squash mixture and broth around the chicken.

cook's tip: Use the vegetables listed here as a guideline when you make this stew. You can use about 4 cups of almost any hardy vegetables you have on hand, such as sweet potatoes, bell peppers, turnips, rutabagas, or leeks.

■ ■ ■

2 tablespoons fresh lime juice

¼ cup snipped fresh cilantro

per serving

Calories 196	Cholesterol 76 mg	Dietary Exchanges
Total Fat 3.5 g	Sodium 314 mg	1 starch, 3 lean meat
Saturated Fat 1.0 g	Carbohydrates 15 g	
Trans Fat 0.0 g	Fiber 2 g	
Polyunsaturated Fat 1.0 g	Sugars 3 g	
Monounsaturated Fat 1.0 g	Protein 26 g	

slow-roasted tarragon chicken

serves 6
3½ ounces chicken
per serving

slow cooker size/shape
3- to 4½-quart round or oval

slow cooking time
1 hour on high plus 3½ to
4 hours on low

Cooking spray

¼ **cup snipped fresh parsley**

2 **tablespoons olive oil**

1 **tablespoon grated lemon zest**

2 **teaspoons dried tarragon,
crumbled**

1½ **teaspoons smoked paprika**

1 **teaspoon dried thyme,
crumbled**

½ **teaspoon garlic powder**

1 **4-pound roasting chicken (with
skin), all visible fat and giblets
discarded**

1 **medium lemon, quartered**

For succulent, savory, and rich-tasting "roasted" chicken, stuff the seasonings under the skin so their flavors permeate the chicken as it slow cooks. Side dishes such as sweet potatoes and asparagus go well with this chicken.

Lightly spray the slow cooker with cooking spray. Set aside.

In a small bowl, stir together the parsley, oil, lemon zest, tarragon, paprika, thyme, and garlic powder.

Carefully loosen the skin from the breast and drumsticks by gently inserting your fingers between the skin and the meat, making a pocket for the parsley mixture. Don't break the skin. Discard any fat beneath the skin. Still working carefully, spread the parsley mixture under the loosened skin as well as possible.

Put the lemon wedges in the cavity. Place the chicken with the breast side up in the slow cooker. Cook, covered, on high for 1 hour. Change the setting to low. Cook for 3½ to 4 hours, or until the internal temperature at the thickest part of the breast reaches 165°F.

Transfer the chicken to a cutting board, leaving the pan drippings in the slow cooker. Let stand for 15 minutes so the juices can redistribute. (The chicken will cook a little more during the standing time.) Before carving the chicken, carefully remove the skin so the seasonings remain in place.

Meanwhile, pour the drippings into a 2-cup glass measuring cup. Place in the freezer for 15 minutes to cool slightly.

Pour the drippings into a quart-size resealable plastic bag. Hold the bag so that one of the bottom ends points down over a medium bowl (forming a "pastry bag"). This will let the fat rise to the top. Snip the pointed end. Let the drippings flow into the bowl, stopping just before the layer of fat gets to the point. Discard the fat. If the juices are too cool, transfer them to a small saucepan. Bring to a boil over medium-high heat. Serve the juices with the chicken.

cook's tip on smoked paprika: Made from ground smoked sweet peppers, smoked paprika adds a wonderful wood-smoked flavor to food. Try sprinkling some on soups, salads, or fish, or use it to enhance salsa, dips, rice dishes, marinades, and many other foods that would work well with a smoky flavor.

per serving

Calories 218	Cholesterol 100 mg	Dietary Exchanges
Total Fat 9.0 g	Sodium 118 mg	3½ lean meat
Saturated Fat 1.5 g	Carbohydrates 1 g	
Trans Fat 0.0 g	Fiber 1 g	
Polyunsaturated Fat 1.5 g	Sugars 0 g	
Monounsaturated Fat 4.5 g	Protein 32 g	

chicken and dumplings

serves 4
3 ounces chicken, 1 cup
vegetables, and 1 dumpling
per serving

slow cooker size/shape
3- to 4½-quart round or
oval (preferred)

slow cooking time
4 to 5 hours on high
plus 25 to 30 minutes on high

Cooking spray

3 medium carrots, sliced

2 medium ribs of celery, sliced

**8 ounces frozen shelled
edamame, thawed**

**1 4-ounce jar sliced pimiento,
drained**

**1 teaspoon canola or corn oil and
1 teaspoon canola or corn oil,
divided use**

**4 boneless, skinless chicken
breast halves (about 4 ounces
each), all visible fat discarded**

1 cup finely chopped onion

**2 cups fat-free, low-sodium
chicken broth and ⅔ cup fat-
free, low-sodium chicken broth,
such as on page 31, divided use**

**2 tablespoons no-salt-added
tomato paste**

¼ cup all-purpose flour

**1 tablespoon finely chopped
fresh rosemary**

¼ teaspoon salt

¼ teaspoon pepper

(continued)

Homemade chicken and dumplings is pure comfort food that's worth a little extra hands-on time. (You'll need to prepare the dumpling batter 35 to 40 minutes before serving.) Adding edamame gives this popular dish a contemporary twist and a nutritional boost.

Lightly spray the slow cooker with cooking spray. Put the carrots, celery, edamame, and pimiento in the slow cooker, stirring to combine. Set aside.

In a large nonstick skillet, heat 1 teaspoon oil over medium-high heat, swirling to coat the bottom. Cook the chicken for 3 to 5 minutes on each side, or until lightly browned. Transfer to the slow cooker.

Put the remaining 1 teaspoon oil in the skillet, swirling to coat the bottom. Cook the onion for 3 minutes, or until soft, stirring frequently. Stir in 2 cups broth and the tomato paste. Set aside.

Put ¼ cup flour in a small bowl. Whisk in the rosemary, ¼ teaspoon salt, the pepper, and the remaining ⅔ cup broth. Stir into the onion mixture. Bring to a boil, still over medium-high heat, stirring frequently. Boil for 2 to 3 minutes, or until thickened and bubbly, stirring frequently and adjusting the heat if necessary. Pour over the chicken. Don't stir. Cook, covered, on high for 4 to 5 hours, or until the chicken is no longer pink in the center.

About 10 minutes before the chicken is cooked, prepare the dumpling dough. In a medium bowl, stir together the cornmeal, remaining ⅓ cup flour, the baking powder, onion powder, and remaining ¼ teaspoon salt. Stir in the parsley.

In a small bowl, whisk together the half-and-half and final 2 tablespoons oil. Stir into the cornmeal mixture until the batter is just moistened but no flour is visible.

When the chicken is ready, quickly transfer it to a large plate, leaving the onion mixture in the slow cooker. Stir the onion mixture and re-cover the slow cooker (leave it set on high). Cover the chicken to keep warm until serving time. Set aside. Using a serving spoon, quickly drop four equal portions of the dumpling dough on top of the onion mixture in the slow cooker. Re-cover the slow cooker. Cook on high for 25 to 30 minutes, or until a wooden toothpick inserted in the center of one of the dumplings comes out clean. (Don't remove the lid while cooking the dumplings.) Serve the dumplings and vegetables alongside the chicken.

cook's tip: Don't prepare the dumpling mixture ahead of time; it will lose its leavening ability.

Dumplings

1/3 **cup yellow cornmeal**

1/3 **cup all-purpose flour**

1 **teaspoon baking powder**

1/4 **teaspoon onion powder**

1/4 **teaspoon salt**

2 **tablespoons finely snipped fresh parsley**

1/4 **cup plus 2 tablespoons fat-free half-and-half**

2 **tablespoons canola or corn oil**

per serving

Calories 466
Total Fat 15.5 g
  Saturated Fat 1.5 g
  Trans Fat 0.0 g
  Polyunsaturated Fat 4.5 g
  Monounsaturated Fat 8.0 g

Cholesterol 73 mg
Sodium 653 mg
Carbohydrates 45 g
  Fiber 7 g
  Sugars 10 g
Protein 38 g

Dietary Exchanges
  2 starch, 3 vegetable,
  4 lean meat

athens chicken pinwheels on pasta

serves 4
3 ounces chicken, ½ cup pasta, and 2 tablespoons sauce per serving

slow cooker size/shape
3- to 4½-quart round or oval

slow cooking time
3½ to 4½ hours on low (preferred), **OR**
2 to 2½ hours on high

2 large boneless, skinless chicken breasts (about 8 ounces each), all visible fat discarded, pounded to ¼-inch thickness

1 teaspoon olive oil

¼ cup finely chopped red bell pepper

¼ cup finely chopped onion

¼ cup chopped button mushrooms

2 medium garlic cloves, minced

½ teaspoon dried oregano, crumbled

⅛ teaspoon salt

1 tablespoon balsamic vinegar

½ cup fat-free, low-sodium chicken broth, such as on page 31

■ ■ ■

4 ounces dried whole-grain spaghetti

¾ cup fat-free, low-sodium chicken broth, such as on page 31

(continued)

A light sauce flecked with red bell pepper and parsley tops Greek-inspired chicken pinwheels and whole-grain pasta. Serve this Mediterranean-flavored meal with a dark green leafy salad lightly dressed with a lemon vinaigrette. *(See photo insert.)*

Put the chicken on a large plate. Lightly brush both sides of the chicken with the oil.

In a small bowl, stir together ¼ cup bell pepper, the onion, mushrooms, garlic, oregano, and salt. Spread over each piece of chicken, leaving about a ½-inch border uncovered. Roll up from one of the long ends, jelly-roll style, tucking the ends under. Tie each roll in several places with kitchen twine. Transfer to the slow cooker.

Brush the tops of the rolls with the vinegar. Pour ½ cup broth around, not over, the chicken. Cook, covered, on low for 3½ to 4½ hours or on high for 2 to 2½ hours.

About 20 minutes before serving time, prepare the pasta using the package directions, omitting the salt. Drain well in a colander.

Meanwhile, transfer the rolls to a cutting board. Let stand, covered, for 10 minutes for easier slicing. Cut the rolls crosswise into slices about ¾ inch thick.

While the pasta boils and the rolls stand, in a small saucepan, stir together the remaining ¾ cup broth, remaining 2 table-spoons bell pepper, and the pepper. Cook over medium-high heat for 6 to 8 minutes, or until reduced to about ½ cup. Remove the sauce from the heat. Stir in the parsley and lemon juice.

Toss the pasta with about ¼ cup of the sauce. Spoon the pasta onto a serving platter. Arrange the pinwheels on the pasta. Drizzle with the remaining sauce.

cook's tip: Larger chicken breasts are better than small for slow cooker chicken rolls since there is more area to accommodate the filling. Because you'll cut the cooked rolls before arranging the slices on the pasta, every-one will get the same amount, even though you use two breasts for four servings.

cook's tip: Replace the pasta with whole-wheat couscous or brown rice for a change.

2 tablespoons finely chopped red bell pepper

¼ teaspoon pepper

1 tablespoon snipped Italian (flat-leaf) parsley

½ teaspoon fresh lemon juice

per serving

Calories 260	Cholesterol 73 mg	Dietary Exchanges
Total Fat 5.0 g	Sodium 224 mg	1½ starch, 3 very lean
Saturated Fat 1.0 g	Carbohydrates 25 g	meat
Trans Fat 0.0 g	Fiber 4 g	
Polyunsaturated Fat 1.0 g	Sugars 3 g	
Monounsaturated Fat 2.0 g	Protein 29 g	

mediterranean chicken

serves 4
3 ounces chicken and 1½ cups vegetables per serving

slow cooker size/shape
3- to 4½-quart round or oval

slow cooking time
4 to 6 hours on low

Cooking spray

1½ **pounds red potatoes, peeled and cut into ¾-inch cubes**

3 **medium green onions, white and green parts thinly sliced on the diagonal and kept separated, divided use**

1 **medium garlic clove, minced**

¼ **teaspoon dried oregano, crumbled; ¼ teaspoon dried oregano, crumbled; and ½ teaspoon dried oregano, crumbled, divided use**

¼ **teaspoon salt**

¼ **teaspoon pepper**

1 **medium lemon, peel cut into strips, juice reserved; and 1 medium lemon, cut crosswise into 8 slices, divided use**

4 **boneless, skinless chicken breast halves (about 4 ounces each), all visible fat discarded**

2 **medium tomatoes, chopped**

¼ **cup crumbled low-fat feta cheese**

Ingredients commonly used in cooking throughout the Mediterranean area—lemon, garlic, and oregano—permeate the chicken breasts and vegetables in this aromatic dish. Fresh tomatoes, green onions, and feta cheese add the finishing touch.

Lightly spray the slow cooker with cooking spray. Make a layer of half the potatoes. Sprinkle with half the white parts of the green onions (reserve the green parts), half the garlic, ¼ teaspoon oregano, half the salt, and half the pepper. Top with half the lemon peel strips and 2 lemon slices. Repeat with another layer of the same ingredients. Don't stir.

Place the chicken on the vegetables. Sprinkle with the final ½ teaspoon oregano. Top each piece of chicken with 1 of the remaining 4 lemon slices.

Pour the reserved lemon juice around, not over, the chicken, so the seasonings stay in place. Cook, covered, on low for 4 to 6 hours, or until the chicken is no longer pink in the center.

Serve the chicken with the potato mixture and cooking liquid. Garnish with the tomatoes, feta, and reserved green parts of the green onions.

cook's tip on cutting lemon peel: Use a potato peeler or sharp knife to remove strips of lemon peel. Don't cut deep enough to get the white pith—it's bitter. Cut the strips to the desired size.

per serving

Calories 290	Cholesterol 76 mg	Dietary Exchanges
Total Fat 4.5 g	Sodium 439 mg	2 starch, 1 vegetable,
Saturated Fat 1.5 g	Carbohydrates 33 g	3 lean meat
Trans Fat 0.0 g	Fiber 5 g	
Polyunsaturated Fat 0.5 g	Sugars 5 g	
Monounsaturated Fat 1.0 g	Protein 30 g	

artichoke-lemon chicken

serves 4
3 ounces chicken and ¾ cup vegetable mixture per serving

slow cooker size/shape
4- to 6-quart round or oval (preferred)

slow cooking time
5 to 6 hours on low (preferred), **OR**
4 to 5 hours on high

16 ounces frozen artichoke hearts, thawed

1 small lemon, thinly sliced

1 medium garlic clove, minced

1 teaspoon chopped fresh rosemary and 2 teaspoons chopped fresh rosemary, divided use

⅛ teaspoon salt and ⅛ teaspoon salt, divided use

⅛ teaspoon pepper and ⅛ teaspoon pepper, divided use

¾ cup fat-free, low-sodium chicken broth, such as on page 31

4 boneless, skinless chicken breast halves (about 4 ounces each), all visible fat discarded

2 teaspoons olive oil

Tart fresh lemon pairs perfectly with chicken and artichokes in this dish. Serve it with brown rice, whole-grain pasta, or whole-wheat couscous to soak up all the delicious broth.

Put the artichokes, lemon, garlic, 1 teaspoon rosemary, ⅛ teaspoon salt, and ⅛ teaspoon pepper in the slow cooker, tossing to combine. Pour in the broth. Set aside.

In a small bowl, stir together the remaining 2 teaspoons rosemary, remaining ⅛ teaspoon salt, and remaining ⅛ teaspoon pepper. Sprinkle over both sides of the chicken. Using your fingertips, gently press the seasonings so they adhere to the chicken.

In a large nonstick skillet, heat the oil over medium heat, swirling to coat the bottom. Cook the chicken for 3 to 5 minutes on each side, or until lightly browned. Place the chicken on the artichoke mixture. Don't stir. Cook, covered, on low for 5 to 6 hours or on high for 4 to 5 hours, or until the chicken is no longer pink in the center and the artichokes and lemon are tender.

cook's tip: You can use a round slow cooker, but you'll need to stack the chicken breasts.

cook's tip on frozen artichoke hearts: Make artichoke hearts a staple in your freezer. No salt is added during packaging, so they contain less sodium than the canned variety.

per serving

Calories 211	Cholesterol 73 mg	Dietary Exchanges
Total Fat 5.0 g	Sodium 348 mg	2 vegetable, 3 lean
Saturated Fat 1.0 g	Carbohydrates 13 g	meat
Trans Fat 0.0 g	Fiber 9 g	
Polyunsaturated Fat 0.5 g	Sugars 1 g	
Monounsaturated Fat 2.5 g	Protein 27 g	

white chicken chili

serves 4
1⅓ cups chili plus 1 tablespoon sour cream and 1 tablespoon cheese per serving

slow cooker size/shape
3- to 4½-quart round or oval

slow cooking time
5 to 6 hours on low
plus 30 minutes on high, **OR**
2½ to 3 hours on high
plus 30 minutes on high

1 teaspoon olive oil

1 pound boneless, skinless chicken breasts, all visible fat discarded, cut into 1-inch cubes

1 15.5-ounce can no-salt-added Great Northern beans, rinsed and drained

1¾ cups fat-free, low-sodium chicken broth, such as on page 31

1 large sweet onion, chopped

1 4-ounce can diced green chiles, drained

1 tablespoon dried minced garlic

1 teaspoon ground cumin

½ teaspoon dried oregano, crumbled

⅛ teaspoon cayenne

■ ■ ■

⅔ cup frozen whole-kernel corn, thawed

¼ cup fat-free sour cream

¼ cup shredded low-fat Monterey Jack cheese

1 tablespoon plus 1 teaspoon snipped fresh cilantro

Score big by serving this chili after the game. It will provide a change of pace from the more common ground beef, red beans, and tomato.

In a large nonstick skillet, heat the oil over medium-high heat, swirling to coat the bottom. Cook the chicken for 4 to 5 minutes, or just until very lightly browned, stirring frequently. Drain if necessary. Transfer to the slow cooker.

Add the beans, broth, onion, green chiles, garlic, cumin, oregano, and cayenne, stirring to combine. Cook, covered, on low for 5 to 6 hours or on high for 2½ to 3 hours.

If using the low setting, change it to high. Quickly stir in the corn and re-cover the slow cooker. Cook for 30 minutes. Serve the chili topped with the sour cream, Monterey Jack cheese, and cilantro.

cook's tip: In addition to the garnishes called for, you may want to offer chopped white or green onions and sliced fresh jalapeños for those craving more heat.

per serving

Calories 326	Cholesterol 80 mg	Dietary Exchanges
Total Fat 7.0 g	Sodium 354 mg	1½ starch, 1 vegetable,
Saturated Fat 2.0 g	Carbohydrates 32 g	4 lean meat
Trans Fat 0.0 g	Fiber 9 g	
Polyunsaturated Fat 0.5 g	Sugars 5 g	
Monounsaturated Fat 2.0 g	Protein 34 g	

pepper-pineapple chicken

serves 4
3 ounces chicken, ½ cup fruit and vegetable mixture, and ½ cup rice per serving

slow cooker size/shape
3- to 4½-quart round or oval

slow cooking time
4 to 5 hours on low plus 10 to 15 minutes on high

2 boneless, skinless chicken breasts (about 8 ounces each), all visible fat discarded, halved

1 8-ounce can pineapple chunks in their own juice, drained and juice reserved

1 8-ounce can sliced water chestnuts, rinsed and drained

1 medium red bell pepper, cut into 1-inch cubes

½ cup fat-free, no-salt-added chicken broth, such as on page 31

1 teaspoon minced peeled gingerroot

1 medium garlic clove, minced

■ ■ ■

2 tablespoons cornstarch

2 tablespoons plain rice vinegar

1 tablespoon soy sauce (lowest sodium available)

1 cup uncooked instant brown rice

¼ cup thinly sliced green onions (green and white parts), cut on the diagonal

Sliced water chestnuts provide extra crunch to this leisurely, low-fat take on classic sweet-and-sour chicken.

Place the chicken in the slow cooker. Top with the pineapple, water chestnuts, and bell pepper. Don't stir.

In a small bowl, whisk together the broth, gingerroot, garlic, and reserved pineapple juice. Pour into the slow cooker. Don't stir. Cook, covered, on low for 4 to 5 hours, or until the chicken is no longer pink in the center.

Using a slotted spoon, quickly transfer the chicken to a large plate, leaving the pineapple mixture in the slow cooker. Re-cover the slow cooker. Cover the plate to keep warm. Set aside.

Change the slow cooker setting to high. Put the cornstarch in a small bowl. Add the vinegar and soy sauce, whisking to dissolve. Quickly stir into the pineapple mixture in the slow cooker. Re-cover the slow cooker. Cook for 10 to 15 minutes, or until the sauce has thickened. Return the chicken to the slow cooker, turning to coat with the sauce.

Meanwhile, prepare the rice using the package directions, omitting the salt and margarine. Spoon onto plates. Top with the chicken mixture. Sprinkle with the green onions.

per serving

Calories 298	Cholesterol 73 mg	Dietary Exchanges
Total Fat 4.0 g	Sodium 250 mg	1½ starch, ½ fruit,
Saturated Fat 0.5 g	Carbohydrates 37 g	1 vegetable, 3 very lean
Trans Fat 0.0 g	Fiber 4 g	meat
Polyunsaturated Fat 1.0 g	Sugars 10 g	
Monounsaturated Fat 1.0 g	Protein 28 g	

curry-rubbed chicken

serves 4
3 ounces chicken, ⅓ cup sauce, and ½ cup couscous per serving

slow cooker size/shape
3- to 4½-quart round or oval

slow cooking time
4 to 5 hours on low (preferred), **OR**
2½ to 3 hours on high

¼ **cup chopped dried apricots**

¼ **cup finely chopped onion**

½ **teaspoon curry powder**

½ **teaspoon ground ginger**

¼ **teaspoon ground cinnamon**

¼ **teaspoon ground cumin**

⅛ **teaspoon cayenne**

2 **boneless, skinless chicken breasts (about 8 ounces each), all visible fat discarded, halved**

1 **8-ounce can no-salt-added tomato sauce**

¼ **cup fresh orange juice**

1 **tablespoon honey**

■ ■ ■

1 **cup uncooked whole-wheat couscous**

¼ **cup snipped fresh parsley**

A medley of spices gives this dish so much over-the-top flavor that you'll never miss the salt shaker.

Put the apricots and onion in the slow cooker. Set aside.

In a small bowl, stir together the curry powder, ginger, cinnamon, cumin, and cayenne. Sprinkle over both sides of the chicken. Using your fingertips, gently press the seasonings so they adhere to the chicken. Place the chicken on the apricot mixture. Don't stir.

In the same small bowl, whisk together the tomato sauce, orange juice, and honey. Pour over the chicken. Don't stir. Cook, covered, on low for 4 to 5 hours or on high for 2½ to 3 hours, or until the chicken is no longer pink in the center.

About 10 minutes before serving time, prepare the couscous using the package directions, omitting the salt. Spoon the chicken and sauce over the couscous. Sprinkle with the parsley.

cook's tip: To serve eight, double all the ingredients and add 1 hour to the cooking time if you're using the high setting or 2 hours for the low setting.

cook's tip on cutting sticky foods: To cut dried apricots or other sticky foods easily, use kitchen shears lightly sprayed with cooking spray.

per serving

Calories 362	Cholesterol 73 mg	Dietary Exchanges
Total Fat 4.0 g	Sodium 147 mg	2½ starch, ½ fruit,
Saturated Fat 0.5 g	Carbohydrates 53 g	1 vegetable, 3 very lean
Trans Fat 0.0 g	Fiber 6 g	meat
Polyunsaturated Fat 0.5 g	Sugars 14 g	
Monounsaturated Fat 1.0 g	Protein 31 g	

rosemary chicken with bell peppers

serves 6
3 ounces chicken and ½ cup bell pepper mixture per serving

slow cooker size/shape
3- to 4½-quart round or oval

slow cooking time
3 to 5 hours on low (preferred), **OR**
1½ to 2½ hours on high

¼ **teaspoon salt**

¼ **teaspoon pepper**

6 boneless, skinless chicken breast halves (about 4 ounces each), all visible fat discarded

2 teaspoons olive oil

1 large onion, halved, then sliced

3 large garlic cloves, minced

3 medium bell peppers, each a different color, cut lengthwise into ½-inch strips

1 tablespoon finely chopped fresh rosemary

Chicken breasts cook in a colorful mélange of bell peppers seasoned with fresh rosemary. Steam some fresh broccoli and toss a salad to serve alongside.

Sprinkle the salt and pepper over both sides of the chicken. Using your fingertips, gently press the seasonings so they adhere to the chicken.

In a large nonstick skillet, heat the oil over medium-high heat, swirling to coat the bottom. Cook the chicken for 3 to 5 minutes on each side, or until browned. Transfer the chicken to a large plate. Set aside.

In the same skillet, cook the onion for 3 minutes, or until soft, stirring frequently. Stir in the garlic. Cook for 30 seconds, stirring constantly. Transfer to the slow cooker. Stir in the bell peppers.

Arrange the chicken on the onion mixture. Don't stir. Sprinkle with the rosemary. Cook, covered, on low for 3 to 5 hours or on high for 1½ to 2½ hours, or until the chicken is no longer pink in the center. Serve the chicken topped with the bell pepper mixture. Spoon the cooking liquid over all.

per serving

Calories 167	Cholesterol 73 mg	Dietary Exchanges
Total Fat 4.5 g	Sodium 232 mg	1 vegetable, 3 lean
Saturated Fat 1.0 g	Carbohydrates 6 g	meat
Trans Fat 0.0 g	Fiber 2 g	
Polyunsaturated Fat 0.5 g	Sugars 3 g	
Monounsaturated Fat 2.0 g	Protein 25 g	

chicken, mushrooms, and pearl onions in red wine

serves 6
3 ounces chicken and
¾ cup vegetables per serving

slow cooker size/shape
3- to 4½-quart round or oval

slow cooking time
4 to 6 hours on low

1 teaspoon olive oil and 1 teaspoon olive oil, divided use

12 ounces medium button mushrooms, quartered

3 medium garlic cloves, minced

16 ounces frozen pearl onions, thawed

4 medium Italian plum (Roma) tomatoes, seeded and chopped

2 tablespoons uncooked instant, or quick-cooking, tapioca

1 medium dried bay leaf

6 boneless, skinless chicken breast halves (about 4 ounces each), all visible fat discarded

½ cup fat-free, low-sodium chicken broth, such as on page 31

½ cup dry red wine (regular or nonalcoholic)

¼ cup no-salt-added tomato paste

2 tablespoons snipped fresh parsley

1½ teaspoons dried thyme, crumbled

¼ teaspoon salt

¼ teaspoon pepper

Impressive enough to serve when entertaining but easy to prepare, this dish is inspired by the French classic *coq au vin*. Add *haricots verts* (or even regular green beans) and fingerling potatoes as side dishes.

In a large nonstick skillet, heat 1 teaspoon oil over medium-high heat, swirling to coat the bottom. Cook the mushrooms for 4 minutes, or until browned, stirring frequently. Stir in the garlic. Cook for 30 seconds, stirring constantly. Transfer to the slow cooker.

Stir in the onions and tomatoes. Sprinkle the tapioca over all. Add the bay leaf. Set aside.

In the same skillet, heat the remaining 1 teaspoon oil, still over medium-high heat, swirling to coat the bottom. Cook the chicken for 3 to 5 minutes on each side, or until browned. Place the chicken on the mushroom mixture. Don't stir.

In a small bowl, whisk together the remaining ingredients. Pour over the chicken. Don't stir. Cook, covered, on low for 4 to 6 hours, or until the chicken is no longer pink in the center. Discard the bay leaf. Transfer the chicken to plates. Spoon the mushroom mixture and sauce on top.

per serving

Calories 255	Cholesterol 73 mg	Dietary Exchanges
Total Fat 5.0 g	Sodium 258 mg	4 vegetable,
Saturated Fat 1.0 g	Carbohydrates 21 g	3 lean meat
Trans Fat 0.0 g	Fiber 2 g	
Polyunsaturated Fat 1.0 g	Sugars 7 g	
Monounsaturated Fat 2.0 g	Protein 28 g	

chicken with black beans and sweet potatoes

QUICK
PREP

serves 4
3 ounces chicken and 1 cup vegetable mixture per serving

slow cooker size/shape
4- to 6-quart round or oval

slow cooking time
7 to 8 hours on low (preferred), **OR**
3½ to 4 hours on high

The rich depth of flavor in this stewlike chicken dish largely comes from chipotle peppers in adobo sauce and from smoked paprika. The result is south-of-the-border comfort food at its best. *(See photo insert.)*

In the slow cooker, make one layer each, in order, of the sweet potatoes, onion, and beans. Place the chicken on top.

In a small bowl, whisk together the broth, salsa, chipotle peppers, tapioca, paprika, garlic powder, pepper, allspice, and salt. Pour over the chicken. Don't stir. Cook, covered, on low for 7 to 8 hours or on high for 3½ to 4 hours, or until the chicken is no longer pink in the center. Ladle onto plates. Sprinkle with the cilantro. Serve with the lime wedges to squeeze over all.

2 small sweet potatoes (about 1 pound total), cut into 1-inch cubes

1 cup chopped onion

1 15.5-ounce can no-salt-added black beans, rinsed and drained

4 boneless, skinless chicken breast halves (about 4 ounces each), all visible fat discarded

1 cup fat-free, low-sodium chicken broth, such as on page 31

½ cup mild salsa (lowest sodium available)

3 tablespoons chopped chipotle peppers canned in adobo sauce

1 tablespoon uncooked instant, or quick-cooking, tapioca

1 teaspoon smoked paprika

1 teaspoon garlic powder

½ teaspoon pepper

½ teaspoon ground allspice

¼ teaspoon salt

■ ■ ■

¼ cup snipped fresh cilantro

1 medium lime, cut into 4 wedges

per serving

Calories 375
Total Fat 3.5 g
  Saturated Fat 0.5 g
  Trans Fat 0.0 g
  Polyunsaturated Fat 0.5 g
  Monounsaturated Fat 1.0 g

Cholesterol 73 mg
Sodium 621 mg
Carbohydrates 50 g
  Fiber 9 g
  Sugars 11 g
  Protein 33 g

Dietary Exchanges
  3 starch, 1 vegetable,
  3½ lean meat

chicken and tomato stew with kalamata olives

serves 4
1 slightly heaping cup
per serving

slow cooker size/shape
3- to 4½-quart round or oval

slow cooking time
3½ to 4 hours on low
(preferred), **OR**
1 hour 45 minutes to
2 hours on high

Ingredients popular all around the Mediterranean Sea shine in this vibrant stew. Serve it in bowls so you can scrape up every drop of the wonderful sauce.

Lightly spray the slow cooker with cooking spray. Put the chicken and tomatoes in the slow cooker.

In a small bowl, whisk together the wine, tomato paste, garlic powder, and red pepper flakes until smooth. Pour over the chicken mixture. Don't stir. Cook, covered, on low for 3½ to 4 hours or on high for 1 hour 45 minutes to 2 hours, or until the chicken is no longer pink in the center.

About 20 minutes before serving time, prepare the pasta using the package directions, omitting the salt. Drain well in a colander.

When the chicken is ready, leave it in the slow cooker and coarsely shred using one or two forks.

Stir the spinach, olives, oregano, oil, and salt into the shredded chicken. Ladle over the pasta.

Cooking spray

2 boneless, skinless chicken breasts (about 6 ounces each) or 3 boneless, skinless chicken breast halves (about 4 ounces each), all visible fat discarded

4 medium tomatoes, chopped

½ cup dry white wine (regular or nonalcoholic)

¼ cup no-salt-added tomato paste

½ teaspoon garlic powder

¼ teaspoon crushed red pepper flakes

■ ■ ■

3 ounces whole-grain egg noodles or whole-grain linguine, broken into thirds if using linguine

2 ounces (about 2 cups) fresh spinach, coarsely chopped

16 kalamata olives, coarsely chopped

3 tablespoons chopped fresh oregano

1½ tablespoons olive oil (extra virgin preferred)

⅛ teaspoon salt

per serving

Calories 323
Total Fat 12.5 g
  Saturated Fat 1.5 g
  Trans Fat 0.0 g
  Polyunsaturated Fat 1.5 g
  Monounsaturated Fat 7.5 g

Cholesterol 54 mg
Sodium 451 mg
Carbohydrates 26 g
  Fiber 5 g
  Sugars 6 g
Protein 23 g

Dietary Exchanges
  1 starch, 2 vegetable,
  2½ lean meat, 1 fat

cajun-sauced drumsticks

serves 4
2 drumsticks, ⅓ cup sauce, and ½ cup rice per serving

slow cooker size
3- to 4½-quart round or oval

slow cooking time
6 hours on low, **OR**
3 hours on high

Cooking spray

8 chicken drumsticks (about 5 ounces each), skin and all visible fat discarded

1 8-ounce can no-salt-added tomato sauce

1 tablespoon mild Louisiana-style hot-pepper sauce (lowest sodium available)

2 teaspoons Worcestershire sauce (lowest sodium available)

1½ teaspoons dried oregano, crumbled

1 teaspoon dried thyme, crumbled

½ teaspoon garlic powder

¼ teaspoon salt

10 ounces frozen brown rice

Take a break from chicken breasts and serve up some "Cajun comfort" with these drumsticks and their slightly spicy tomato sauce. This dish uses one of the milder versions of hot-pepper sauce, providing flavor rather than heat.

Lightly spray the slow cooker with cooking spray. Put the chicken in the slow cooker.

In a small bowl, stir together the remaining ingredients except the rice. Pour over the chicken. Cook, covered, on low for 6 hours or on high for 3 hours, or until the chicken is no longer pink in the center. Be careful not to overcook.

About 5 minutes before serving time, prepare the rice using the package directions. Serve the chicken and sauce over the rice.

cook's tip on removing the skin from poultry. To remove the skin from the poultry easily, use paper towels. The towels let you get a firmer grip on the skin and keep your fingers from slipping.

per serving

Calories 308	Cholesterol 108 mg	Dietary Exchanges
Total Fat 7.5 g	Sodium 292 mg	1 starch, 1 vegetable,
Saturated Fat 1.5 g	Carbohydrates 22 g	4 lean meat
Trans Fat 0.0 g	Fiber 2 g	
Polyunsaturated Fat 1.5 g	Sugars 3 g	
Monounsaturated Fat 2.0 g	Protein 36 g	

moroccan chicken thighs with raisin-and-carrot couscous

serves 4
1 thigh and ½ cup couscous
per serving

slow cooker size/shape
1½- to 2½-quart round or oval

slow cooking time
4 to 6 hours on low, **OR**
2 to 3 hours on high

2 teaspoons smoked paprika

1 teaspoon ground cumin

1 teaspoon ground cinnamon

¼ teaspoon pepper

¼ teaspoon ground turmeric

Dash of ground allspice

4 bone-in, skinless chicken thighs
(about 5 ounces each)

1 teaspoon olive oil

¼ cup water

■ ■ ■

1 cup water

¾ cup uncooked whole-wheat
couscous

¼ cup dark raisins

¼ cup shredded carrot

Cinnamon and a touch of allspice add a background hint of sweetness, giving the chicken a rich, complex flavor. Couscous is the perfect side dish.

In a small bowl, stir together the paprika, cumin, cinnamon, pepper, turmeric, and allspice. Sprinkle over both sides of the chicken. Using your fingertips, gently press the seasonings so they adhere to the chicken.

In a medium nonstick skillet, heat the oil over medium-high heat, swirling to coat the bottom. Cook the chicken for 3 to 5 minutes on each side, or until browned, turning once halfway through. Transfer to the slow cooker.

Pour ¼ cup water into the skillet. Bring to a boil, scraping to dislodge any browned bits. Pour over the chicken. Cook, covered, on low for 4 to 6 hours or on high for 2 to 3 hours, or until the chicken is no longer pink in the center.

About 10 minutes before serving time, in a small saucepan, bring the remaining 1 cup water to a boil over high heat. Stir in the couscous, raisins, and carrot. Remove from the heat. Let stand, covered, for 5 minutes, or until the water is absorbed and the couscous is tender. Fluff with a fork.

Spoon the couscous onto plates. Place the chicken on the couscous. Spoon the cooking liquid over the couscous if desired.

per serving

Calories 364
Total Fat 10.0 g
  Saturated Fat 2.5 g
  Trans Fat 0.0 g
  Polyunsaturated Fat 2.5 g
  Monounsaturated Fat 4.0 g

Cholesterol 72 mg
Sodium 70 mg
Carbohydrates 44 g
  Fiber 7 g
  Sugars 7 g
  Protein 27 g

Dietary Exchanges
2½ starch, ½ fruit,
3 lean meat

chicken cacciatore

serves 6
3 ounces chicken, ½ cup sauce, and ⅔ cup pasta per serving

slow cooker size/shape
3- to 4½-quart round or oval

slow cooking time
6 to 7 hours on low
plus 15 minutes on high, **OR**
3 to 3½ hours on high
plus 15 minutes on high

6 ounces medium button mushrooms, quartered (about 2 cups)

1 14.5-ounce can no-salt-added diced tomatoes, undrained

1 medium onion, chopped

1 medium rib of celery, sliced

1 medium carrot, chopped

½ cup fat-free, low-sodium chicken broth, such as on page 31, or water

2 medium garlic cloves, minced

1 teaspoon dried Italian seasoning, crumbled

¼ teaspoon salt

¼ teaspoon pepper

1 medium dried bay leaf

6 boneless, skinless chicken thighs (about 4 ounces each), all visible fat discarded

■ ■ ■

1 6-ounce can no-salt-added tomato paste

1 tablespoon balsamic vinegar

6 ounces dried whole-grain fettuccine

¼ cup shredded fresh basil

Although you can use any whole-grain pasta you prefer in this Italian classic, we recommend ribbons of fettuccine to support the thick, chunky sauce.

In the slow cooker, stir together the mushrooms, tomatoes with liquid, onion, celery, carrot, broth, garlic, Italian seasoning, salt, pepper, and bay leaf. Add the chicken thighs, spooning the sauce over them. Cook, covered, on low for 6 to 7 hours or on high for 3 to 3½ hours, or until the chicken is no longer pink in the center and the vegetables are tender.

If using the low setting, change it to high. Quickly stir in the tomato paste and vinegar and re-cover the slow cooker. Cook for 15 minutes. Discard the bay leaf.

Meanwhile, prepare the pasta using the package directions, omitting the salt. Drain well in a colander. Serve the chicken mixture over the pasta. Sprinkle with the basil.

per serving

Calories 338	Cholesterol 74 mg	Dietary Exchanges
Total Fat 9.5 g	Sodium 225 mg	1½ starch, 3 vegetable,
Saturated Fat 2.5 g	Carbohydrates 36 g	3 lean meat
Trans Fat 0.0 g	Fiber 6 g	
Polyunsaturated Fat 2.5 g	Sugars 11 g	
Monounsaturated Fat 3.5 g	Protein 28 g	

turkey breast with gravy

serves 15
3 ounces turkey and
2 tablespoons gravy
per serving

slow cooker size/shape
5- to 7-quart oval

slow cooking time
8 to 10 hours on low, **OR**
5 to 6 hours on high

1 teaspoon dried sage

½ teaspoon salt

¼ teaspoon pepper

1 5½-pound whole bone-in
turkey breast, skin and all
visible fat discarded

¼ cup fat-free, low-sodium
chicken broth, such as on
page 31

■ ■ ■

¾ to 1 cup fat-free, low-sodium
chicken broth, such as on
page 31

¼ cup all-purpose flour

¼ cup cold water

¼ teaspoon dried sage

¼ teaspoon salt

¼ teaspoon pepper

If you're intimidated by the prospect of roasting a whole turkey, this recipe offers a delicious and easy option: Slow cook a whole breast.

In a small bowl, stir together 1 teaspoon sage, ½ teaspoon salt, and ¼ teaspoon pepper. Sprinkle all over the turkey. Using your fingertips, gently press the seasonings so they adhere to the turkey.

Pour ¼ cup broth into the slow cooker. Add the turkey. Cook, covered, on low for 8 to 10 hours or on high for 5 to 6 hours, or until the thickest part of the breast registers 160°F on an instant-read thermometer. Transfer the turkey to a cutting board. Cover loosely. Let stand for 10 to 15 minutes to finish cooking (it should reach a minimum of 165°F) before slicing.

Pour the cooking liquid through a strainer into a 2-cup glass measuring cup, discarding any solids. Pour in enough of the remaining ¾ to 1 cup broth to make 2 cups of liquid. Pour into a medium saucepan. Set aside.

Put the flour in a small bowl. Pour in the water, whisking to dissolve. Whisk the flour mixture, remaining ¼ teaspoon sage, remaining ¼ teaspoon salt, and remaining ¼ teaspoon pepper into the broth mixture. Cook over medium-high heat for 3 minutes, or until the gravy comes to a boil and thickens, whisking frequently. Serve with the turkey.

per serving

Calories 155	Cholesterol 82 mg	Dietary Exchanges
Total Fat 1.0 g	Sodium 185 mg	3 lean meat
Saturated Fat 0.5 g	Carbohydrates 2 g	
Trans Fat 0.0 g	Fiber 0 g	
Polyunsaturated Fat 0.0 g	Sugars 0 g	
Monounsaturated Fat 0.0 g	Protein 33 g	

barbecue-spiced turkey breast

serves 6
3 ounces turkey per serving

slow cooker size/shape
3- to 3½-quart round or
oval (preferred)

slow cooking time
6 to 8 hours on low, **OR**
3 to 4 hours on high

2 teaspoons smoked paprika

1 teaspoon paprika

1 teaspoon dried sage

1 teaspoon firmly packed light or
dark brown sugar

½ teaspoon chili powder

½ teaspoon garlic powder

½ teaspoon onion powder

½ teaspoon pepper

1 bone-in turkey breast half
(about 2 pounds), skin and all
visible fat discarded

There's no need to fire up the barbecue grill when you can turn to this recipe instead. Smoky paprika and chili, garlic, and onion powders add the taste of the grill without the fuss. Serve with corn on the cob or a refreshing salad of cucumber and tomatoes.

In a small bowl, stir together all the ingredients except the turkey. Sprinkle all over the turkey. Using your fingertips, gently press the seasonings so they adhere to the turkey. Transfer with the meaty side up to the slow cooker.

Cook, covered, on low for 6 to 8 hours or on high for 3 to 4 hours, or until the thickest part of the breast registers 160°F on an instant-read thermometer.

Transfer the turkey to a cutting board. Cover loosely. Let stand for 10 to 15 minutes to finish cooking (it should reach a minimum of 165°F) before slicing. Serve with the cooking juices if desired.

cook's tip on turkey doneness: The USDA recommends cooking turkey (whole, pieces, or ground) to a minimum of 165°F (at the end of any standing time). If you prefer to cook your turkeys a bit more, up to about 175°F, adjust the time and temperature accordingly.

per serving

Calories 142	Cholesterol 74 mg	Dietary Exchanges
Total Fat 1.0 g	Sodium 64 mg	4 lean meat
Saturated Fat 0.5 g	Carbohydrates 2 g	
Trans Fat 0.0 g	Fiber 1 g	
Polyunsaturated Fat 0.5 g	Sugars 1 g	
Monounsaturated Fat 0.0 g	Protein 30 g	

turkey meat loaf with creamy chicken gravy

Cooking spray

12 ounces ground skinless turkey breast

1 3.5-ounce sweet Italian turkey breakfast sausage link, casing discarded

½ medium red or orange bell pepper, chopped

½ cup snipped fresh parsley

2 large egg whites

⅓ cup uncooked quick-cooking oatmeal

¾ teaspoon dried sage

½ teaspoon dried thyme, crumbled

¼ teaspoon dried fennel seeds, crushed

Paprika to taste

■ ■ ■

1 tablespoon olive oil

1 tablespoon all-purpose flour

¾ cup fat-free milk

1 packet (1 teaspoon) salt-free chicken bouillon

⅛ teaspoon salt

Seasoned with a bit of turkey sausage and sage, this loaf is comfort food at its best.

Lightly spray the slow cooker with cooking spray.

In a large bowl, using your hands or a spoon, combine the turkey, sausage, bell pepper, parsley, egg whites, oatmeal, sage, thyme, and fennel seeds. Transfer the mixture to the slow cooker. Depending on the shape of your slow cooker, shape into an oval or round loaf that is 2 inches thick, leaving a ½-inch border between it and the side of the crock. Sprinkle with the paprika. Cook, covered, on low for 4 hours or on high for 2 hours, or until the meat loaf registers 160°F on an instant-read thermometer and is no longer pink in the center.

Using a flat spatula, transfer the meat loaf to a cutting board. Let stand for 5 minutes to finish cooking (it should reach a minimum of 165°F) before slicing or cutting into wedges.

While the meat loaf stands, in a medium nonstick skillet, heat the oil over medium heat, swirling to coat the bottom. Whisk in the flour. Cook for 1 minute, whisking constantly. Gradually whisk in the milk, bouillon, and salt. Cook for 4 minutes, or until thickened and reduced to ½ cup. Serve over the meat loaf.

cook's tip: Leaving space between the meat loaf and the side of the crock helps the meat loaf retain its shape and makes it easier to remove the loaf from the slow cooker.

per serving

Calories 252
Total Fat 9.0 g
  Saturated Fat 1.5 g
  Trans Fat 0.0 g
  Polyunsaturated Fat 2.0 g
  Monounsaturated Fat 4.0 g

Cholesterol 93 mg
Sodium 312 mg
Carbohydrates 11 g
  Fiber 2 g
  Sugars 3 g
  Protein 30 g

Dietary Exchanges
  ½ starch, 4 lean meat

turkey and sweet potato stew

serves 4
1½ cups per serving

slow cooker size/shape
3- to 4½-quart round or oval

slow cooking time
5 to 6 hours on low
plus 30 minutes on high, **OR**
2½ to 3 hours on high
plus 30 minutes on high

1 **1-pound turkey tenderloin, all visible fat discarded, cut into 1-inch cubes**

1¾ **cups fat-free, low-sodium chicken broth, such as on page 31**

4 **medium carrots, cut crosswise into medium slices**

1 **large Vidalia, Maui, Oso Sweet, or other sweet onion, coarsely chopped**

2 **medium sweet potatoes (10 to 11 ounces each), peeled and cut into 1-inch cubes**

1 **tablespoon dried minced garlic**

1 **teaspoon ground cumin**

½ **teaspoon curry powder**

¼ **teaspoon ground ginger**

¼ **teaspoon pepper**

■ ■ ■

2 **tablespoons all-purpose flour**

2 **tablespoons cold water**

Classic fall ingredients—sweet potatoes and turkey—are highlighted in this stew. The seasonings add a hint of heat to help chase away the chill of a cool evening.

In the slow cooker, stir together the turkey, broth, carrots, onion, sweet potatoes, garlic, cumin, curry powder, ginger, and pepper. Cook, covered, on low for 5 to 6 hours or on high for 2½ to 3 hours.

Put the flour in a small bowl. Pour in the water, whisking to dissolve. Quickly whisk into the stew and re-cover the slow cooker. If using the low setting, change it to high. Cook for 30 minutes.

cook's tip: Sweet potatoes cook a little more quickly in the slow cooker than carrots do, so this recipe calls for cutting the sweet potatoes into larger cubes and slicing the carrots thinly to even out the cooking time.

per serving

Calories 314	Cholesterol 70 mg	Dietary Exchanges
Total Fat 1.0 g	Sodium 210 mg	2 starch, 3 vegetable,
Saturated Fat 0.5 g	Carbohydrates 42 g	3 lean meat
Trans Fat 0.0 g	Fiber 8 g	
Polyunsaturated Fat 0.5 g	Sugars 14 g	
Monounsaturated Fat 0.0 g	Protein 33 g	

pulled turkey tostadas with cucumber guacamole

serves 6
1 tostada per serving

slow cooker size/shape
3- to 3½-quart round or oval (preferred)

slow cooking time
5 to 8 hours on low, **OR**
2½ to 4 hours on high

---

1 teaspoon olive oil

1 bone-in turkey breast half (about 2 pounds), skin and all visible fat discarded

2 cups chopped tomatoes

½ cup chopped green bell pepper

½ cup chopped onion

1 teaspoon chopped serrano pepper, seeds and ribs discarded

1 medium garlic clove, minced

1 tablespoon snipped fresh cilantro

■ ■ ■

6 6-inch corn tortillas

Cooking spray

½ medium avocado, chopped and mashed

⅓ cup finely chopped peeled cucumber

1 tablespoon chopped onion

1 tablespoon snipped fresh cilantro

(continued)

Turkey breast slow cooked in salsa and then shredded partners with more salsa and guacamole to top crisp tortillas. Cucumber adds a pleasing crunch to traditional guacamole.

In a medium or large nonstick skillet, heat the oil over medium-high heat, swirling to coat the bottom. Cook the turkey for 5 to 7 minutes, or until browned, turning once halfway through. Transfer with the meaty side up to the slow cooker. Set aside.

Meanwhile, for the salsa, in a small bowl, stir together the tomatoes, bell pepper, ½ cup onion, 1 teaspoon serrano pepper, and garlic. Stir in 1 tablespoon cilantro. Spoon 1 cup salsa into a small airtight container. Refrigerate until needed. Pour the remaining salsa over the turkey.

Cook the turkey, covered, on low for 5 to 8 hours or on high for 2½ to 4 hours, or until the thickest part of the breast registers about 155°F on an instant-read thermometer. Transfer the turkey to a cutting board, leaving the salsa in the slow cooker. Let stand for 15 minutes to continue cooking. The breast should reach a minimum of 165°F. Cut the turkey into ½-inch slices. Using your hands or two forks, pull the meat apart into long shreds. Transfer to a medium bowl.

Using a slotted spoon, transfer the solid salsa ingredients from the slow cooker to the bowl with the turkey, stirring to combine. Discard the liquid remaining in the slow cooker.

Meanwhile, preheat the oven to 425°F.

Arrange the tortillas in a single layer on a baking sheet. Lightly spray both sides of the tortillas with cooking spray.

Bake the tortillas for 7 to 10 minutes, or until crisp and lightly browned on the edges. Transfer to a large plate to keep from overcooking. Set aside.

For the guacamole, in a medium bowl, stir together the avocado, cucumber, remaining 1 tablespoon onion, remaining 1 tablespoon cilantro, and remaining ½ teaspoon serrano pepper.

At serving time, spoon the turkey mixture over the tortillas. Top with the reserved 1 cup salsa and the guacamole. Spoon a dollop of sour cream on each tostada and serve with the lime wedges to squeeze over all.

cook's tip: For crisper tortillas, arrange the tortillas on the baking sheet and let stand for 30 minutes before baking. The edges of the tortillas will curl slightly as they begin to dry.

½ teaspoon chopped serrano pepper, seeds and ribs discarded if desired

¼ cup plus 2 tablespoons fat-free sour cream (optional)

1 large lime, cut into 6 wedges (optional)

per serving

Calories 219	Cholesterol 74 mg	Dietary Exchanges
Total Fat 4.5 g	Sodium 87 mg	½ starch, 1 vegetable,
Saturated Fat 1.0 g	Carbohydrates 13 g	4 lean meat
Trans Fat 0.0 g	Fiber 3 g	
Polyunsaturated Fat 1.0 g	Sugars 3 g	
Monounsaturated Fat 2.5 g	Protein 31 g	

per serving (with optional toppings)

Calories 234	Cholesterol 77 mg	Dietary Exchanges
Total Fat 4.5 g	Sodium 99 mg	½ starch, 1 vegetable,
Saturated Fat 1.0 g	Carbohydrates 15 g	4 lean meat
Trans Fat 0.0 g	Fiber 3 g	
Polyunsaturated Fat 1.0 g	Sugars 4 g	
Monounsaturated Fat 2.5 g	Protein 32 g	

turkey cassoulet with gremolata

serves 4
3 ounces turkey and
1 cup beans and vegetables
per serving

slow cooker size/shape
3- to 4½-quart round or oval

slow cooking time
4 to 5 hours on low, **OR**
2 to 2½ hours on high

1 15.5-ounce can no-salt-added cannellini beans, rinsed and drained

1 large red bell pepper, chopped

1 large leek (white and light green parts), sliced (about 1½ cups)

1 cup fat-free, low-sodium chicken broth, such as on page 31

1 teaspoon dried thyme, crumbled

¼ teaspoon salt

¼ teaspoon pepper

1 pound turkey tenderloin, all visible fat discarded, cut crosswise into 4 pieces

1 teaspoon olive oil

■ ■ ■

⅓ cup snipped fresh parsley

1 tablespoon grated lemon zest

2 or 3 medium garlic cloves, minced

Gremolata is a fresh seasoning mixture of parsley, garlic, and lemon zest. It adds color and brings a bright flavor to this hearty one-dish meal.

In the slow cooker, stir together the beans, bell pepper, leek, and broth. Set aside.

Sprinkle the thyme, salt, and pepper all over the turkey. Using your fingertips, gently press the seasonings so they adhere to the turkey.

In a large nonstick skillet, heat the oil over medium-high heat, swirling to coat the bottom. Cook the turkey for 2 minutes on each side, or until browned. Place on the bean mixture. Don't stir. Cook, covered, on low for 4 to 5 hours or on high for 2 to 2½ hours, or until the turkey is no longer pink in the center.

Just before serving time, in a small bowl, stir together the parsley, lemon zest, and garlic. Set the gremolata aside.

Using a slotted spoon, transfer the turkey and the bean mixture to plates. Discard the cooking liquid. Sprinkle the turkey and the bean mixture with the gremolata.

cook's tip: If turkey breast "steaks" are available at your supermarket, you can substitute them for the tenderloin. You'll need four 4-ounce pieces.

per serving

Calories 255	Cholesterol 70 mg	Dietary Exchanges
Total Fat 3.0 g	Sodium 258 mg	1 starch, 1 vegetable,
Saturated Fat 0.5 g	Carbohydrates 21 g	4 lean meat
Trans Fat 0.0 g	Fiber 6 g	
Polyunsaturated Fat 0.5 g	Sugars 4 g	
Monounsaturated Fat 1.0 g	Protein 35 g	

southwestern turkey meatballs

1 pound ground skinless turkey breast

1 large egg white

¼ cup whole-wheat bread crumbs (lowest sodium available)

¼ cup minced onion and ¼ cup minced onion, divided use

½ medium fresh jalapeño, seeds and ribs discarded, minced

1 teaspoon chili powder and 1 teaspoon chili powder, divided use

½ teaspoon ground cumin and ½ teaspoon ground cumin, divided use

1 medium garlic clove, minced, and 1 medium garlic clove, minced, divided use

⅛ teaspoon salt and ⅛ teaspoon salt, divided use

2 teaspoons olive oil

1 14.5-ounce can no-salt-added diced tomatoes, undrained

1 8-ounce can no-salt-added tomato sauce

■ ■ ■

¼ cup snipped fresh cilantro

These jalapeño-spiked meatballs are delicious on their own and over whole-grain spaghetti, brown rice, or whole-wheat couscous as well. Steamed broccoli or green beans make a colorful accompaniment.

In a medium bowl, using your hands or a spoon, combine the turkey, egg white, bread crumbs, ¼ cup onion, the jalapeño, 1 teaspoon chili powder, ½ teaspoon cumin, 1 garlic clove, and ⅛ teaspoon salt. Shape into 16 balls.

In a large nonstick skillet, heat the oil over medium-high heat, swirling to coat the bottom. Cook the meatballs for 6 minutes, or until lightly browned, turning frequently.

Meanwhile, in the slow cooker, stir together the tomatoes with liquid, tomato sauce, remaining ¼ cup onion, remaining 1 teaspoon chili powder, remaining ½ teaspoon cumin, remaining 1 garlic clove, and remaining ⅛ teaspoon salt. Set aside.

When the meatballs are ready, add to the sauce. Cook, covered, on low for 8 to 10 hours or on high for 5 to 6 hours. Just before serving, stir in the cilantro.

cook's tip on leftover bread: When you have heels or leftover slices of bread, make bread crumbs. Put coarsely torn pieces of bread in the food processor and process until they reach the desired size and texture. Use right away for soft crumbs, or spread the pieces in a single layer on a plate and let stand overnight for dried crumbs. Freeze in airtight plastic freezer bags for up to two months.

per serving

Calories 237	Cholesterol 70 mg	Dietary Exchanges
Total Fat 3.5 g	Sodium 285 mg	½ starch, 2 vegetable,
Saturated Fat 0.5 g	Carbohydrates 17 g	3 lean meat
Trans Fat 0.0 g	Fiber 3 g	
Polyunsaturated Fat 0.5 g	Sugars 8 g	
Monounsaturated Fat 2.0 g	Protein 32 g	

beer barrel turkey chili

serves 8
1 cup per serving

slow cooker size/shape
3- to 4½-quart round or oval

slow cooking time
7½ to 8 hours on low, **OR**
3 hours 45 minutes to
4 hours on high

Cooking spray

1 teaspoon olive oil

8 ounces ground skinless turkey breast

4 ounces low-fat turkey breakfast sausage

1 14.5-ounce can no-salt-added diced tomatoes, undrained

12 ounces light beer

1 medium onion, chopped

3 tablespoons no-salt-added ketchup

3 tablespoons chili powder

1 tablespoon sugar

1 tablespoon smoked paprika

2 teaspoons ground cumin

1 teaspoon dried oregano, crumbled

2 medium garlic cloves, minced

½ teaspoon salt

■ ■ ■

1 tablespoon olive oil

1 teaspoon ground cumin

1 cup fat-free sour cream

½ cup snipped fresh cilantro

4 medium green onions, finely chopped

Heavily seasoned with chili powder, smoked paprika, cumin, and beer, this chili will satisfy poultry lovers—and even people who think chili *has* to be beefy. Use the leftover chili as a topping for baked potatoes or serve it over whole-grain no-yolk egg noodles or brown rice for an easy weeknight meal.

Lightly spray the slow cooker with cooking spray. Set aside.

In a large skillet, heat 1 teaspoon oil over medium-high heat, swirling to coat the bottom. Cook the ground turkey and sausage for 3 minutes, or until no longer pink on the outside, stirring frequently. Transfer to the slow cooker.

Stir in the tomatoes with liquid, beer, onion, ketchup, chili powder, sugar, paprika, 2 teaspoons cumin, oregano, garlic, and salt. Cook, covered, on low for 7½ to 8 hours or on high for 3 hours 45 minutes to 4 hours, or until the onion is very soft.

Stir in the remaining 1 tablespoon oil and remaining 1 teaspoon cumin. Serve topped with the sour cream, cilantro, and green onions.

cook's tip on beer: Beer adds a richer flavor to chili and enhances the spices. The hops add bitterness, while the malt adds sweetness. The alcohol will evaporate during the cooking process. The darker the brew, the more flavor it will impart.

per serving

Calories 157	Cholesterol 33 mg	Dietary Exchanges
Total Fat 4.0 g	Sodium 283 mg	1 vegetable, ½ other
Saturated Fat 0.5 g	Carbohydrates 15 g	carbohydrate, 1½ lean
Trans Fat 0.0 g	Fiber 2 g	meat
Polyunsaturated Fat 0.5 g	Sugars 8 g	
Monounsaturated Fat 2.0 g	Protein 13 g	

hot stuffed peppers

serves 4
1 stuffed pepper per serving

slow cooker size/shape
3½- to 5-quart round or oval

slow cooking time
5½ to 6 hours on low, **OR**
2 hours 45 minutes to
3 hours on high

Cooking spray

1 8-ounce can no-salt-added tomato sauce

1½ teaspoons minced chipotle pepper canned in adobo sauce

1 teaspoon sugar

½ teaspoon dry mustard

¼ teaspoon salt

8 ounces extra-lean ground beef

1 small onion, diced

2 large egg whites

⅓ cup yellow cornmeal

1 3.5-ounce sweet Italian turkey breakfast sausage link, casing discarded

1 medium fresh jalapeño, seeds and ribs discarded, finely chopped

1 teaspoon ground cumin

4 medium bell peppers, any color or combination, tops, seeds, and ribs discarded

Stuffed peppers became really popular in the 1950s, and variations of the original have remained family favorites ever since. This version uses a mixture of sweet Italian turkey breakfast sausage and ground beef, flavored with jalapeño and chipotle peppers, cornmeal, and cumin for a little taste of Mexico in every bite. Try a variety of bell peppers for a more colorful dish.

Lightly spray the slow cooker with cooking spray. Set aside.

In a small bowl, stir together the tomato sauce, chipotle pepper, sugar, mustard, and salt.

In a large bowl, using your hands or a spoon, combine half the tomato sauce mixture with the remaining ingredients except the bell peppers. Stuff the peppers with the mixture.

Arrange the peppers in the slow cooker. Spoon the remaining tomato sauce mixture on top of the peppers. Cook, covered, on low for 5½ to 6 hours or on high for 2 hours 45 minutes to 3 hours, or until the stuffing registers 160°F on an instant-read thermometer.

Turn off the slow cooker. Let the peppers stand, uncovered, for 15 minutes so the stuffing continues to cook to the minimum safe temperature of 165°F. The cornmeal will thicken during the standing time, firming up the stuffing, and the flavors will blend more.

per serving

Calories 253	Cholesterol 71 mg	Dietary Exchanges
Total Fat 8.0 g	Sodium 398 mg	½ starch, 3 vegetable,
Saturated Fat 2.0 g	Carbohydrates 25 g	2½ lean meat
Trans Fat 0.0 g	Fiber 4 g	
Polyunsaturated Fat 1.5 g	Sugars 9 g	
Monounsaturated Fat 2.5 g	Protein 21 g	

peach-glazed cornish hen for two

A Cornish hen is an elegant entrée for two, and the slow cooker makes an easy job of cooking it to tender perfection. Seasoned with soy sauce, mustard, garlic, and ginger, this hen is finished with a quick peach glaze that has a hint of ginger. Serve it with fingerling potatoes and sautéed broccolini.

serves 2
½ hen per serving

slow cooker size/shape
1½- to 2½-quart round or oval (preferred)

slow cooking time
4 to 6 hours on low, **OR**
2 to 3 hours on high

Cooking spray

2 teaspoons soy sauce (lowest sodium available)

1 teaspoon Dijon mustard

½ teaspoon garlic powder

¼ teaspoon ground ginger

1 24-ounce Cornish hen, halved lengthwise, all visible fat, tail, and giblets discarded

■ ■ ■

¼ cup all-fruit peach spread

¼ teaspoon plain rice vinegar

Dash of ground ginger

cook's tip: Ask the butcher to cut the Cornish hen in half lengthwise for you. If that isn't possible, you can cut it yourself. Place the hen with the breast side down on a cutting board. Using kitchen shears, start at the bottom near the thigh and cut on either side of the backbone up to the neck. Discard the backbone. Cut through the breastbone in the center of the hen to separate it into halves.

Lightly spray the slow cooker with cooking spray. Set aside.

In a small bowl, stir together the soy sauce, mustard, garlic powder, and ¼ teaspoon ginger. Spoon over both sides of the hen halves. Using your fingertips, gently rub the soy sauce mixture into the hen. Transfer with the breast side up to the slow cooker. Cook, covered, on low for 4 to 6 hours or on high for 2 to 3 hours, or until the thickest part of the breast registers 165°F on an instant-read thermometer. Discard the skin. Transfer the hen halves to plates, reserving the cooking liquid.

Pour the liquid into a medium saucepan. Bring to a boil over high heat. Boil for 1 to 2 minutes, or until reduced by half. Transfer to a small bowl.

Meanwhile, in a small microwaveable bowl, whisk together the fruit spread, vinegar, and remaining dash of ginger. Microwave on high for 30 to 50 seconds, or until the fruit spread is melted. Spoon the glaze over the hen halves. Serve with the cooking liquid.

per serving

Calories 260	Cholesterol 133 mg	Dietary Exchanges
Total Fat 5.0 g	Sodium 281 mg	1½ other
Saturated Fat 1.5 g	Carbohydrates 22 g	carbohydrate, 4 lean
Trans Fat 0.0 g	Fiber 0 g	meat
Polyunsaturated Fat 1.0 g	Sugars 16 g	
Monounsaturated Fat 1.5 g	Protein 30 g	

meats

swiss steak with melting tomatoes and onions

serves 6
3 ounces beef and ½ cup sauce per serving

slow cooker size/shape
3- to 4½-quart oval
(oval is necessary)

slow cooking time
6 to 8 hours on low, **OR**
3 to 4 hours on high

- **1 tablespoon chopped fresh thyme and 2 teaspoons chopped fresh thyme, divided use**
- **3 medium garlic cloves, minced**
- **½ teaspoon salt**
- **¼ teaspoon pepper**
- **1½ pounds boneless top round steak, all visible fat discarded**
- **2 tablespoons all-purpose flour**
- **1 teaspoon olive oil and ½ teaspoon olive oil, divided use**
- **2 large onions, cut into 1-inch wedges**
- **3 large tomatoes, cut into ½-inch wedges (about 3 cups)**

■ ■ ■

- **2 tablespoons cornstarch**
- **2 tablespoons water**

The long slow cooking process is perfect not only for making round steak fork-tender but also for blending fresh tomato and onion wedges into a savory "melted" topping for the steak.

Sprinkle 1 tablespoon thyme, the garlic, salt, and pepper over both sides of the beef. Using your fingertips, gently press the seasonings so they adhere to the beef. Put the flour on a large plate. Add the beef, turning to coat. Using your fingertips, gently press the flour so as much as possible adheres to the beef.

In a large nonstick skillet, heat 1 teaspoon oil over medium-high heat, swirling to coat the bottom. Cook the beef for 3 to 5 minutes, or until browned, turning once halfway through. Transfer to a separate large plate.

Reduce the heat to medium low. Add the remaining ½ teaspoon oil to the skillet, swirling to coat the bottom. Cook the onions for 2 minutes, stirring frequently. Transfer to the slow cooker. Top with the beef. Pile the tomatoes on the beef. Sprinkle with the remaining 2 teaspoons thyme. Don't stir. Cook, covered, on low for 6 to 8 hours or on high for 3 to 4 hours, or until the beef is fork-tender.

Transfer the beef to a large plate. Let stand, loosely covered, for 10 minutes before slicing. Pour the onion mixture into a colander held over a medium skillet. Set the onion mixture and the liquid aside separately.

After slicing the beef, bring the strained liquid to a boil over medium-high heat. Put the cornstarch in a small bowl. Pour in the water, whisking to dissolve. Whisk into the sauce. Boil for 1 minute, stirring frequently. Spoon the onion mixture over the beef. Serve with the sauce.

per serving

Calories 211	Cholesterol 57 mg	Dietary Exchanges
Total Fat 4.5 g	Sodium 233 mg	3 vegetable, 3 lean
Saturated Fat 1.5 g	Carbohydrates 15 g	meat
Trans Fat 0.0 g	Fiber 3 g	
Polyunsaturated Fat 0.5 g	Sugars 7 g	
Monounsaturated Fat 2.5 g	Protein 27 g	

brisket with exotic-mushroom and onion gravy

serves 8
3 ounces beef and ¼ cup gravy
per serving

slow cooker size/shape
3- to 4½-quart round or
oval (preferred)

slow cooking time
8 to 10 hours on low

1 ounce dried sliced mushrooms,
such as shiitake, porcini, or
chanterelle, or a combination
(about 1 cup)

1 cup warm water

2 tablespoons chopped fresh
thyme or 2 teaspoons dried
thyme, crumbled

¼ teaspoon salt

¼ teaspoon pepper

1 2-pound flat-end brisket, all
visible fat discarded

1 teaspoon olive oil and ½ teaspoon olive oil, divided use

2 cups cubed onions (1-inch
pieces) (about 2 large)

3 large garlic cloves, minced

½ cup fat-free, low-sodium beef
broth, such as on page 32

■ ■ ■

2 tablespoons all-purpose flour

2 tablespoons water

Brisket is a flavorful cut of beef that lends itself
to long and slow moist cooking. In this recipe,
it's topped with a pile of onions and dried
mushrooms that season the cooking broth; it in
turn becomes the gravy base.

In a small bowl, soak the dried mushrooms in 1 cup warm water for 20 to 30 minutes, or until they are soft. In a small sieve,
drain the mushrooms, reserving the soaking water. Strain the
soaking water through a fine sieve or coffee filter to remove
any dirt. Set the mushrooms and soaking water aside.

Sprinkle the thyme, salt, and pepper over both sides of the
beef. Using your fingertips, gently press the seasonings so
they adhere to the beef.

In a large skillet, heat 1 teaspoon oil over medium-high
heat, swirling to coat the bottom. Cook the beef for 4 to
6 minutes, or until browned, turning once halfway through.
Transfer to a large plate. Set aside.

Reduce the heat to medium. Add the remaining ½ teaspoon
oil, swirling to coat the bottom. Cook the onions and garlic
for 1 minute, stirring frequently. Transfer to the slow cooker.
Stir in the mushrooms.

Place the brisket on top of the onion mixture. Don't stir.
Set aside.

Pour the broth and reserved soaking water into the skillet.
Increase the heat to high and bring to a boil, scraping to
dislodge any browned bits. Pour over the brisket.

Cook, covered, on low for 8 to 10 hours, or until very tender. Transfer the beef to a separate large plate, reserving the onion mixture. Cover the beef loosely. Let stand for 10 minutes before slicing.

During the standing time, put the flour in a small bowl. Add the remaining 2 tablespoons water, whisking to dissolve. Pour the onion mixture from the slow cooker into a large skillet. Bring to a boil over high heat.

Slowly whisk about half the flour mixture into the gravy. Bring to a boil, whisking constantly. Whisk in the remaining flour mixture 1 teaspoon at a time until the desired consistency. Boil for 1 minute, whisking constantly. Serve the gravy over the beef.

cook's tip: Be sure to buy the flat end of the brisket. It is the leanest part and slices well.

per serving

Calories 188	Cholesterol 74 mg	Dietary Exchanges
Total Fat 5.5 g	Sodium 165 mg	1 vegetable, 3 lean
Saturated Fat 2.0 g	Carbohydrates 8 g	meat
Trans Fat 0.0 g	Fiber 1 g	
Polyunsaturated Fat 0.5 g	Sugars 2 g	
Monounsaturated Fat 2.5 g	Protein 26 g	

cabernet-simmered beef roast with rosemary

serves 8
3 ounces beef and 2 tablespoons sauce per serving

slow cooker size/shape
3- to 4½-quart round or
oval (preferred)

slow cooking time
7 to 9 hours on low, **OR**
3½ to 4½ hours on high

**2 tablespoons finely chopped
fresh rosemary or 2 teaspoons
dried rosemary, crushed**

3 large garlic cloves, minced

¼ teaspoon salt

¼ teaspoon pepper

**1 2-pound boneless sirloin tip
roast, any netting or kitchen
string and all visible fat
discarded**

**1 teaspoon olive oil and ½ tea-
spoon olive oil, divided use**

1 large onion, coarsely chopped

**1 cup cabernet sauvignon or
other hearty red wine (regular
or nonalcoholic) or fat-free,
low-sodium beef broth, such as
on page 32**

■ ■ ■

1½ teaspoons cornstarch

2 teaspoons water

The hearty wine not only helps tenderize and flavor the roast but also creates a rich-tasting, intense sauce for this elegant entrée.

In a small bowl, stir together the rosemary, garlic, salt, and pepper. Sprinkle over both sides of the beef. Using your fingertips, gently press the seasonings so they adhere to the beef.

In a medium skillet, heat 1 teaspoon oil over medium-high heat, swirling to coat the bottom. Cook the beef for 6 to 8 minutes, turning to brown on all sides. Transfer to a large plate.

Reduce the heat to medium. Heat the remaining ½ teaspoon oil in the skillet, swirling to coat the bottom. Cook the onion for 3 minutes, or until beginning to soften, stirring frequently. Transfer the onion to the slow cooker. Place the beef on top. Don't stir. Set aside.

Pour the wine into the skillet. Increase the heat to high and bring to a boil. Boil for 1 minute, scraping to dislodge any browned bits. Pour over the beef.

Cook, covered, on low for 7 to 9 hours or on high for 3½ to 4½ hours, or until the beef is tender when pierced with a knife and registers 155°F on an instant-read ther-mometer for medium doneness. Transfer the beef to a cutting board, leaving the cooking liquid in the slow cooker. Cover the beef loosely. Let stand for 10 minutes before slic-ing. The temperature will rise about 5 degrees.

During the standing time, using a fine-mesh strainer, strain the cooking liquid into a large skillet. Discard the solids. Bring the liquid to a boil over high heat. Boil for 3 to 5 minutes, or until reduced by one-third, to about 1 cup, stirring occasionally.

Meanwhile, put the cornstarch in a small bowl. Pour in the water, whisking to dissolve. Set aside.

When the sauce is reduced, slowly whisk about half the cornstarch mixture into the gravy. Bring to a boil, whisking constantly. Whisk in the remaining cornstarch mixture 1 teaspoon at a time until the desired consistency. Boil for 1 minute, whisking constantly. Serve the gravy over the beef.

per serving

Calories 181
Total Fat 5.0 g
 Saturated Fat 2.0 g
 Trans Fat 0.0 g
 Polyunsaturated Fat 0.5 g
 Monounsaturated Fat 3.0 g

Cholesterol 56 mg
Sodium 116 mg
Carbohydrates 2 g
 Fiber 0 g
 Sugars 0 g
Protein 24 g

Dietary Exchanges
 3 lean meat

coffee kettle pot roast

serves 8
3 ounces beef, ½ cup noodles, and ¼ cup sauce per serving

slow cooker size/shape
3- to 4½-quart round or oval

slow cooking time
8 hours on low, **OR**
3 hours 45 minutes to 4 hours on high

Cooking spray

1 8-ounce can no-salt-added tomato sauce

1 tablespoon instant coffee granules

2 tablespoons dark molasses

3 packets (1 tablespoon) salt-free instant beef bouillon

1 teaspoon onion powder

1 teaspoon garlic powder

½ teaspoon pepper (coarsely ground preferred)

¼ teaspoon salt

1 teaspoon canola or corn oil

1 2-pound boneless chuck shoulder roast, all visible fat discarded, cut to fit in slow cooker if necessary

½ cup water

■ ■ ■

8 ounces dried whole-grain no-yolk noodles

This sounds interesting

Molasses and instant coffee add deep flavor to this very tender roast, which will remind you of Sunday dinner at Grandma's house.

Lightly spray the slow cooker with cooking spray. Set aside.

In a medium bowl, stir together the tomato sauce, coffee granules, molasses, bouillon, onion and garlic powders, pepper, and salt. Set aside.

In a large nonstick skillet, heat the oil over medium-high heat, swirling to coat the bottom. Cook the beef on one side for 3 minutes, or until browned. Put the beef with the browned side up in the slow cooker.

Pour the water into the skillet, scraping the bottom and side to dislodge any browned bits. Pour over the beef.

Stir in the tomato sauce mixture. Cook, covered, on low for 8 hours or on high for 3 hours 45 minutes to 4 hours, or until the beef is tender. You won't need to cut the roast—it will fall apart.

About 20 minutes before serving time, prepare the pasta using the package directions, omitting the salt. Drain well in a colander. Serve the beef and sauce over the pasta.

cook's tip on whole-grain no-yolk noodles: Although they are similar in texture, whole-grain no-yolk noodles contain more fiber than the traditional no-yolk noodles.

per serving

Calories 299	Cholesterol 65 mg	Dietary Exchanges
Total Fat 8.0 g	Sodium 149 mg	2 starch, 3 lean meat
Saturated Fat 2.5 g	Carbohydrates 29 g	
Trans Fat 0.0 g	Fiber 4 g	
Polyunsaturated Fat 0.5 g	Sugars 6 g	
Monounsaturated Fat 3.0 g	Protein 28 g	

indonesian beef with couscous

serves 8
½ cup beef mixture and ½ cup couscous per serving

slow cooker size/shape
3- to 4½-quart round or oval

slow cooking time
8 to 8½ hours on low, **OR**
4 hours to 4 hours 15 minutes on high

Cooking spray

1 teaspoon canola or corn oil and 1 tablespoon canola or corn oil, divided use

2 pounds lean boneless chuck roast, all visible fat discarded, cut into 1-inch cubes

1 medium onion, cut into 8 wedges

2 medium Italian plum (Roma) tomatoes

4 medium garlic cloves

1 tablespoon crushed red pepper flakes

1½ teaspoons grated peeled gingerroot

1 cup water and 1 cup water, divided use

2 packets (2 teaspoons) salt-free instant beef bouillon

1 tablespoon sugar

1 teaspoon salt

■ ■ ■

1 cup uncooked whole-wheat couscous

½ cup finely chopped green onions

Cooking a paste of herbs, spices, and chiles in hot oil is the key to this international dish.

Lightly spray the slow cooker with cooking spray. Set aside.

In a large nonstick skillet, heat 1 teaspoon oil over medium-high heat, swirling to coat the bottom. Cook one-third of the beef for 2 to 3 minutes, or until browned on all sides, stirring frequently. Drain on paper towels. Brown the remaining beef in two batches. Transfer to the slow cooker.

Meanwhile, in a food processor or blender, process the onion, tomatoes, garlic, red pepper flakes, and gingerroot until smooth. Set aside.

In the same skillet, heat the remaining 1 tablespoon oil over medium-high heat, swirling to coat the bottom. Cook the onion mixture for 8 minutes, or until thickened to a paste-like consistency, stirring constantly. Transfer to the slow cooker. Pour 1 cup water into the skillet. Bring to a boil over medium-high heat. Boil for 1 minute, scraping to dislodge any browned bits. Pour into the slow cooker. Stir in the bouillon, sugar, salt, and remaining 1 cup water. Cook, covered, on low for 8 to 8½ hours or on high for 4 hours to 4 hours 15 minutes, or until the beef is tender.

Just before serving, prepare the couscous using the package directions, omitting the salt. Fluff with a fork. Stir in the green onions. Spoon onto plates. Top with the beef mixture.

per serving

Calories 281	Cholesterol 44 mg	Dietary Exchanges
Total Fat 7.5 g	Sodium 335 mg	2 starch, 3 lean meat
Saturated Fat 2.0 g	Carbohydrates 28 g	
Trans Fat 0.0 g	Fiber 4 g	
Polyunsaturated Fat 1.0 g	Sugars 4 g	
Monounsaturated Fat 3.5 g	Protein 26 g	

sauerbraten with red cabbage and apples

serves 12
3 ounces beef, ½ cup cabbage mixture, and 3 tablespoons gravy per serving

slow cooker size/shape
5- to 7-quart oval

slow cooking time
4 to 5 hours on low plus 4 to 5 hours on low plus 15 minutes on warm or low (preferred), **OR** 2 to 2½ hours on high plus 2 to 2½ hours on high plus 15 minutes on warm or low

2 cups fat-free, low-sodium beef broth, such as on page 32

1 cup water

1 cup cider vinegar

½ cup firmly packed light brown sugar

1 teaspoon ground allspice

1 teaspoon ground ginger

½ teaspoon ground cloves

1 4-pound top round roast or eye-of-round roast, all visible fat discarded

■ ■ ■

2 teaspoons canola or corn oil

1 medium Vidalia, Maui, Oso Sweet, or other sweet onion, thinly sliced and quartered (about 2 cups)

Marinating the beef overnight tenderizes and flavors this famous German dish, so be sure to plan ahead when making it. Red cabbage and apples cook with the beef and become a perfectly complementary side dish to the meal.

In a glass or other nonmetallic bowl large enough to hold the beef, stir together the broth, 1 cup water, the vinegar, sugar, allspice, ginger, and cloves. Add the beef, turning to coat. Cover and refrigerate for 8 to 24 hours, turning occasionally. At cooking time, drain the beef and pat dry, reserving the marinade.

In a large nonstick skillet, heat the oil over medium-high heat, swirling to coat the bottom. Cook the beef for 10 minutes, or until browned on all sides.

Spread the onion in the slow cooker. Place the beef on the onion. Pour 2 cups of the reserved marinade over the beef. Cover and refrigerate the remaining marinade.

Cook, covered, on low for 4 to 5 hours or on high for 2 to 2½ hours.

Quickly arrange the cabbage and apples around the beef and re-cover the slow cooker. Cook on low for 4 to 5 hours or on high for 2 to 2½ hours, or until the beef is tender and registers 155°F to 160°F on an instant-read thermometer.

(continued)

If using the high setting, change it to low. Quickly transfer the beef to a cutting board, leaving the cabbage mixture in the slow cooker. Re-cover the slow cooker. Let the beef stand, covered, for about 15 minutes, or until it registers 160°F to 165°F on the thermometer. Slice the beef.

During the standing time, pour the 2 cups refrigerated marinade into a medium saucepan. Bring to a rolling boil over high heat. Boil for 5 minutes. Pour into a liquid measuring cup. Add enough water to measure 1¾ cups. Pour into the pan. Reduce the heat to medium.

Put the cornstarch in a small bowl. Add the remaining ¼ cup cold water, whisking to dissolve. Gradually stir into the gravy. Cook for 1 minute, stirring constantly. Whisk in the ginger snaps.

Transfer the sliced beef and cabbage mixture to plates. Spoon the gravy over the beef.

■ ■ ■

5 cups shredded red cabbage (about 15 ounces)

2 large semitart apples, such as Gala or Jonathan, diced

2 tablespoons cornstarch

Water as needed plus ¼ cup cold water, divided use

⅓ cup crushed low-fat ginger snaps

per serving

Calories 276	Cholesterol 77 mg	Dietary Exchanges
Total Fat 5.0 g	Sodium 127 mg	1 fruit, 1 vegetable,
Saturated Fat 1.5 g	Carbohydrates 21 g	5 lean meat
Trans Fat 0.0 g	Fiber 2 g	
Polyunsaturated Fat 0.5 g	Sugars 16 g	
Monounsaturated Fat 2.5 g	Protein 35 g	

asian lettuce wraps

serves 4
2 wraps per serving

slow cooker size
3- to 4½-quart round or oval

slow cooking time
8 to 10 hours on low, **OR**
4 to 5 hours on high

1 1-pound flank steak or flat-end brisket, all visible fat discarded, cut to fit if necessary

1 cup matchstick-size strips of peeled jícama (about 1 small)

2 tablespoons plain rice vinegar

1 tablespoon soy sauce (lowest sodium available)

1 teaspoon minced peeled gingerroot

¼ to ½ teaspoon crushed red pepper flakes

∎ ∎ ∎

1 tablespoon cornstarch and (if needed) 1 tablespoon cornstarch, divided use

1 tablespoon plain rice vinegar

1 tablespoon water (if needed)

½ cup matchstick-size strips of red bell pepper

¼ cup sliced green onions

8 Bibb or Boston lettuce leaves

Eat these wraps with your hands, or shred the lettuce and serve the beef mixture on top.

Put the beef in the slow cooker. Top with the jícama.

In a small bowl, whisk together 2 tablespoons vinegar, the soy sauce, gingerroot, and red pepper flakes. Pour over the beef. Cook, covered, on low for 8 to 10 hours or on high for 4 to 5 hours, or until the beef is tender and the desired doneness. Transfer the beef to a cutting board, leaving the jícama mixture in the slow cooker. Set aside.

Put 1 tablespoon cornstarch in a small bowl. Add the remaining 1 tablespoon vinegar, whisking to dissolve. Stir into the jícama mixture. If the sauce still seems watery (more likely if cooking on low), put the remaining 1 tablespoon cornstarch in the same small bowl. Add 1 tablespoon water, whisking to dissolve. Stir into the jícama mixture. Stir in the bell pepper and green onions. Set aside.

Slice the beef diagonally across the grain if making wraps, or use one or two forks to shred it if serving on top of the lettuce. Return the beef to the slow cooker, stirring to coat.

To make wraps, spoon the filling down the center of each lettuce leaf. Fold the left and right sides of the lettuce toward the center. Starting from the unfolded end closest to you, roll the wrap toward the other end to enclose the filling. If you prefer, shred the lettuce and serve the beef and sauce on top.

per serving

Calories 202	Cholesterol 48 mg	Dietary Exchanges
Total Fat 6.5 g	Sodium 146 mg	1 vegetable, 3 lean
Saturated Fat 3.0 g	Carbohydrates 9 g	meat
Trans Fat 0.0 g	Fiber 2 g	
Polyunsaturated Fat 0.5 g	Sugars 2 g	
Monounsaturated Fat 3.0 g	Protein 24 g	

flank steak with artichoke ratatouille

QUICK PREP

serves 4
3 ounces beef and ¾ cup ratatouille per serving

slow cooker size/shape
3- to 4½-quart round or oval

slow cooking time
8 to 10 hours on low plus 30 minutes on high, **OR**
4 to 5 hours on high plus 30 minutes on high

- **1 1-pound flank steak, all visible fat discarded, cut to fit in slow cooker if necessary**
- **1 teaspoon dried Italian seasoning, crumbled**
- **¼ teaspoon salt**
- **¼ teaspoon pepper**
- **½ cup finely chopped onion**
- **2 medium garlic cloves, minced**
- **1 14.5-ounce can no-salt-added diced tomatoes, undrained**
- **2 tablespoons red wine vinegar**

■ ■ ■

- **8 ounces frozen artichoke hearts, thawed (about 2 cups)**
- **1 small yellow summer squash or zucchini, halved lengthwise and thinly sliced crosswise (about 1½ cups)**
- **1 medium red or green bell pepper, cut into matchstick-size strips (about 1 cup)**
- **¼ cup snipped fresh parsley**

Frozen artichoke hearts stand in for the traditional eggplant in a ratatouille sauce that accompanies slices of tender flank steak. For variety, use half a yellow summer squash and half a zucchini instead of choosing just one of them. *(See photo insert.)*

Sprinkle both sides of the beef with the Italian seasoning, salt, and pepper. Using your fingertips, gently press the seasonings so they adhere to the beef. Transfer to the slow cooker.

Sprinkle the onion and garlic over the beef. Pour in the tomatoes with liquid and vinegar. Cook, covered, on low for 8 to 10 hours or on high for 4 to 5 hours, or until the beef is tender. Transfer to a cutting board. Set aside.

If using the low setting, change it to high. Quickly stir in the artichoke hearts, squash, and bell pepper and re-cover the slow cooker. Cook for 30 minutes, or until tender.

Meanwhile, slice the beef diagonally across the grain or, using one or two forks, shred it. Cover to keep warm. Set aside until the ratatouille is ready.

Put the beef on plates. Using a slotted spoon, spoon the ratatouille over the beef. If you prefer, spoon the ratatouille alongside the beef. Sprinkle with the parsley.

per serving

Calories 237	Cholesterol 48 mg	Dietary Exchanges
Total Fat 6.5 g	Sodium 234 mg	3 vegetable, 3 lean
Saturated Fat 3.0 g	Carbohydrates 16 g	meat
Trans Fat 0.0 g	Fiber 6 g	
Polyunsaturated Fat 0.5 g	Sugars 6 g	
Monounsaturated Fat 3.0 g	Protein 27 g	

flank steak fajitas

serves 5
3 ounces beef, ½ cup vegetable
mixture, and 1 tortilla
per serving

slow cooker size/shape
2- to 3½-quart oval

slow cooking time
4 to 6 hours on low, **OR**
2 to 3 hours on high

½ **teaspoon olive oil and 1 teaspoon olive oil, divided use**

2 **medium to large onions, sliced
crosswise**

1 **teaspoon ground cumin**

1 **teaspoon chili powder**

½ **teaspoon garlic powder**

¼ **teaspoon salt**

¼ **teaspoon pepper**

⅛ **teaspoon ground chipotle**

1¼ **pounds flank steak, all visible
fat discarded**

2 **large tomatoes, chopped**

▪ ▪ ▪

3 **tablespoons snipped fresh
cilantro**

2 **teaspoons olive oil**

1 **large green bell pepper, sliced
lengthwise**

1 **large red bell pepper, sliced
lengthwise**

5 **8-inch fat-free whole-wheat
tortillas (lowest sodium
available)**

The mixture of spices is key to the success of these great-tasting fajitas. If you wish, dress them up with additional toppings, such as hot chiles, green onions, and lime wedges to squeeze over the filling.

In a medium nonstick skillet, heat ½ teaspoon oil over medium heat, swirling to coat the bottom. Cook the onions for 1 to 2 minutes, or until barely beginning to soften, stirring frequently. Transfer to the slow cooker. Set aside.

In a small bowl, stir together the cumin, chili powder, garlic powder, salt, pepper, and ground chipotle. Sprinkle over both sides of the beef. Using your fingertips, gently press the seasonings so they adhere to the beef.

In the same skillet, heat 1 teaspoon oil over medium-high heat, swirling to coat the bottom. Cook the beef for 4 to 6 minutes, or until browned, turning once halfway through. Place the beef on the onions. Top with the tomatoes. Don't stir. Cook, covered, on low for 4 to 6 hours or on high for 2 to 3 hours, or until the beef is tender.

Transfer the beef to a cutting board, leaving the onion mixture in the slow cooker. Let the beef stand, loosely covered, for 10 minutes before thinly slicing.

Meanwhile, using a slotted spoon, transfer the onions and tomatoes to a medium bowl, discarding any liquid remaining in the slow cooker. Stir in the cilantro and beef slices, discarding any juices that remain.

Meanwhile, in a medium skillet over medium heat, heat the remaining 2 teaspoons oil, swirling to coat the bottom. Cook the bell peppers over medium heat for 2 minutes, or until beginning to soften. Increase the heat to medium high. Cook for 1 to 3 minutes, or until the peppers are lightly browned and tender-crisp, stirring frequently.

Just before serving time, warm the tortillas using the package directions. Spoon the beef mixture onto the tortillas. Top with the bell pepper mixture. Roll up jelly-roll style.

cook's tip on chili powder: Most bottled chili powder contains salt, so check the labels for the brand with the least amount. Or, in a pinch, substitute a mixture of two parts paprika to one part ground cumin.

per serving

Calories 371	Cholesterol 48 mg	Dietary Exchanges
Total Fat 12.0 g	Sodium 516 mg	1½ starch, 2 vegetable,
Saturated Fat 3.5 g	Carbohydrates 37 g	3 lean meat, ½ fat
Trans Fat 0.0 g	Fiber 7 g	
Polyunsaturated Fat 1.5 g	Sugars 11 g	
Monounsaturated Fat 6.0 g	Protein 29 g	

chunky chili con carne

serves 4
scant 1¾ cups per serving

slow cooker size/shape
3- to 4½-quart round or oval

slow cooking time
6 to 8 hours on low
plus 30 minutes on low, **OR**
4 to 5 hours on high
plus 30 minutes on high

1 tablespoon chili powder

1 teaspoon ground cumin

½ teaspoon salt

¼ teaspoon dried oregano, crumbled

¼ teaspoon pepper

1 pound boneless top sirloin steak, all visible fat discarded, cut into ½-inch cubes

2 teaspoons olive oil

2 14.5-ounce cans no-added-salt diced tomatoes, undrained

1 medium onion, chopped

1 medium green bell pepper, chopped

¼ cup water

2 tablespoons no-salt-added tomato paste

2 medium garlic cloves, minced

▪ ▪ ▪

1 15.5-ounce can no-salt-added kidney beans, rinsed and drained

2 medium green onions, thinly sliced

Cubes of browned, spice-coated sirloin enhance this chili. All you need to serve on the side is a wedge of jalapeño cornbread.

In a small bowl, stir together the chili powder, cumin, salt, oregano, and pepper. Sprinkle 1 teaspoon over both sides of the beef. Using your fingertips, gently press the seasonings so they adhere to the beef. Set the remaining mixture aside.

In a large nonstick skillet, heat the oil over medium-high heat, swirling to coat the bottom. Cook the beef for 5 minutes, or until browned on all sides, stirring frequently. Transfer to the slow cooker.

Stir in the tomatoes with liquid, onion, bell pepper, water, tomato paste, garlic, and reserved chili powder mixture. Cook, covered, on low for 6 to 8 hours or on high for 4 to 5 hours, or until the beef is tender.

Quickly stir in the beans and re-cover the slow cooker. Cook for 30 minutes. Serve sprinkled with the green onions.

per serving

Calories 335	Cholesterol 60 mg	Dietary Exchanges
Total Fat 7.0 g	Sodium 409 mg	1 starch, 3 vegetable,
Saturated Fat 2.0 g	Carbohydrates 33 g	4 lean meat
Trans Fat 0.0 g	Fiber 12 g	
Polyunsaturated Fat 0.5 g	Sugars 12 g	
Monounsaturated Fat 4.0 g	Protein 35 g	

beef and brew stew

serves 4
1½ cups per serving

serves 4
1½ cups per serving

slow cooker size/shape
3- to 4½-quart round or oval

slow cooking time
8 to 10 hours on low
plus 10 minutes on high, **OR**
5 to 6 hours on high
plus 10 minutes on high

Dark beer gives this stew its complex flavor. You'll definitely want to soak up all the sauce, so serve the stew over whole-wheat no-yolk noodles, brown rice, or mashed potatoes made with heart-healthy ingredients.

Spread the beef on a large plate. Sprinkle the salt and pepper over the beef. Toss to coat.

In a large nonstick skillet, heat the oil over medium-high heat, swirling to coat the bottom. Cook the beef and onion for 5 minutes, or until the beef is browned on all sides, stirring frequently. Transfer to the slow cooker.

Stir in the broth, beer, turnips, carrots, celery, garlic, and thyme. Cook, covered, on low for 8 to 10 hours or on high for 5 to 6 hours, or until the beef and vegetables are tender.

Put the flour in a small bowl. Add the water, whisking to dissolve. Quickly pour into the beef mixture, stirring until well combined, and re-cover the slow cooker. If using the low setting, change it to high. Cook for 10 minutes, or until the sauce is slightly thickened. Stir in the parsley and vinegar.

cook's tip: If you don't care for dark beer, you can use light beer instead, or for a nonalcoholic alternative, substitute an additional 1½ cups of fat-free, low-sodium beef broth for the beer.

1 pound boneless sirloin steak, all visible fat discarded, cut into ½-inch cubes

¼ teaspoon salt

¼ teaspoon pepper

2 teaspoons olive oil

1 small onion, chopped

1¼ cups fat-free, low-sodium beef broth, such as on page 32

12 ounces dark beer

2 medium turnips or potatoes (about 1 pound total), peeled and cut into ½-inch cubes

2 medium carrots, halved lengthwise and cut crosswise into ½-inch slices

1 medium rib of celery, chopped

2 medium garlic cloves, minced

¼ teaspoon dried thyme, crumbled

■ ■ ■

2 tablespoons all-purpose flour

2 tablespoons cold water

2 tablespoons snipped fresh parsley (optional)

1 tablespoon balsamic vinegar

per serving

Calories 263
Total Fat 5.5 g
  Saturated Fat 1.5 g
  Trans Fat 0.0 g
  Polyunsaturated Fat 0.5 g
  Monounsaturated Fat 3.0 g

Cholesterol 58 mg
Sodium 312 mg
Carbohydrates 19 g
  Fiber 3 g
  Sugars 7 g
Protein 28 g

Dietary Exchanges
½ starch, 2 vegetable, 3 lean meat

beef goulash with lemon

serves 6
1½ cups per serving

slow cooker size/shape
3- to 4½-quart round or oval

slow cooking time
8 to 10 hours on low
plus 30 minutes on high, **OR**
4 to 5 hours on high
plus 30 minutes on high

- 2 cups baby carrots, halved crosswise
- 1 large onion, diced
- 1½ pounds boneless top round roast or eye-of-round roast, all visible fat discarded, cut into 1-inch cubes
- 1 pound unpeeled red potatoes, cut into 1-inch cubes
- 2 tablespoons uncooked instant, or quick-cooking, tapioca
- 1 cup fat-free, low-sodium beef broth, such as on page 32
- ¼ cup no-salt-added tomato paste
- 1 tablespoon paprika (1½ teaspoons Hungarian sweet and 1½ teaspoons hot preferred)
- 2 medium garlic cloves, minced
- ½ teaspoon caraway seeds, crushed
- ½ teaspoon dried marjoram, crumbled
- ¼ teaspoon dried thyme, crumbled
- ¼ teaspoon salt

Caraway seeds, marjoram, thyme, and lots of paprika help season this one-dish meal, but it's the addition of lemon zest that sets it apart. Tapioca, better known as a dessert, is used in this entrée recipe to thicken the stew.

In the slow cooker, make one layer each, in order, of the carrots, onion, beef, and potatoes. Sprinkle with the tapioca. Don't stir.

In a small bowl, whisk together the broth, tomato paste, paprika, garlic, caraway seeds, marjoram, thyme, and salt. Pour over the vegetables and beef in the slow cooker. Don't stir. Cook, covered, on low for 8 to 10 hours or on high for 4 to 5 hours.

Quickly stir the beans and lemon zest into the goulash and re-cover the slow cooker. If using the low setting, change it to high. Cook for 30 minutes, or until the beans are tender. Ladle into bowls. Top each serving with a dollop of sour cream.

(continued)

cook's tip on caraway seeds: The fruit of an herb in the carrot family, caraway seeds are very popular in German, Austrian, and Hungarian foods. To release their flavor, crush them using a mortar and pestle.

cook's tip on citrus zest: A microplane makes quick work of removing and grating the peel, or zest, of citrus fruit. Be careful to avoid cutting into any of the pith, the bitter white covering just beneath the peel. Measuring will be easy if you work over a sheet of wax paper, which you can fold to pour the zest into a measuring spoon. Any remaining zest can be frozen for later use.

12 ounces green beans, trimmed, cut into bite-size pieces (about 2 cups)

2 tablespoons finely chopped lemon zest, or to taste

2 tablespoons fat-free sour cream (optional)

per serving

Calories 268	Cholesterol 58 mg	Dietary Exchanges
Total Fat 3.5 g	Sodium 223 mg	1 starch, 3 vegetable,
Saturated Fat 1.5 g	Carbohydrates 30 g	3 very lean meat
Trans Fat 0.0 g	Fiber 6 g	
Polyunsaturated Fat 0.5 g	Sugars 9 g	
Monounsaturated Fat 1.5 g	Protein 30 g	

beef stew with fresh mango

serves 6
1 cup stew and ½ cup couscous
per serving

slow cooker size/shape
5- to 7-quart round or oval

slow cooking time
8 to 9 hours on low, **OR**
5 to 5½ hours on high

1½ pounds lean stew meat (1-inch cubes), all visible fat discarded

2 14.5-ounce cans no-salt-added diced tomatoes, drained

1 medium onion, cut into 6 wedges

1 large red bell pepper, cut lengthwise into ½-inch strips

2 tablespoons Worcestershire sauce (lowest sodium available)

1 tablespoon chili powder

2 medium garlic cloves, minced

½ teaspoon ground cinnamon

¼ teaspoon salt

¼ teaspoon pepper

■ ■ ■

1 cup uncooked whole-wheat couscous

1½ cups fat-free, low-sodium beef broth, such as on page 32, or fat-free, low-sodium vegetable broth, such as on page 33

1 medium mango, cut into bite-size pieces

½ cup snipped fresh cilantro

Fresh mango and cilantro add the perfect balance to this beef stew, full-flavored complements of lots of Worcestershire sauce and chili powder and just a bit of cinnamon. Serving it over whole-wheat couscous is an easy way to boost your fiber intake.

In the slow cooker, stir together the beef, tomatoes, onion, bell pepper, Worcestershire sauce, chili powder, garlic, cinnamon, salt, and pepper. Cook, covered, on low for 8 to 9 hours or on high for 5 to 5½ hours, or until the beef is tender.

About 10 minutes before serving time, prepare the couscous using the package directions, omitting the salt and substituting the broth for the water. Spoon into bowls. Ladle the stew onto the couscous. Top with the mango and cilantro.

cook's tip: If you have any stew and couscous left over, make tacos! Combine the stew and couscous, warm the mixture in the microwave, spoon onto warmed corn tortillas, and top each with a dollop of fat-free sour cream and a little shredded low-fat Cheddar cheese. Roll up jelly-roll style or eat using a knife and fork.

per serving

Calories 395
Total Fat 9.0 g
  Saturated Fat 3.0 g
  Trans Fat 0.0 g
  Polyunsaturated Fat 0.5 g
  Monounsaturated Fat 3.5 g

Cholesterol 71 mg
Sodium 224 mg
Carbohydrates 50 g
  Fiber 8 g
  Sugars 15 g
Protein 30 g

Dietary Exchanges
  2 starch, 2 vegetable,
  ½ fruit, 3 lean meat

country cassoulet

serves 4
1½ cups per serving

slow cooker size
3- to 4½-quart round or oval

slow cooking time
8 to 10 hours on low, **OR**
4 to 5 hours on high

1 cup dried navy beans (about 6 ounces), sorted for stones and shriveled beans, rinsed and drained

1 teaspoon olive oil

1 pound lean stew meat (1-inch cubes), all visible fat discarded

4 cups fat-free, low-sodium beef broth, such as on page 32

2 medium carrots, sliced crosswise

1 medium onion, cut into 16 wedges

1 medium rib of celery, sliced crosswise

2 medium garlic cloves, minced

1 medium dried bay leaf

1 teaspoon dried herbes de Provence, crumbled

¼ teaspoon salt

¼ teaspoon pepper

■ ■ ■

¼ cup snipped fresh parsley

With its coarse textures and aromatic flavors, this beef and bean dish is evocative of the French countryside.

Fill a large saucepan three-fourths full of water. Bring to a boil over high heat. Stir in the beans. Return to a boil. Reduce the heat and simmer for 15 minutes. Pour the beans into a colander and rinse. Pour into the slow cooker. Set aside.

In a large nonstick skillet, heat the oil over medium-high heat, swirling to coat the bottom. Cook the beef for 4 to 6 minutes, or until browned on all sides, stirring frequently. Transfer to the slow cooker.

Stir in the remaining ingredients except the parsley. Cook, covered, on low for 8 to 10 hours or on high for 4 to 5 hours, or until the beans are tender. Discard the bay leaf. Ladle into bowls. Sprinkle with the parsley.

cook's tip on herbes de provence: Herbes de Provence is a standout seasoning blend containing dried herbs commonly found in southern France, such as basil, lavender, marjoram, rosemary, sage, and thyme. Try this mixture for seasoning soups, stews, vinaigrettes, and roasted or grilled pork, poultry, and vegetables.

per serving

Calories 382	Cholesterol 71 mg	Dietary Exchanges
Total Fat 10.0 g	Sodium 295 mg	2 starch, 2 vegetable,
Saturated Fat 3.0 g	Carbohydrates 39 g	3½ lean meat
Trans Fat 0.0 g	Fiber 15 g	
Polyunsaturated Fat 1.0 g	Sugars 5 g	
Monounsaturated Fat 4.5 g	Protein 34 g	

molasses-glazed beef and veggie meat loaf

QUICK PREP

serves 4
1 slice or wedge per serving

slow cooker size/shape
3- to 4½-quart round or oval (preferred)

slow cooking time
3 hours 45 minutes to 5 hours 45 minutes on low plus
5 to 10 minutes on high, **OR**
1 hour 45 minutes to
2 hours 45 minutes on high plus 5 to 10 minutes on high

Cooking spray

1 pound extra-lean ground beef

1 medium onion, finely chopped

⅔ cup shredded carrots

⅔ cup shredded cabbage

⅔ cup finely chopped broccoli florets

½ cup plain panko (Japanese bread crumbs)

2 large egg whites

½ teaspoon garlic powder

½ teaspoon dried thyme, crumbled

¼ teaspoon salt

¼ teaspoon pepper

■ ■ ■

2 tablespoons no-salt-added ketchup

1 tablespoon light molasses

Shredded carrots, cabbage, and broccoli make this meat loaf lighter and healthier than most. The glaze adds color and a final layer of flavor.

Fold an 18-inch-long piece of aluminum foil lengthwise in thirds. Place the foil in the slow cooker so it runs the length of the cooker and hangs over the two short sides (assuming use of an oval cooker). The foil will help you remove the cooked meat loaf from the slow cooker later. Lightly spray the foil and the inside of the slow cooker with cooking spray. Set aside.

Crumble the beef into a large bowl. Add the onion, carrots, cabbage, and broccoli. Using your hands or a spoon, gently combine.

Work in the panko, egg whites, garlic powder, thyme, salt, and pepper. Depending on the shape of your slow cooker, shape into an oval or round loaf 2½ to 3 inches thick. Place in the slow cooker so the foil strip is under the middle of the meat loaf. Cook, covered, on low for 3 hours 45 minutes to 5 hours 45 minutes or on high for 1 hour 45 minutes to 2 hours 45 minutes, or until the internal temperature of the meat loaf reaches 160°F on an instant-read thermometer.

About 30 minutes before serving time, in a small bowl, stir together the ketchup and molasses. Set aside.

When the meat loaf is ready, quickly spread the glaze over the top and re-cover the slow cooker. If using the low setting, change it to high. Cook for 5 to 10 minutes, or until the glaze is hot. Grasping the ends of the foil, carefully lift the meat loaf from the slow cooker. Transfer to a cutting board. Cover loosely. Let stand for 10 minutes before slicing or cutting into wedges.

per serving

Calories 231	Cholesterol 62 mg	Dietary Exchanges
Total Fat 6.0 g	Sodium 296 mg	½ starch, 2 vegetable,
Saturated Fat 2.5 g	Carbohydrates 18 g	3 lean meat
Trans Fat 0.5 g	Fiber 2 g	
Polyunsaturated Fat 0.5 g	Sugars 9 g	
Monounsaturated Fat 2.5 g	Protein 28 g	

picadillo beef

serves 4
¾ cup beef mixture per serving

slow cooker size/shape
3- to 4½-quart round or oval

slow cooking time
6 hours on low, **OR**
3 hours on high

Cooking spray

12 ounces extra-lean ground beef

1 14.5-ounce can no-salt-added diced tomatoes, undrained

1 medium onion, diced

⅓ cup dark or golden raisins

2 medium dried bay leaves

1 medium fresh serrano pepper or jalapeño with seeds, finely chopped

2 teaspoons sugar

¾ teaspoon ground cinnamon

½ teaspoon ground cumin

½ teaspoon ground nutmeg

½ teaspoon garlic powder

½ teaspoon dried thyme, crumbled

¼ teaspoon ground allspice

■ ■ ■

10 ounces frozen brown rice

¼ cup slivered almonds, dry-roasted (about 1 ounce)

¼ teaspoon salt

¼ teaspoon pepper

A spicy favorite in Spanish-speaking countries and the Philippines (where it is known as *giniling*), picadillo (pee-kah-DEE-yoh) usually contains ground beef and tomatoes, with the other ingredients varying by region. Our version features raisins, almonds, and a number of spices and is served over brown rice. Keep the ribs and seeds in the pepper so you'll get the full effect of the heat.

Lightly spray the slow cooker with cooking spray. Set aside.

In a large nonstick skillet, cook the beef over medium-high heat for 3 to 5 minutes, or until browned on the outside and no longer pink in the center, stirring occasionally to turn and break up the beef. Remove the skillet from the heat.

Stir in the tomatoes with liquid, onion, raisins, bay leaves, serrano pepper, sugar, cinnamon, cumin, nutmeg, garlic powder, thyme, and allspice. Transfer to the slow cooker. Cook, covered, on low for 6 hours or on high for 3 hours, or until the onion is very soft.

About 5 minutes before serving time, prepare the rice using the package directions.

Discard the bay leaves from the picadillo. Stir in the almonds, salt, and pepper. Spoon over the rice.

per serving

Calories 320	Cholesterol 47 mg	Dietary Exchanges
Total Fat 8.5 g	Sodium 228 mg	1 starch, 1 fruit,
Saturated Fat 2.0 g	Carbohydrates 40 g	2 vegetable, 2½ lean
Trans Fat 0.5 g	Fiber 5 g	meat
Polyunsaturated Fat 1.5 g	Sugars 16 g	
Monounsaturated Fat 4.0 g	Protein 23 g	

five-way cincinnati-style chili

serves 6
1 cup chili and 1 cup pasta
per serving

slow cooker size/shape
3- to 4½-quart round or oval

slow cooking time
5 to 7 hours on low, **OR**
3 to 3½ hours on high

1 pound extra-lean ground beef

1 15.5-ounce can no-salt-added kidney beans, rinsed and drained

1 14.5-ounce can no-salt-added diced tomatoes, undrained

⅔ cup chopped onion

3 tablespoons cider vinegar

2 teaspoons chili powder

1 teaspoon ground cinnamon

1 teaspoon dried minced garlic

1 teaspoon ground cumin

½ teaspoon ground allspice

¼ teaspoon salt

¼ teaspoon pepper

■ ■ ■

12 ounces dried whole-grain spaghetti

2 tablespoons semisweet chocolate chips

¼ cup plus 2 tablespoons diced onion

¾ cup low-fat shredded sharp Cheddar cheese

You don't have to be from Ohio to enjoy the aroma and distinctive taste of Cincinnati chili, which features cinnamon, allspice, and chocolate or cocoa. The typical version is called "five-way" because the chili (1) is served over spaghetti (2) and garnished with beans (3), raw onion (4), and cheese (5), although we veered from tradition a bit by cooking the beans in the chili. *(See photo insert.)*

In a large nonstick skillet, cook the beef over medium-high heat for 3 to 5 minutes, or until browned on the outside and no longer pink in the center, stirring occasionally to turn and break up the beef. Drain if needed. Transfer to the slow cooker.

Stir in the beans, tomatoes with liquid, ⅔ cup onion, vinegar, chili powder, cinnamon, garlic, cumin, allspice, salt, and pepper. Cook, covered, on low for 5 to 7 hours or on high for 3 to 3½ hours.

About 15 minutes before serving time, prepare the pasta using the package directions, omitting the salt. Drain well in a colander.

Add the chocolate chips to the chili, stirring until melted.

Spoon the pasta onto plates. Top with the chili, remaining ¼ cup plus 2 tablespoons onion, and the Cheddar.

per serving

Calories 447	Cholesterol 45 mg	Dietary Exchanges
Total Fat 8.0 g	Sodium 269 mg	4 starch, 1 vegetable,
Saturated Fat 3.0 g	Carbohydrates 64 g	3 lean meat
Trans Fat 0.0 g	Fiber 11 g	
Polyunsaturated Fat 1.0 g	Sugars 9 g	
Monounsaturated Fat 2.5 g	Protein 33 g	

jerk pork loin with mango salsa

serve 8
3 ounces pork and ¼ cup salsa per serving

slow cooker size/shape
3- to 4½-quart round or oval

slow cooking time
6 to 7 hours on low, **OR**
3 to 3½ hours on high

1 cup water

½ medium onion, sliced

1 sprig of fresh thyme

1 teaspoon salt-free Jamaican jerk seasoning blend

1 2-pound boneless pork loin roast, any netting or kitchen twine and all visible fat discarded

1 tablespoon fresh lime juice

■ ■ ■

2 medium mangoes, chopped

½ cup finely chopped red bell pepper

¼ cup chopped green onions (green and white parts)

¼ cup snipped fresh cilantro

2 tablespoons fresh lime juice

¼ teaspoon crushed red pepper flakes

Mango salsa makes a colorful pairing for this delectable, spicy pork dish. Once the pork roast is slow cooking, you can make and refrigerate the salsa, or toss it together just before serving the meal. *(See photo insert.)*

In the slow cooker, stir together the water, onion, and thyme. Set aside.

Sprinkle the seasoning blend all over the pork. Using your fingertips, gently press the seasoning so it adheres to the pork. Transfer to the slow cooker.

Drizzle 1 tablespoon lime juice over the pork. Cook, covered, on low for 6 to 7 hours or on high for 3 to 3½ hours, or until the pork registers 145°F on an instant-read thermometer.

Transfer the pork to a cutting board. Let stand for about 10 minutes. Cut the pork into thin slices or shred it using one or two forks.

Meanwhile, in a medium bowl, stir together the remaining ingredients. Cover and refrigerate until needed if made in advance, or prepare shortly before serving time and set aside.

When the pork is ready, spoon the salsa on top or serve alongside.

per serving

Calories 221	Cholesterol 65 mg	Dietary Exchanges
Total Fat 7.0 g	Sodium 50 mg	1 fruit, 3 lean meat
Saturated Fat 2.5 g	Carbohydrates 14 g	
Trans Fat 0.0 g	Fiber 2 g	
Polyunsaturated Fat 0.5 g	Sugars 12 g	
Monounsaturated Fat 3.5 g	Protein 25 g	

cuban-style pork with orange

serves 6
3 ounces pork per serving

slow cooker size/shape
3- to 4½-quart round or oval

slow cooking time
6 to 8 hours on low, **OR**
3 to 4 hours on high

1 medium orange, cut into
   8 wedges

½ teaspoon pepper

½ teaspoon salt

1 1½-pound boneless pork loin
   roast, any netting or kitchen
   twine and all visible fat
   discarded

1 teaspoon olive oil

2 tablespoons minced onion

1 tablespoon chopped fresh
   oregano

1½ teaspoons cumin seeds

2 medium garlic cloves, minced

½ teaspoon grated orange zest

Many of the seasonings found in a typical Cuban adobo—a piquant sauce including garlic, cumin, oregano, and orange—are used to flavor this pork roast. In this recipe, the pork cooks on orange wedges, which provide moisture and act as a cooking rack, allowing the fat to drain away from the roast.

Lightly squeeze the orange wedges to release only some of their juice into the slow cooker. Add the wedges, each with one flat side down.

Sprinkle the pepper and salt all over the pork. Using your fingertips, gently press the seasonings so they adhere to the pork. In a medium nonstick skillet, heat the oil over medium-high heat, swirling to coat the bottom. Cook the pork for 4 to 6 minutes, turning to brown on all sides. Transfer to a large plate.

Reduce the heat to medium. Add the remaining ingredients to the skillet, stirring to combine. Cook for 2 minutes, or until the onion begins to soften and the ingredients are fragrant. Spread over the pork. Place the pork on the orange wedges. Cook, covered, on low for 6 to 8 hours or on high for 3 to 4 hours, or until the pork registers 145°F on an instant-read thermometer.

Transfer the pork to a cutting board. Discard the orange wedges. Let the pork stand, loosely covered, for 10 minutes before slicing.

per serving

Calories 183	Cholesterol 65 mg	Dietary Exchanges
Total Fat 7.5 g	Sodium 242 mg	3 lean meat
Saturated Fat 3.0 g	Carbohydrates 3 g	
Trans Fat 0.0 g	Fiber 0 g	
Polyunsaturated Fat 0.5 g	Sugars 1 g	
Monounsaturated Fat 4.0 g	Protein 25 g	

four-seed pork loin

QUICK
PREP

serve 8
3 ounces pork and 2 tablespoons sauce per serving

slow cooker size/shape
3- to 4½-quart round or oval

slow cooking time
6 to 7 hours on low, **OR**
3 to 3½ hours on high

⅔ cup unsweetened apple cider
   or apple juice

½ medium onion, sliced

1 teaspoon fennel seeds, crushed

1 teaspoon caraway seeds,
   crushed

1 teaspoon dill seeds, crushed

1 teaspoon celery seeds, crushed

1 tablespoon spicy brown
   mustard

1 2-pound boneless pork loin
   roast, any netting or kitchen
   twine and all visible fat
   discarded

■ ■ ■

1 tablespoon cornstarch

1 tablespoon unsweetened apple
   cider or apple juice

The slow cooker mellows a combination of spices
to create an extremely flavorful pork roast.

In the slow cooker, stir together ⅔ cup cider and the onion.
Set aside.

On a large piece of wax paper, combine the fennel, caraway,
dill, and celery seeds. Spread them in a single layer. Set aside.

Brush the mustard all over the pork loin. Gently roll the
pork in the seeds to coat. Place the pork in the slow cooker.
Cook, covered, on low for 6 to 7 hours or on high for
3 to 3½ hours, or until the pork registers 145°F on
an instant-read thermometer.

Leaving the cooking liquid in the slow cooker, transfer the
pork to a cutting board. Let the pork stand for about
10 minutes. Slice the pork. Cover to keep warm.

While the pork is standing, strain the cooking liquid into
a small saucepan.

Put the cornstarch in a small bowl. Add the remaining
1 tablespoon cider, whisking to dissolve. Whisk into the
cooking liquid. Cook over medium heat for 2 minutes, or
until the sauce is thickened and bubbly, whisking constantly.
Serve spooned over the pork.

cook's tip on crushing seeds: You can crush seeds by using a mortar
and pestle or spreading them in a single layer on a cutting board and
either pressing them with the side of a chef's knife blade or rolling over
them with a rolling pin.

per serving

Calories 188	Cholesterol 65 mg	Dietary Exchanges
Total Fat 7.0 g	Sodium 68 mg	½ other carbohydrate,
Saturated Fat 2.5 g	Carbohydrates 5 g	3 lean meat
Trans Fat 0.0 g	Fiber 1 g	
Polyunsaturated Fat 0.5 g	Sugars 3 g	
Monounsaturated Fat 3.5 g	Protein 25 g	

tuscan pork and beans

serves 6
3 ounces pork and ⅓ cup beans per serving

slow cooker size/shape
2- to 3-quart round or oval

slow cooking time
8 to 12 hours on low, **OR**
4 to 6 hours on high

½ cup dried Great Northern beans, sorted for stones and shriveled beans, rinsed, and drained

1 large red bell pepper, chopped

¾ cup fat-free, low-sodium chicken broth, such as on page 31

1 teaspoon olive oil

1 1½-pound boneless pork loin roast, any netting or kitchen twine and all visible fat discarded

½ teaspoon salt

¼ teaspoon pepper

2 tablespoons finely chopped fresh rosemary

4 medium garlic cloves, minced

1 teaspoon dried fennel seeds, crushed

As the pork loin, with its crust of rosemary, garlic, and fennel, slowly cooks atop the beans, it infuses them with robust flavor.

Fill a small saucepan three-fourths full of water. Bring to a boil over high heat. Stir in the beans. Return to a boil. Reduce the heat and simmer for 15 minutes. Pour the beans into a colander and rinse. Pour into the slow cooker. Stir in the bell pepper and broth.

Meanwhile, in a medium nonstick skillet, heat the oil over medium-high heat, swirling to coat the bottom. Cook the pork for 4 to 6 minutes, turning to brown all sides. Transfer to a large plate. Sprinkle the salt and pepper over the top side of the pork. Using your fingertips, gently press the seasonings so they adhere to the pork.

In a small bowl, stir together the rosemary, garlic, and fennel seeds. Sprinkle over the top of the pork. Place the pork with the seasoned side up on the beans. Cook, covered, on low for 8 to 12 hours or on high for 4 to 6 hours, or until the pork is fork-tender and the beans are creamy and very tender.

Transfer the pork to a cutting board, leaving the bean mixture in the slow cooker. Let the pork stand, loosely covered, for 10 minutes before slicing. Serve over the beans or with the beans on the side.

cook's tip: For this recipe, you don't need to test the pork for doneness with a thermometer. It will cook past the minimum internal temperature needed for food safety (145°F) to get to the fork-tender stage.

per serving

Calories 230	Cholesterol 65 mg	Dietary Exchanges
Total Fat 8.0 g	Sodium 250 mg	½ starch, 3½ lean meat
Saturated Fat 3.0 g	Carbohydrates 10 g	
Trans Fat 0.0 g	Fiber 4 g	
Polyunsaturated Fat 1.0 g	Sugars 1 g	
Monounsaturated Fat 4.0 g	Protein 28 g	

pork tenderloin with cherry and peach salsa

serves 4
3 ounces pork and ⅓ cup salsa per serving

slow cooker size/shape
3- to 4½-quart round or oval

slow cooking time
2 hours to 2 hours
15 minutes on low plus
15 minutes on high, **OR**
1 hour to 1 hour 10 minutes on high plus 15 minutes on high

Cooking spray

2 teaspoons chili powder

½ teaspoon ground cinnamon

½ teaspoon garlic powder

¼ teaspoon ground allspice

¼ teaspoon salt

⅛ teaspoon cayenne

1 1-pound pork tenderloin, all visible fat discarded

1 teaspoon canola or corn oil

¼ cup water

■ ■ ■

1 cup frozen dark sweet cherries, thawed, coarsely chopped

1 cup frozen unsweetened peach slices, thawed, diced

1 medium fresh jalapeño, seeds and ribs discarded, finely chopped

1 tablespoon sugar

1½ teaspoons balsamic vinegar

1 teaspoon grated peeled gingerroot

The unusually flavored salsa, with its blend of fruity, spicy, and tangy notes, is a worthy accompaniment for the delicious, succulent pork.

Lightly spray the slow cooker with cooking spray. Set aside.

In a small bowl, stir together the chili powder, cinnamon, garlic powder, allspice, salt, and cayenne. Sprinkle over both sides of the pork. Using your fingertips, gently press the seasonings so they adhere to the pork.

In a large nonstick skillet, heat the oil over medium-high heat, swirling to coat the bottom. Cook the pork for 4 minutes, or until browned, turning once halfway through. Remove the skillet from the heat. Transfer the pork to the slow cooker.

Pour the water into the skillet, scraping the bottom and side to dislodge any browned bits. Pour around, not over, the pork. Cook, covered, on low for 2 hours to 2 hours 15 minutes or on high for 1 hour to 1 hour 10 minutes, or until the pork registers 145°F on an instant-read thermometer. Quickly transfer the pork to a cutting board. Discard the cooking liquid.

If using the low setting, change it to high. Put the remaining ingredients except the gingerroot in the slow cooker, stirring to combine. Cook, covered, for 15 minutes, or until heated through. Meanwhile, let the pork stand for about 10 minutes before slicing.

When the salsa is hot, stir in the gingerroot. Serve the salsa with the pork.

cook's tip: It's important not to overcook pork tenderloin—or it won't be tender! Season it, brown it a bit, and cook it in the slow cooker just for a while.

per serving

Calories 198	Cholesterol 74 mg	Dietary Exchanges
Total Fat 4.0 g	Sodium 229 mg	1 fruit, 3 lean meat
Saturated Fat 1.0 g	Carbohydrates 15 g	
Trans Fat 0.0 g	Fiber 3 g	
Polyunsaturated Fat 1.0 g	Sugars 10 g	
Monounsaturated Fat 2.0 g	Protein 25 g	

salad greens with lime and herb pulled pork

QUICK PREP

A mild version of pico de gallo dresses a bed of fresh salad greens topped with herb-rubbed pork. Squeeze fresh lime juice over the salad for some extra zing.

In the slow cooker, stir together the onion, water, jalapeño, and 3 garlic cloves. Set aside.

In a small bowl, stir together the cumin, oregano, pepper, and salt. Sprinkle all over the pork. Using your fingertips, gently press the seasonings so they adhere to the pork.

Place the pork in the slow cooker. Drizzle the lime juice over the pork. Cook, covered, on low for 7 to 8 hours or on high for 3½ to 4 hours, or until the pork is fork-tender. (The pork will be past the minimum internal temperature of 145°F at this point.)

Meanwhile, in a medium bowl, stir together the tomatoes, red onion, cilantro, and remaining garlic clove. If you make the pico de gallo 1 hour or more in advance, cover and refrigerate until needed. If less than 1 hour, set the uncovered pico de gallo aside.

1 medium onion, cut into 12 wedges

½ cup water

1 medium fresh jalapeño, seeds and ribs discarded, chopped

3 medium garlic cloves, minced

1 teaspoon ground cumin

1 teaspoon dried oregano, crumbled

¼ teaspoon pepper

¼ teaspoon salt

1 1-pound pork tenderloin, all visible fat discarded

1 tablespoon fresh lime juice

■ ■ ■

1 cup chopped seeded tomatoes (2 medium)

2 tablespoons finely chopped red onion

2 tablespoons snipped fresh cilantro

1 medium garlic clove, minced

6 cups torn fresh lettuces, spinach, or a combination

1 small lime, cut into 4 wedges

Transfer the pork to a cutting board, leaving the onion mixture in the slow cooker. Let the pork stand for 3 minutes. Using your hands or two forks, pull the meat apart into long shreds. Stir into the onion mixture to "wet" the pork.

Just before serving, arrange the lettuce on plates. Using a slotted spoon or tongs, put the pork on the lettuce, discarding the onion mixture. Top with the pico de gallo. Serve with the lime wedges for squeezing over all.

cook's tip on seeding tomatoes: To seed tomatoes easily, cut the tomato crosswise and squeeze out the seeds and liquid.

per serving

Calories 170	Cholesterol 74 mg	Dietary Exchanges
Total Fat 3.0 g	Sodium 223 mg	2 vegetable, 3 lean
Saturated Fat 1.0 g	Carbohydrates 11 g	meat
Trans Fat 0.0 g	Fiber 3 g	
Polyunsaturated Fat 0.5 g	Sugars 6 g	
Monounsaturated Fat 1.0 g	Protein 26 g	

pork and butternut stew

serves 4
1¼ cups per serving

slow cooker size/shape
3- to 4½-quart round or oval

slow cooking time
5 to 6 hours on low

1½ **pounds butternut squash,
peeled, seeds and strings
discarded, cut into 1-inch
cubes, or 16 to 18 ounces
refrigerated cubes**

1 **medium onion, chopped**

1 **pound pork tenderloin, all
visible fat discarded, cut into
1-inch cubes**

1 **medium green or red bell
pepper, diced**

2 **tablespoons uncooked instant,
or quick-cooking, tapioca**

½ **cup fat-free, low-sodium
chicken broth, such as on
page 31**

¼ **cup no-salt-added tomato
paste**

2 **tablespoons honey**

2 **tablespoons balsamic vinegar**

1 **teaspoon ground cumin**

½ **to 1 teaspoon ground chipotle
powder**

¼ **teaspoon salt**

¼ **teaspoon pepper**

■ ■ ■

1½ **cups uncooked instant brown
rice**

¼ **cup snipped fresh cilantro
(optional)**

Ground chipotle pepper is a great ingredient to have on hand to add subtle smokiness and kick up the heat of an everyday dish. It and honey are the "secret" ingredients that make this stew special.

In the slow cooker, make one layer each, in order, of the squash, onion, pork, and bell pepper, sprinkling about 1½ teaspoons tapioca over each layer as you go.

In a small bowl, whisk together the broth, tomato paste, honey, vinegar, cumin, chipotle powder, salt, and pepper. Pour into the slow cooker. Don't stir. Cook, covered, on low for 5 to 6 hours.

About 20 minutes before serving time, prepare the rice using the package directions, omitting the salt and margarine.

Serve the stew over the rice. Garnish with the cilantro.

cook's tip on cutting winter squash: To make any raw whole winter squash easier to cut, microwave it first. Pierce the squash in several places with the tip of a knife. Place the squash on a paper towel. For a 1½-pound squash, as in this recipe, microwave on 100 percent power (high) for about 3 minutes. Using a kitchen towel to keep from burning your fingers, transfer the squash to a cutting board. Still using the towel, hold the squash in place and carefully cut it in the desired number of pieces.

per serving

Calories 380	Cholesterol 74 mg	Dietary Exchanges
Total Fat 4.0 g	Sodium 243 mg	3½ starch, 2 vegetable,
Saturated Fat 1.0 g	Carbohydrates 60 g	3 very lean meat
Trans Fat 0.0 g	Fiber 6 g	
Polyunsaturated Fat 1.0 g	Sugars 18 g	
Monounsaturated Fat 1.0 g	Protein 29 g	

sun-dried tomato, kalamata, and tuna tapenade page 15

open-face empanadas page 26

**fresh tomato soup with
goat cheese and basil** page 36

chicken tortilla soup page 51

**countryside beef and
garden vegetable soup** page 56

**salmon fillets with
pineapple-melon relish** page 73

shrimp jambalaya page 83

athens chicken pinwheels on pasta page 96

**chicken with black beans
and sweet potatoes** page 105

**flank steak with
artichoke ratatouille** page 133

five-way cincinnati-style chili   page 145

jerk pork loin with mango salsa   page 146

**italian artichoke-stuffed
bell peppers** page 171

**east indian spiced beans
with apricot rice** page 174

balsamic-glazed beets with toasted walnuts page 194

vegetable and mixed-rice pilaf page 208

**cinnamon quinoa
with peaches** page 229

pears with raspberry-orange sauce   page 238

pork-and-beans chili

serves 4
1½ cups per serving

slow cooker size/shape
4- to 6-quart round or oval

slow cooking time
5 to 7 hours on low, **OR**
2 to 3 hours on high

1 **28-ounce can no-salt-added diced or whole peeled tomatoes, undrained, diced if whole**

1 **pound boneless lean pork loin roast or chops, any netting or kitchen twine and all visible fat discarded, cut into 1½-inch cubes**

1 **15.5-ounce can no-salt-added black beans or no-salt-added pinto beans, rinsed and drained**

1 **medium onion, chopped**

1 **medium fresh jalapeño, seeds and ribs discarded, chopped**

3 **tablespoons red wine vinegar**

2 **teaspoons dried minced garlic**

2 **teaspoons chili powder**

1 **teaspoon ground cumin**

1 **teaspoon dried oregano, crumbled**

¼ **teaspoon salt**

¼ **teaspoon pepper**

■ ■ ■

¼ **cup fat-free sour cream (optional)**

¼ **cup shredded or grated fat-free sharp Cheddar cheese (optional)**

Snipped fresh cilantro (optional)

If your idea of chili means ground beef and red beans, try this quick-to-fix pork-and-black-bean version instead. It's guaranteed to change your way of thinking about your usual bowl of red.

In the slow cooker, stir together the tomatoes with liquid, pork, beans, onion, jalapeño, vinegar, garlic, chili powder, cumin, oregano, salt, and pepper. Cook, covered, on low for 5 to 7 hours or on high for 2 to 3 hours. Ladle into bowls. Top each serving with the sour cream, Cheddar, and cilantro.

per serving

Calories 326	Cholesterol 64 mg	Dietary Exchanges
Total Fat 8.0 g	Sodium 239 mg	1 starch, 3 vegetable,
Saturated Fat 3.0 g	Carbohydrates 31 g	3½ lean meat
Trans Fat 0.0 g	Fiber 7 g	
Polyunsaturated Fat 0.5 g	Sugars 12 g	
Monounsaturated Fat 3.5 g	Protein 31 g	

per serving (with optional toppings)

Calories 352	Cholesterol 68 mg	Dietary Exchanges
Total Fat 8.0 g	Sodium 321 mg	1½ starch, 3 vegetable,
Saturated Fat 3.0 g	Carbohydrates 34 g	3½ lean meat
Trans Fat 0.0 g	Fiber 7 g	
Polyunsaturated Fat 0.5 g	Sugars 13 g	
Monounsaturated Fat 3.5 g	Protein 34 g	

alsatian pork-and-potato casserole

serves 8
3 ounces pork and 1 cup vegetables per serving

slow cooker size/shape
5- to 7-quart round or oval

slow cooking time
6 to 7 hours on low plus 20 to 30 minutes on low

Cooking spray

1 teaspoon olive oil and 1 teaspoon olive oil, divided use

8 boneless center-cut pork chops (about 4 ounces each), all visible fat discarded, patted dry

2 medium onions, cut crosswise into ¼-inch slices

2 pounds red potatoes, peeled, cut crosswise into ¼-inch slices

2 medium garlic cloves, minced

1½ teaspoons caraway seeds

1½ teaspoons dried thyme, crumbled

½ teaspoon salt

¼ teaspoon pepper

1 cup fat-free, low-sodium chicken broth, such as on page 31, and ½ cup fat-free, low-sodium chicken broth, divided use

2 tablespoons cornstarch

■ ■ ■

1 medium red bell pepper, cut into ¼-inch rings

Reminiscent of a dish you might enjoy in Alsace, where the cuisine is more German than French, this casserole uses everyday ingredients to create a satisfying meal. The low heat is needed for tenderness and moistness. Serve it with green beans, followed with fresh fruit for dessert.

Lightly spray the slow cooker with cooking spray. Set aside.

In a large skillet, heat 1 teaspoon oil over medium-high heat, swirling to coat the bottom. Cook the pork for 3 to 4 minutes on each side, or until browned. Transfer to a large plate. Set aside.

Add the remaining 1 teaspoon oil to the skillet, swirling to coat the bottom. Cook the onions for 8 to 10 minutes, or until softened and golden, stirring frequently and adjusting the heat as necessary so they don't burn.

In the slow cooker, make one layer each of half the potatoes and half the onions. Sprinkle with half the garlic and all the caraway seeds, thyme, salt, and pepper. Arrange the pork on the onions. Repeat with the remaining potatoes, onions, and garlic. Don't stir.

Pour 1 cup broth into the skillet. Cook over medium heat for 5 minutes, or until hot.

Put the cornstarch in a small bowl. Add the remaining ½ cup broth, whisking to dissolve. Whisk into the broth in the skillet. Cook for 1 minute, or until thickened, whisking constantly. Pour over the ingredients in the slow cooker. Cook, covered, on low for 6 to 7 hours, or until the pork is slightly pink in the center.

Quickly arrange the bell pepper on top of the casserole and re-cover the slow cooker. Cook for 20 to 30 minutes, or until the bell pepper is tender.

cook's tip: Mandolines and inexpensive v-blade slicers make quick work of slicing potatoes and onions to uniform thickness.

per serving

Calories 266	Cholesterol 60 mg	Dietary Exchanges
Total Fat 7.0 g	Sodium 234 mg	1½ starch, 3 lean meat
Saturated Fat 2.0 g	Carbohydrates 25 g	
Trans Fat 0.0 g	Fiber 3 g	
Polyunsaturated Fat 1.0 g	Sugars 4 g	
Monounsaturated Fat 3.0 g	Protein 25 g	

pork chops with grape tomatoes and fresh basil

serves 4
1 pork chop and ¼ cup sauce per serving

slow cooker size/shape
2½- to 3½-quart round or oval

slow cooking time
2½ to 3½ hours on low, **OR**
1½ to 2 hours on high

3 medium garlic cloves, minced

¼ teaspoon salt

¼ teaspoon pepper

4 lean bone-in pork rib chops (about 6 ounces each), all visible fat discarded

1 teaspoon olive oil

⅓ cup white wine (regular or nonalcoholic) or fat-free low-sodium, chicken broth, such as on page 31

1½ cups grape tomatoes, halved

■ ■ ■

2 tablespoons loosely packed chopped fresh basil

For an easy Italian meal, serve this dish, beautiful with its vibrant topping of red tomatoes and deep green basil, with whole-wheat orzo and broccoli rabe.

Sprinkle the garlic, salt, and pepper over both sides of the pork. Using your fingertips, gently press the seasonings so they adhere to the pork.

In a large skillet, heat the oil over medium-high heat, swirling to coat the bottom. Cook the pork for 4 to 6 minutes, or until browned, turning once halfway through. Arrange in a single layer in the slow cooker (the ends of the chops may slightly overlap).

Pour the wine into the skillet. Increase the heat to high and bring to a boil, scraping the bottom and side to dislodge any browned bits. Boil for 30 seconds to 1 minute, or until the mixture is reduced by about half. Pour over the pork.

Spread the tomatoes over the pork. Cook, covered, on low for 2½ to 3½ hours or on high for 1½ to 2 hours, or until the pork is tender and slightly pink in the very center.

Transfer the pork to plates. Using a slotted spoon, spoon the tomatoes over the pork. Set aside. Pour the cooking liquid into a medium skillet. Bring to a boil over high heat. Boil for 2 to 4 minutes, or until reduced by one-third (to about ¼ cup). Pour over the pork and tomatoes. Sprinkle with the basil.

per serving

Calories 222
Total Fat 9.5 g
  Saturated Fat 2.5 g
  Trans Fat 0.0 g
  Polyunsaturated Fat 1.0 g
  Monounsaturated Fat 3.5 g

Cholesterol 68 mg
Sodium 216 mg
Carbohydrates 5 g
  Fiber 1 g
  Sugars 2 g
Protein 26 g

Dietary Exchanges
  1 vegetable, 3 lean meat

garlicky lamb steaks with green olive and tomato relish

3 medium garlic cloves, minced

¼ **teaspoon salt**

¼ **teaspoon pepper**

4 boneless top round lamb steaks
(about 4 ounces each), all
visible fat discarded

1 teaspoon olive oil

1 large onion, cut into ½-inch
wedges

½ cup fat-free, low-sodium
chicken broth, such as on
page 31

■ ■ ■

¼ cup pitted green olives or
pimiento-stuffed olives,
chopped

¼ cup chopped grape tomatoes

1 tablespoon slivered almonds,
chopped

1 tablespoon chopped fresh basil

1½ teaspoons chopped fresh mint

⅛ teaspoon minced garlic

⅛ teaspoon pepper

A lively relish of tangy green olives, sweet grape tomatoes, crunchy almonds, and fragrant basil and mint tops these rich-tasting lamb steaks.

Sprinkle the garlic, salt, and ¼ teaspoon pepper over both sides of the lamb. Using your fingertips, gently press the seasonings so they adhere to the lamb.

In a large skillet, heat the oil over medium-high heat, swirl-ing to coat the bottom. Cook the lamb for 3 to 5 minutes, or until browned, turning once halfway through. Transfer to a large plate. Set aside.

In the same skillet, still over medium-high heat, cook the onion for 3 minutes, or until soft, stirring frequently. Transfer the onion to the slow cooker. Place the lamb on the onion.

Pour the broth into the skillet. Increase the heat to high and bring to a boil, scraping the bottom and side to dislodge any browned bits. Pour over the lamb. Cook, covered, on low for 3 to 5 hours or on high for 1½ to 2½ hours, or until the lamb is tender.

Just before serving time, in a small bowl, stir together the remaining ingredients. Spoon the relish over the lamb.

per serving

Calories 212	Cholesterol 68 mg	Dietary Exchanges
Total Fat 11.0 g	Sodium 381 mg	1 vegetable, 3 lean
Saturated Fat 3.0 g	Carbohydrates 7 g	meat, ½ fat
Trans Fat 0.0 g	Fiber 2 g	
Polyunsaturated Fat 1.0 g	Sugars 4 g	
Monounsaturated Fat 5.5 g	Protein 22 g	

vegetarian entrées

"baked" potatoes stuffed with blue cheese and soy crumbles

serves 4
1 potato, ¼ cup soy crumble mixture, and 2 tablespoons cheese per serving

slow cooker size/shape
3- to 4½-quart round or oval

slow cooking time
5½ to 6 hours on low, **OR**
2 hours 45 minutes to 3 hours on high

4 6-ounce Yukon Gold or red potatoes, each pierced with a fork in several places

■ ■ ■

2 teaspoons canola or corn oil

6 ounces frozen soy crumbles

1½ teaspoons dried dillweed, crumbled

¼ teaspoon pepper (coarsely ground preferred)

2 medium green onions, finely chopped

½ cup reduced-fat blue cheese

Simply wrap potatoes in aluminum foil, pop them in the slow cooker, and know they'll be waiting for you at mealtime. You can make the filling in about 5 minutes.

Wrap each potato tightly in aluminum foil. Place in the slow cooker. Cook, covered, on low for 5½ to 6 hours or on high for 2 hours 45 minutes to 3 hours, or until the potatoes are tender when pierced with a fork. Remove the potatoes from the slow cooker. Set aside, still wrapped.

About 5 minutes before serving time, in a medium nonstick skillet, heat the oil over medium heat, swirling to coat the bottom. Cook the soy crumbles, dillweed, and pepper for 3 minutes, or until heated through and beginning to brown, stirring frequently. Remove from the heat. Stir in the green onions, saving a small amount to sprinkle over the potatoes if desired.

Split the potatoes almost in half lengthwise. Fluff with a fork. Spoon the blue cheese onto each potato. Top with the soy crumble mixture. Sprinkle with any remaining green onions.

cook's tip: Wrapping the potatoes in aluminum foil keeps the moisture in and prevents the skins from drying out. Using Yukon Gold or red potatoes will ensure that you'll have a moister potato after baking.

per serving

Calories 254	Cholesterol 8 mg	Dietary Exchanges
Total Fat 5.0 g	Sodium 353 mg	2½ starch, 2 lean meat
Saturated Fat 2.0 g	Carbohydrates 36 g	
Trans Fat 0.0 g	Fiber 6 g	
Polyunsaturated Fat 1.0 g	Sugars 2 g	
Monounsaturated Fat 2.0 g	Protein 16 g	

mexican-style barley and black beans

serves 4
1¼ cups per serving

slow cooker size/shape
3- to 4½-quart round or oval

slow cooking time
3 hours on low, **OR**
1½ hours on high

Cooking spray

2 cups water

1 cup quick-cooking barley

1 medium red bell pepper, chopped

1 medium onion, chopped

■ ■ ■

½ 15.5-ounce can no-salt-added black beans, rinsed and drained

1 medium poblano pepper, seeds and ribs discarded, thinly sliced lengthwise and cut crosswise into 2-inch strips

2 tablespoons fresh lime juice

2 tablespoons olive oil (extra virgin preferred)

2 medium garlic cloves, minced

½ teaspoon salt

¼ cup snipped fresh cilantro

Take a break from the expected by making this barley dish instead of rice the next time you want to eat Mexican. It's a stick-to-your-ribs entrée, so come to the table hungry!

Lightly spray the slow cooker with cooking spray. Stir in the water, barley, bell pepper, and onion. Cook, covered, on low for 3 hours or on high for 1½ hours, or until the barley is tender. Transfer to a large bowl.

Stir in the remaining ingredients except the cilantro. Gently stir in the cilantro.

per serving

Calories 261	Cholesterol 0 mg	Dietary Exchanges
Total Fat 7.5 g	Sodium 301 mg	2½ starch, 1 vegetable,
Saturated Fat 1.0 g	Carbohydrates 43 g	1 fat
Trans Fat 0.0 g	Fiber 8 g	
Polyunsaturated Fat 1.0 g	Sugars 6 g	
Monounsaturated Fat 5.0 g	Protein 8 g	

barley risotto with mushrooms and spinach

2 teaspoons olive oil

8 ounces button mushrooms, sliced

1 small onion, diced

3½ cups fat-free, low-sodium vegetable broth, such as on page 33

1½ cups uncooked pearl barley (not quick-cooking or instant)

2 medium garlic cloves, minced

¼ teaspoon salt

¼ teaspoon pepper

■ ■ ■

2 ounces spinach (about 2 cups), chopped

¼ cup fat-free, low-sodium vegetable broth, such as on page 33

½ cup shredded or grated Parmesan cheese

2 tablespoons fresh lemon juice

Although most often used in soups, barley can be the main ingredient of a satisfying entrée, as it is here. You can also serve this risotto in half-cup portions as a healthy side to simply prepared seafood, poultry, or beef. Either way, wait until serving time to add the Parmesan and lemon juice so you'll get the maximum effect.

In a large nonstick skillet, heat the oil over medium-high heat, swirling to coat the bottom. Cook the mushrooms and onion for 6 to 8 minutes, or until the mushrooms are soft, stirring frequently. Transfer to the slow cooker.

Stir in 3½ cups broth, the barley, garlic, salt, and pepper. Cook, covered, on high for 2 hours, or until the barley is tender.

Stir in the spinach and remaining ¼ cup broth. Cook, covered, on high for 15 minutes, or until the spinach is wilted.

Stir in the Parmesan and lemon juice.

cook's tip: Instead of using spinach, try other quick-cooking greens, such as chopped Swiss chard, escarole, or arugula, for a change.

per serving

Calories 361	Cholesterol 7 mg	Dietary Exchanges
Total Fat 6.0 g	Sodium 385 mg	4 starch, 1 vegetable,
Saturated Fat 2.5 g	Carbohydrates 65 g	½ lean meat
Trans Fat 0.0 g	Fiber 13 g	
Polyunsaturated Fat 1.0 g	Sugars 5 g	
Monounsaturated Fat 2.5 g	Protein 14 g	

zucchini and tomato risotto

serves 5
1½ cups per serving

slow cooker size/shape
3- to 4½-quart round or oval

slow cooking time
1 hour on high plus
45 minutes on high

2 teaspoons olive oil

1 small onion, chopped

1½ cups uncooked arborio rice

1 medium garlic clove, minced

3 cups fat-free, low-sodium
vegetable broth, such as on
page 33

½ teaspoon salt

¼ teaspoon pepper

■ ■ ■

1½ cups diced zucchini

1¼ cups fat-free, low-sodium
vegetable broth, such as on
page 33

■ ■ ■

1 large tomato, chopped

½ cup shredded or grated
Parmesan cheese

¼ cup chopped fresh basil

If you love the creaminess of risotto but not all the stirring it requires, try making it in your slow cooker. Our version, which cooks for an hour with no stirring involved, adds fresh zucchini, tomato, and basil for color, flavor, and texture.

In a large nonstick skillet, heat the oil over medium-high heat, swirling to coat the bottom. Cook the onion, covered, for 6 minutes, or until tender, stirring occasionally. Stir in the rice and garlic. Cook, covered, for 1 minute. Transfer to the slow cooker.

Stir in 3 cups broth, the salt, and pepper. Cook, covered, on high for 1 hour.

Quickly stir in the zucchini and remaining 1¼ cups broth and re-cover the slow cooker. Cook on high for 45 minutes, or until the rice is tender. Turn off the slow cooker.

Stir in the tomato, Parmesan, and basil. Let stand, covered, for 5 minutes before serving.

per serving

Calories 269	Cholesterol 6 mg	Dietary Exchanges
Total Fat 4.0 g	Sodium 418 mg	3 starch, 1 vegetable
Saturated Fat 1.5 g	Carbohydrates 49 g	
Trans Fat 0.0 g	Fiber 3 g	
Polyunsaturated Fat 0.5 g	Sugars 3 g	
Monounsaturated Fat 2.0 g	Protein 8 g	

nutty brown rice and arugula toss

serves 4
1⅓ cups per serving

slow cooker size/shape
3- to 4½-quart round or oval

slow cooking time
3 hours on low, **OR**
1½ hours on high

Cooking spray

2 cups water

1 cup uncooked converted brown rice

1 medium onion, diced

■ ■ ■

2 cups arugula, coarsely chopped (2 ounces)

½ 15.5-ounce can no-salt-added chickpeas, rinsed and drained

¾ cup crumbled reduced-fat blue cheese

½ cup pine nuts, dry-roasted

¼ cup chopped fresh basil

1 tablespoon finely chopped fresh rosemary or 1 teaspoon dried rosemary, crushed

2 teaspoons grated lemon zest

1 medium garlic clove, minced

¼ teaspoon salt

Blue cheese, pine nuts, and fresh basil, rosemary, and lemon zest all play major roles in flavoring this chickpea and rice dish. A smart choice as a meatless entrée, the versatile recipe also makes a great side to serve 12 people. Not a blue cheese fan? Use low-fat feta cheese instead.

Lightly spray the slow cooker with cooking spray. Put the water, rice, and onion in the slow cooker, stirring to combine. Cook, covered, on low for 3 hours or on high for 1½ hours, or until the rice is fluffy and the water is absorbed. Transfer to a large bowl.

Add the remaining ingredients to the slow cooker. Using two utensils, toss gently. Let stand for 15 minutes under a tented piece of aluminum foil to keep warm while the flavors blend. (Don't cover tightly. You don't want to steam the food.)

per serving

Calories 381
Total Fat 13.5 g
  Saturated Fat 4.0 g
  Trans Fat 0.0 g
  Polyunsaturated Fat 4.0 g
  Monounsaturated Fat 4.5 g

Cholesterol 11 mg
Sodium 459 mg
Carbohydrates 52 g
  Fiber 8 g
  Sugars 5 g
  Protein 17 g

Dietary Exchanges
3½ starch, 1½ lean meat, 1 fat

rustic two-cheese ratatouille

serves 4
¾ cup vegetable mixture and
½ cup pasta per serving

slow cooker size
3- to 3½-quart round or oval

slow cooking time
6 to 7 hours on low, **OR**
3 to 3½ hours on high

Cooking spray

6 ounces eggplant, unpeeled, cut into 1-inch cubes (about 3 cups)

7 ounces grape tomatoes (about 1½ cups)

1 medium green bell pepper, cut into 1-inch squares

1 medium zucchini, halved lengthwise and cut crosswise into 1-inch slices

½ cup chopped onion

2 tablespoons water

2 teaspoons dried oregano, crumbled

1 teaspoon dried basil, crumbled

⅛ teaspoon crushed red pepper flakes

■ ■ ■

1 tablespoon balsamic vinegar

¼ teaspoon salt

4 ounces dried whole-grain penne (about 1⅓ cups)

16 kalamata olives, coarsely chopped

¾ cup shredded low-fat mozzarella cheese

2 tablespoons shredded or grated Parmesan cheese

This meatless one-dish meal provides both fiber—7 grams of it—and the heady flavors of Italian herbs and kalamata olives.

Lightly spray the slow cooker with cooking spray. Put the eggplant, tomatoes, bell pepper, zucchini, onion, water, oregano, basil, and red pepper flakes in the slow cooker, stirring to combine. Cook, covered, on low for 6 to 7 hours or on high for 3 to 3½ hours, or until the bell pepper is very soft. Stir in the vinegar and salt.

About 20 minutes before serving, prepare the pasta using the package directions, omitting the salt. Drain well in a colander.

Serve the eggplant mixture over the pasta. Top with the olives, mozzarella, and Parmesan.

cook's tip: The flavor of the kalamata olives is more pronounced if they're served on top of, rather than stirred into, the eggplant mixture.

cook's tip on eggplant: The flesh of an eggplant darkens quickly once it is exposed to the air, so cut the eggplant just before cooking it.

per serving

Calories 245	Cholesterol 9 mg	Dietary Exchanges
Total Fat 8.0 g	Sodium 595 mg	1½ starch, 2 vegetable,
Saturated Fat 2.0 g	Carbohydrates 34 g	1 lean meat, 1 fat
Trans Fat 0.0 g	Fiber 7 g	
Polyunsaturated Fat 1.0 g	Sugars 7 g	
Monounsaturated Fat 4.5 g	Protein 12 g	

veggies and pasta with blue cheese

serves 4
1¼ cups per serving

slow cooker size/shape
5- to 7-quart round or oval

slow cooking time
4½ to 5 hours on low, **OR**
2 hours 15 minutes to
2½ hours on high

Cooking spray

1 medium red bell pepper, cut into 1-inch squares

1 medium green bell pepper, cut into 1-inch squares

1 medium yellow summer squash, cut lengthwise into 8 wedges and crosswise into 1-inch pieces

1 medium onion, cut into 8 wedges

¼ to ½ teaspoon dried fennel seeds

1 tablespoon olive oil

■ ■ ■

4 ounces dried whole-grain penne (about 1⅓ cups)

1 medium garlic clove, minced

¼ teaspoon salt

¾ cup crumbled low-fat blue cheese

¼ cup chopped fresh basil

This one-dish wonder is packed with slow-roasted veggies, whole-grain penne, and creamy blue cheese, plus a hint of fennel. All you need to do before turning on the slow cooker is cut the vegetables.

Lightly spray the slow cooker with cooking spray. Put the bell peppers, squash, and onion in the slow cooker. Sprinkle with the fennel seeds. Drizzle with the oil. Don't stir. Cook, covered, on low for 4½ to 5 hours or on high for 2 hours 15 minutes to 2½ hours, or until the onion is soft.

About 20 minutes before the vegetables finish cooking, prepare the pasta using the package directions, omitting the salt. Drain well in a colander.

Stir the garlic and salt into the cooked bell pepper mixture. Gently stir in the pasta, blue cheese, and basil.

per serving

Calories 227	Cholesterol 11 mg	Dietary Exchanges
Total Fat 8.0 g	Sodium 435 mg	1½ starch, 2 vegetable,
Saturated Fat 3.0 g	Carbohydrates 30 g	1 lean meat, 1 fat
Trans Fat 0.0 g	Fiber 6 g	
Polyunsaturated Fat 1.0 g	Sugars 6 g	
Monounsaturated Fat 3.5 g	Protein 10 g	

white and greens lasagna

serves 8
1½ cups per serving

slow cooker size/shape
3- to 4½-quart round or
oval (preferred)

slow cooking time
4 to 6 hours on low
plus 10 minutes on low, **OR**
2 to 3 hours on high
plus 10 minutes on high

Cooking spray

3 medium garlic cloves, minced,
  and 3 medium garlic cloves,
  minced, divided use

36 ounces fat-free evaporated
  milk

3 tablespoons cornstarch

3 tablespoons water

⅓ cup chopped fresh tarragon

¼ teaspoon salt

⅛ teaspoon pepper and ⅛
  teaspoon pepper, divided use

1 tablespoon olive oil

1 large onion, chopped

4 cups loosely packed sliced Swiss
  chard leaves (½-inch slices)

10 ounces frozen chopped spinach,
  thawed, drained, and squeezed
  until very dry

1 cup low-fat ricotta

1 large egg white

½ cup shredded low-fat
  4-cheese Italian blend and
  ½ cup shredded low-fat
  4-cheese Italian blend,
  divided use

(continued)

Full of the goodness of greens in the form of Swiss chard and spinach, this lasagna is cooked with a white sauce flavored with fresh tarragon and garlic. There's no need to pre-cook the whole-wheat lasagna noodles—just make sure they're well coated with the sauce as you layer the ingredients.

Lightly spray the slow cooker and a large saucepan with cooking spray. Set the slow cooker aside.

In the pan, cook 3 minced garlic cloves over medium heat for 1 minute, stirring constantly. Pour the evaporated milk into the pan. Bring to a boil, still over medium heat, stirring frequently.

Put the cornstarch in a small bowl. Add the water, whisking to dissolve. Whisk into the evaporated milk mixture. Return to a boil, still over medium heat. Boil for 1 minute, whisking constantly. Remove from the heat. Whisk in the tarragon, salt, and ⅛ teaspoon pepper. Set the sauce aside.

In a large nonstick skillet, heat the oil over medium heat, swirling to coat the bottom. Cook the onion for 3 minutes, or until slightly softened, stirring frequently. Stir in the chard. Cook for 2 minutes, or until almost wilted, stirring constantly. Stir in the spinach and remaining 3 minced garlic cloves. Cook for 1 minute, or until the spinach is hot, the garlic is fragrant, and the chard is wilted, stirring constantly. Stir in the remaining ⅛ teaspoon pepper. Remove the skillet from the heat. Set aside.

In a small bowl, whisk together the ricotta and egg white until smooth. Whisk in ½ cup 4-cheese Italian blend and the Parmesan.

Spread 1 cup sauce in the slow cooker. Arrange 3 noodles on the sauce, breaking them to fit as needed. (They won't fit perfectly. There may be some overlap or gaps.) Spoon one-third of the ricotta mixture over the noodles, spreading gently. Sprinkle one-third of the onion mixture over the ricotta. Top with one-third of the tomatoes. Pour in 1 cup sauce, spreading to cover. Repeat the layers twice, beginning with the noodles. Sprinkle with the remaining ½ cup 4-cheese Italian blend.

Cook, covered, on low for 4 to 6 hours or on high for 2 to 3 hours, or until the noodles are tender. Quickly sprinkle the remaining ½ cup 4-cheese blend over the lasagna and re-cover the slow cooker. Cook for 10 minutes, or until the cheese has melted. Let stand, uncovered, for 15 to 20 minutes, or until set.

cook's tip on swiss chard: To cut Swiss chard leaves easily, stack several leaves and tightly roll them lengthwise. Cut crosswise into the desired width (½ inch for this recipe). One bunch will give you more than enough chard for this recipe.

¼ cup shredded or grated Parmesan cheese

9 dried oven-ready whole-wheat lasagna noodles

1½ cups grape tomatoes, halved

■ ■ ■

½ cup shredded low-fat 4-cheese Italian blend

per serving

Calories 356	Cholesterol 26 mg	Dietary Exchanges
Total Fat 8.0 g	Sodium 550 mg	1½ starch, 1½ fat-free
Saturated Fat 4.0 g	Carbohydrates 44 g	milk, 1 vegetable, 1½
Trans Fat 0.0 g	Fiber 3 g	lean meat
Polyunsaturated Fat 0.5 g	Sugars 21 g	
Monounsaturated Fat 2.0 g	Protein 26 g	

layered pasta casserole

serves 4
1½ cups per serving

slow cooker size/shape
4- to 5-quart round or oval

slow cooking time
4 to 4½ hours on low, **OR**
2 hours to 2 hours 15 minutes
on high

Cooking spray

1 tablespoon canola or corn oil

1 medium green bell pepper,
chopped

6 ounces button mushrooms,
sliced

1 small onion, diced

1½ cups meatless spaghetti sauce
(lowest sodium available)

2 medium tomatoes, diced

1 cup fat-free cottage cheese

½ cup snipped fresh parsley

2 large egg whites

2 teaspoons dried oregano,
crumbled

¼ teaspoon dried fennel seeds
(optional)

4 ounces dried whole-grain rotini
(about 1⅓ cups)

¼ cup shredded low-fat
mozzarella cheese

2 tablespoons shredded or
grated Parmesan cheese

■ ■ ■

¼ cup shredded low-fat
mozzarella cheese

2 tablespoons shredded or
grated Parmesan cheese

No need to cook the pasta ahead of time for this hunger-buster cheese-and-veggie–packed meal. Just add the pasta straight from the box or bag and let the slow cooker work its magic!

Lightly spray the slow cooker with cooking spray. Set aside.

In a large nonstick skillet, heat the oil over medium-high heat, swirling to coat the bottom. Cook the bell pepper, mushrooms, and onion for 3 minutes, or until the onion is soft, stirring frequently. Remove from the heat. Stir in the spaghetti sauce and tomatoes. Set aside.

In a medium bowl, stir together the cottage cheese, parsley, egg whites, oregano, and fennel seeds.

In the slow cooker, layer the casserole as follows: one-third (about 1⅓ cups) of the bell pepper mixture, half the pasta, half the cottage cheese mixture, ¼ cup mozzarella cheese, and 2 tablespoons Parmesan. Make another layer each of one-third of the bell pepper mixture, the remaining pasta, and the remaining cottage cheese mixture. Spoon the final one-third of the bell pepper mixture over all. Cook, covered, on low for 4 to 4½ hours or on high for 2 hours to 2 hours 15 minutes, or until the pasta is tender.

Sprinkle with the remaining ¼ cup mozzarella and remaining 2 tablespoons Parmesan. Turn off the slow cooker. Let the casserole stand, uncovered, for 15 minutes so the flavors blend, the pasta absorbs additional moisture, and the cheeses melt.

per serving

Calories 357	Cholesterol 22 mg	Dietary Exchanges
Total Fat 11.5 g	Sodium 559 mg	2 starch, 3 vegetable,
Saturated Fat 3.0 g	Carbohydrates 45 g	2 lean meat, ½ fat
Trans Fat 0.0 g	Fiber 8 g	
Polyunsaturated Fat 2.5 g	Sugars 15 g	
Monounsaturated Fat 4.5 g	Protein 19 g	

italian artichoke-stuffed bell peppers

serves 4
1 stuffed bell pepper
per serving

slow cooker size/shape
3½- to 5-quart round or oval

slow cooking time
4 to 6 hours on low, **OR**
2 to 3 hours on high

½ cup uncooked fine- or medium-grind quick-cooking bulgur

¾ cup boiling water

1 teaspoon olive oil

1 medium onion, chopped

1 cup diced zucchini

2 medium garlic cloves, minced

1 teaspoon dried fennel seeds, crushed

1 cup frozen artichokes, thawed, patted dry, and coarsely chopped

1 cup chopped tomato

½ cup loosely packed chopped fresh basil

2 ounces low-fat provolone, diced (about ½ cup)

4 large red bell peppers, tops, seeds, and ribs discarded

½ to ¾ cup water

■ ■ ■

1 tablespoon shredded or grated Parmesan cheese

A highly satisfying entrée, these attractive bell peppers are filled with bulgur mixed with artichokes, provolone cheese, tomatoes, and fresh basil. *(See photo insert.)*

Put the bulgur in a large bowl. Pour ¾ cup boiling water over the bulgur. Let stand, covered, for 30 minutes, or until the water is absorbed and the bulgur is tender. Fluff with a fork.

Meanwhile, in a medium nonstick skillet, heat the oil over medium heat, swirling to coat the bottom. Cook the onion for 2 minutes, stirring frequently.

Stir in the zucchini. Cook for 1½ minutes, stirring constantly.

Stir in the garlic and fennel seeds. Cook for 30 seconds, stirring constantly. Stir into the bulgur.

Gently stir in the artichokes, tomato, and basil. Gently stir in the provolone. Spoon the filling into the bell peppers, mounding as necessary.

Place the bell peppers in the slow cooker. Pour in enough of the ½ to ¾ cup water to cover the bottom of the slow cooker. Cook, covered, on low for 4 to 6 hours or on high for 2 to 3 hours, or until the peppers are tender and the filling is hot. Transfer to plates. Sprinkle with the Parmesan. Let stand for 5 minutes, or until the Parmesan has melted.

per serving

Calories 214	Cholesterol 9 mg	Dietary Exchanges
Total Fat 5.0 g	Sodium 185 mg	1 starch, 4 vegetable,
Saturated Fat 2.0 g	Carbohydrates 34 g	1 fat
Trans Fat 0.0 g	Fiber 11 g	
Polyunsaturated Fat 0.5 g	Sugars 11 g	
Monounsaturated Fat 1.5 g	Protein 10 g	

gingered lentils and quinoa

serves 4
1 cup lentils and ½ cup quinoa
per serving

slow cooker size/shape
3- to 4½-quart round or oval

slow cooking time
4 hours on low, **OR**
2 hours on high

Cooking spray

1 tablespoon canola or corn oil

1 medium onion, diced

3 cups fat-free, low-sodium
vegetable broth, such as on
page 33

1 cup dried lentils, sorted for
stones and shriveled lentils,
rinsed, and drained

1 medium red bell pepper, diced

½ teaspoon curry powder

⅛ to ¼ teaspoon crushed red
pepper flakes

■ ■ ■

½ cup snipped fresh cilantro

1 tablespoon grated peeled
gingerroot

½ teaspoon salt

2 cups water

½ cup uncooked quinoa, rinsed
well under cold running water
and drained

Ginger, curry powder, and red pepper flakes punch up the mild flavor of lentils, served here on a bed of quinoa.

Lightly spray the slow cooker with cooking spray. Set aside.

In a medium nonstick skillet, heat the oil over medium-high heat, swirling to coat the bottom. Cook the onion for 4 to 5 minutes, or until beginning to richly brown, stirring frequently. Transfer to the slow cooker.

Stir in the broth, lentils, bell pepper, curry powder, and red pepper flakes. Cook, covered, on low for 4 hours or on high for 2 hours, or until the lentils are tender. Stir in the cilantro, gingerroot, and salt.

About 15 minutes before the lentils finish cooking, in a small saucepan, bring the water to a boil over high heat. Stir in the quinoa. Reduce the heat and simmer, covered, for 10 to 12 minutes, or until the water is absorbed and the quinoa is tender. Transfer to a fine-mesh strainer. Drain well. Shake off any excess liquid. Spoon onto plates. Spoon the lentils on top.

per serving

Calories 312	Cholesterol 0 mg	Dietary Exchanges
Total Fat 5.0 g	Sodium 338 mg	3 starch, 1 vegetable,
Saturated Fat 0.5 g	Carbohydrates 51 g	1 lean meat
Trans Fat 0.0 g	Fiber 9 g	
Polyunsaturated Fat 1.5 g	Sugars 8 g	
Monounsaturated Fat 2.5 g	Protein 18 g	

greek lentils

serves 6
1 cup per serving

slow cooker size/shape
3- to 4½-quart round or oval

slow cooking time
5 to 6 hours on low, **OR**
2½ to 3 hours on high

4 cups fat-free, low-sodium
vegetable broth, such as on
page 33

2 cups dried lentils, sorted for
stones and shriveled lentils,
rinsed, and drained

2 medium carrots, shredded
(about 1 cup)

1 medium onion, chopped

1 teaspoon salt-free Greek
seasoning blend, crumbled

1 teaspoon dried oregano,
crumbled

1 teaspoon grated lemon zest

¼ teaspoon salt

¼ teaspoon pepper

4 ounces spinach, torn into bite-
size pieces (about 4 cups)

¼ cup crumbled fat-free feta
cheese

With its Greek seasoning blend, oregano, feta cheese, and lemon zest, this easy one-pot meal will almost make you think you're cruising the Mediterranean Sea!

In the slow cooker, stir together the broth, lentils, carrots, onion, seasoning blend, oregano, lemon zest, salt, and pepper. Cook, covered, on low for 5 to 6 hours or on high for 2½ to 3 hours, or until the liquid is absorbed and the lentils are tender.

Just before serving, stir in the spinach. Sprinkle the feta over each serving.

cook's tip: If you have trouble finding salt-free Greek seasoning blend, you can use a brand that contains salt, but be sure to omit the ¼ teaspoon of salt called for in the recipe.

per serving

Calories 248	Cholesterol 0 mg	Dietary Exchanges
Total Fat 1.0 g	Sodium 267 mg	2½ starch, 1 vegetable,
Saturated Fat 0.0 g	Carbohydrates 43 g	2 lean meat
Trans Fat 0.0 g	Fiber 16 g	
Polyunsaturated Fat 0.5 g	Sugars 6 g	
Monounsaturated Fat 0.0 g	Protein 19 g	

east indian spiced beans with apricot rice

serves 4
1 cup bean mixture and
⅔ cup rice per serving

slow cooker size/shape
3-quart round or oval

slow cooking time
3½ to 4 hours on low, **OR**
1 hour 45 minutes to 2 hours
on high

Cooking spray

1 tablespoon canola or corn oil
and 2 teaspoons canola or corn
oil, divided use

1 large onion, diced

1 large yellow bell pepper,
chopped

1 15.5-ounce can no-salt-added
dark kidney beans, rinsed and
drained

1 8-ounce can no-salt-added
tomato sauce

1 cup water

2 tablespoons sugar

1½ teaspoons ground coriander

1 teaspoon ground cumin

½ teaspoon ground cardamom

½ teaspoon ground ginger

½ teaspoon salt

⅛ teaspoon ground cloves or
allspice

⅛ teaspoon cayenne

(continued)

The mélange of spices in this dish provides stellar flavor. Serve the deep-red beans over the crunchy apricot-flecked brown rice, or switch places and put the rice on top. Either way is colorful and delicious. *(See photo insert.)*

Lightly spray the slow cooker with cooking spray. Set aside.

In a large nonstick skillet, heat 1 tablespoon oil over medium-high heat, swirling to coat the bottom. Cook the onion for 3 minutes, or until soft, stirring frequently. Transfer the mixture to the slow cooker.

Stir in the bell pepper, beans, tomato sauce, water, sugar, coriander, cumin, cardamom, ginger, salt, cloves, and cayenne. Cook, covered, on low for 3½ to 4 hours or on high for 1 hour 45 minutes to 2 hours, or until the onion is very soft.

About 15 minutes before serving, prepare the rice using the package directions, adding the turmeric and omitting the salt and margarine. Remove from the heat. Gently stir in the apricots, green onions, pecans, and remaining 2 teaspoons oil. Serve the beans over the rice or the rice over the beans.

cook's tip on coriander: Coriander is considered both an herb and a spice because its leaves, known as cilantro, and seeds are both used as seasonings. The seeds have a mild taste reminiscent of a combination of lemon and sage and are often used in Indian dishes. Store ground coriander in a cool, dark place. It will stay fresh for about four to six months.

cook's tip on cardamom: A member of the ginger family, cardamom adds a wonderfully sweet and pungent flavor to foods. Because cardamom is one of the more expensive spices, and one that you may not use regularly, you can assure a fresh product and probably save money by purchasing a small quantity at a store that sells spices in bulk bins.

■ ■ ■

½ **cup uncooked instant brown rice**

¼ **teaspoon ground turmeric**

⅓ **cup dried apricot halves, diced**

2 **medium green onions, finely chopped**

¼ **cup finely chopped pecans, dry-roasted**

per serving

Calories 345	Cholesterol 0 mg	Dietary Exchanges
Total Fat 11.5 g	Sodium 322 mg	1½ starch, 3 vegetable,
Saturated Fat 1.0 g	Carbohydrates 53 g	1 fruit, 2 fat
Trans Fat 0.0 g	Fiber 14 g	
Polyunsaturated Fat 3.5 g	Sugars 21 g	
Monounsaturated Fat 6.5 g	Protein 11 g	

mexican stuffed squash

serves 4
2 squash halves per serving

slow cooker size/shape
4- to 6-quart round or oval

slow cooking time
5 to 6 hours on low, **OR**
2½ to 3 hours on high

Cooking spray

4 medium yellow summer squash

1 teaspoon canola or corn oil

½ medium onion, diced

1 cup frozen brown rice, thawed

½ 15.5-ounce can no-salt-added black beans, rinsed and drained

¼ cup pickled jalapeño slices, drained and finely chopped

1 teaspoon ground cumin

¼ cup water

1 medium Italian plum (Roma) tomato, diced

■ ■ ■

⅛ teaspoon salt

¼ cup snipped fresh cilantro

¾ cup shredded low-fat sharp Cheddar cheese

Portion control is easy with these squash "boats." Two of the yummy boats, filled with brown rice, black beans, and pickled jalapeño slices, are just the right size for a serving.

Lightly spray the slow cooker with cooking spray. Set aside.

Cut the squash in half lengthwise. Using a teaspoon, scrape the seeds and pulp into a small bowl, leaving a ¼-inch border of the shell all the way around.

In a large nonstick skillet, heat the oil over medium-high heat, swirling to coat the bottom. Cook the reserved squash seeds and pulp and the onion for 3 to 4 minutes, or until the onion is soft, stirring frequently. Remove from the heat. Stir in the rice, beans, jalapeños, and cumin. Spoon into the squash cavities.

Pour the water into the slow cooker. Add the squash. Sprinkle with the tomato. Cook, covered, on low for 5 to 6 hours or on high for 2½ to 3 hours, or until the squash boats are tender when pierced with a fork.

Sprinkle, in order, with the salt, cilantro, and Cheddar. Turn off the slow cooker. Let stand, uncovered, for 15 minutes so the flavors blend and the cheese melts.

per serving

Calories 178	Cholesterol 4 mg	Dietary Exchanges
Total Fat 3.5 g	Sodium 411 mg	1 starch, 2 vegetable,
Saturated Fat 1.0 g	Carbohydrates 27 g	1 lean meat
Trans Fat 0.0 g	Fiber 6 g	
Polyunsaturated Fat 0.5 g	Sugars 8 g	
Monounsaturated Fat 1.0 g	Protein 12 g	

cuban-style black beans and rice

serves 6
1 cup beans and ½ cup rice per serving

slow cooker size/shape
4- to 6-quart round or oval

slow cooking time
4 to 6 hours on high

1 pound dried black beans, sorted for stones and shriveled beans, rinsed, and drained

4 cups water

1 14.5-ounce can no-salt-added diced tomatoes, undrained

1 large green bell pepper, chopped

1 medium onion, diced

1 tablespoon plus 1 teaspoon ground cumin

2 teaspoons dried minced garlic

2 medium dried bay leaves

1 teaspoon olive oil

3 drops red hot-pepper sauce

¼ teaspoon salt

■ ■ ■

1½ cups uncooked instant brown rice

3 tablespoons snipped fresh cilantro

⅓ cup chopped red onion (optional)

Plenty of cumin, bay leaves, onion, and garlic—and not much salt—seasons this hearty, protein-packed dish. Serve a crisp leafy green salad with a light citrus vinaigrette to complete the meal.

Fill a large saucepan three-fourths full of water. Bring to a boil over high heat. Stir in the beans. Return to a boil. Reduce the heat and simmer for 15 minutes. Pour the beans into a colander and rinse. Pour into the slow cooker.

Stir in the water, tomatoes with liquid, bell pepper, onion, cumin, garlic, bay leaves, oil, hot-pepper sauce, and salt. Cook, covered, on high for 4 to 6 hours. Discard the bay leaves.

About 20 minutes before serving time, prepare the rice using the package directions, omitting the salt and margarine. Spoon the rice into bowls. Ladle the bean mixture on top. Sprinkle with the cilantro and red onion.

cook's tip on dried beans: The first slow cooker was actually the classic bean pot, a clay or ceramic vessel that protected beans from a fire-fed oven's high heat. Still perfect for cooking any variety of dried beans, slow cookers yield beans that tend to be creamier than their canned counterparts. Slow cooked beans can be better for you, too, because you get to control the amount of added sodium.

per serving

Calories 400	Cholesterol 0 mg	Dietary Exchanges
Total Fat 3.0 g	Sodium 128 mg	4½ starch, 1 vegetable,
Saturated Fat 0.5 g	Carbohydrates 75 g	2 lean meat
Trans Fat 0.0 g	Fiber 17 g	
Polyunsaturated Fat 1.0 g	Sugars 12 g	
Monounsaturated Fat 1.0 g	Protein 20 g	

red-bean spaghetti

serves 5
¾ cup bean mixture and
¾ cup spaghetti per serving

slow cooker size/shape
3- to 4½-quart round or oval

slow cooking time
6 to 8 hours on low plus
30 to 45 minutes on high, **OR**
3 to 4 hours on high plus
30 to 45 minutes on high

2 cups chopped button
mushrooms

1 15.5-ounce can no-salt-added
dark red kidney beans, rinsed
and drained

1 14.5-ounce can no-salt-added
diced tomatoes, undrained

½ cup chopped green bell pepper

¼ cup finely chopped onion

2 medium garlic cloves, minced

1 teaspoon dried oregano,
crumbled

½ teaspoon ground cumin

½ teaspoon salt

¼ teaspoon crushed red pepper
flakes

■ ■ ■

1½ cups chopped zucchini

¼ cup no-salt-added tomato
paste

8 ounces dried whole-grain
spaghetti

This chunky, hearty bean mixture is great on
pasta and is also very tasty over brown rice.

In the slow cooker, stir together the mushrooms, beans,
tomatoes with liquid, bell pepper, onion, garlic, oregano,
cumin, salt, and red pepper flakes. Cook, covered, on low
for 6 to 8 hours or on high for 3 to 4 hours.

If using the low setting, change it to high. Quickly stir in
the zucchini and tomato paste and re-cover the slow
cooker. Cook for 30 to 45 minutes, or until the zucchini
is tender-crisp.

About 15 minutes before serving time, prepare the spaghetti
using the package directions, omitting the salt. Drain well in
a colander. Serve with the bean mixture spooned on top.

per serving

Calories 279	Cholesterol 0 mg	Dietary Exchanges
Total Fat 1.5 g	Sodium 232 mg	3 starch, 2 vegetable
Saturated Fat 0.0 g	Carbohydrates 55 g	
Trans Fat 0.0 g	Fiber 14 g	
Polyunsaturated Fat 0.5 g	Sugars 8 g	
Monounsaturated Fat 0.5 g	Protein 14 g	

bean and roasted vegetable stew

1 cup dried cannellini, navy, or baby lima beans, sorted for stones and shriveled beans, rinsed, and drained

5 cups fat-free, low-sodium vegetable broth, such as on page 33

1 teaspoon dried sage

2 medium garlic cloves, minced

¼ teaspoon salt

⅛ teaspoon pepper

■ ■ ■

1 medium turnip, peeled and cut into ½-inch cubes, or 1 medium red potato, cut into ½-inch cubes

1 small sweet potato, cut into ½-inch cubes

1 small red bell pepper, cut into ½-inch cubes

1 small onion, chopped

2 teaspoons olive oil

¼ teaspoon salt

⅛ teaspoon pepper

1 14.5-ounce can no-salt-added diced tomatoes, undrained

It's so worth the extra step of roasting the vegetables for this stew. They play a key role in providing the stew's incredibly deep flavor.

Fill a small saucepan three-fourths full of water. Bring to a boil over high heat. Stir in the beans. Return to a boil. Reduce the heat and simmer for 15 minutes. Pour into a colander and rinse. Pour into the slow cooker.

Stir in the broth, sage, garlic, ¼ teaspoon salt, and ⅛ teaspoon pepper. Cook, covered, on low for 8 to 10 hours or on high for 5 to 6 hours, or until the beans are tender.

About 1 hour 15 minutes before the beans are done, preheat the oven to 400°F.

Place the turnip, sweet potato, bell pepper, and onion in a large baking pan. Drizzle with the oil. Sprinkle with the remaining ¼ teaspoon salt and ⅛ teaspoon pepper. Toss to coat. Spread the vegetables in a single layer.

Roast the vegetables for 25 minutes. Stir. Roast for 15 minutes, or until the vegetables are browned and tender.

Quickly stir the roasted vegetables and the tomatoes with liquid into the beans and re-cover the slow cooker. Cook for 30 minutes.

per serving

Calories 225	Cholesterol 0 mg	Dietary Exchanges
Total Fat 2.0 g	Sodium 338 mg	2 starch, 2 vegetable,
Saturated Fat 0.5 g	Carbohydrates 40 g	1 lean meat
Trans Fat 0.0 g	Fiber 9 g	
Polyunsaturated Fat 0.0 g	Sugars 8 g	
Monounsaturated Fat 1.5 g	Protein 12 g	

louisiana vegetable stew

serves 5
1⅔ cups per serving

slow cooker size/shape
4- to 6-quart round or oval

slow cooking time
5½ to 6½ hours on low, **OR**
3 to 3½ hours on high

1 15.5-ounce can no-salt-added red beans, rinsed and drained

1 14.5-ounce can no-salt-added diced tomatoes, undrained

1¾ cups fat-free, low-sodium vegetable broth, such as on page 33

1½ cups frozen sliced okra, thawed

1 medium green bell pepper, finely chopped

1 medium onion, finely chopped

1 cup uncooked brown rice (not instant)

1 cup water

1 teaspoon extra-spicy salt-free all-purpose seasoning blend

½ teaspoon salt

3 to 5 drops red hot-pepper sauce, or to taste

You'll never miss the meat in this thick, spicy stew from bayou country. All you need to add is cornbread on the side.

In the slow cooker, stir together all the ingredients. Cook, covered, on low for 5½ to 6½ hours or on high for 3 to 3½ hours.

cook's tip on seasoning slow-cooked dishes: For the best flavor, you almost always should add dried herbs and seasonings at the beginning of the slow cooking time. Fresh herbs are usually added toward the end. The flavor of some seasonings can diminish during slow cooking, so get in the habit of tasting your dish before serving. (Remember to avoid lifting the lid while the dish cooks because doing so lowers the temperature in the slow cooker.) If the seasonings—except salt and seasonings that include salt—aren't strong enough, you can add more.

per serving

Calories 252	Cholesterol 0 mg	Dietary Exchanges
Total Fat 1.5 g	Sodium 316 mg	2½ starch, 2 vegetable
Saturated Fat 0.5 g	Carbohydrates 50 g	
Trans Fat 0.0 g	Fiber 8 g	
Polyunsaturated Fat 0.5 g	Sugars 7 g	
Monounsaturated Fat 0.5 g	Protein 10 g	

black and red bean chili with peppery sour cream

serves 6
1 cup chili and 2 tablespoons sour cream per serving

slow cooker size/shape
3- to 4½-quart round or oval

slow cooking time
8 hours on low, **OR**
4 hours on high

Cooking spray
- ½ **cup dried pinto beans, sorted for stones and shriveled beans, rinsed, and drained**
- ½ **cup dried black beans, sorted for stones and shriveled beans, rinsed, and drained**
- 3 **cups water**
- 10 **ounces whole grape tomatoes (about 2 cups)**
- 1 **medium yellow bell pepper, chopped**
- 1 **medium onion, chopped**
- 2 **medium poblano peppers, seeds and ribs discarded, chopped**
- 2 **teaspoons chili powder**
- 1½ **teaspoons ground cumin**
- 1½ **teaspoons sugar**
- 2 **medium garlic cloves, minced**
- ¾ **teaspoon salt**
- ¾ **teaspoon dried oregano, crumbled**

■ ■ ■

- 2 **tablespoons fresh lime juice**
- ¾ **cup fat-free sour cream**
- 1 **tablespoon olive oil (extra virgin preferred)**
- 2 to 3 **teaspoons mild Louisiana-style hot-pepper sauce**

This two-bean chili gets additional splashes of color from grape tomatoes and yellow bell pepper. The unusual sour cream topping is an integral part of the dish—be sure to give it a try.

Lightly spray the slow cooker with cooking spray. Set aside.

Fill a large saucepan three-fourths full of water. Bring to a boil over high heat. Stir in the beans. Reduce the heat and simmer for 15 minutes. Pour into a colander and rinse. Pour into the slow cooker.

Stir in the water, tomatoes, bell pepper, onion, poblanos, chili powder, cumin, sugar, garlic, salt, and oregano. Cook, covered, on low for 8 hours or on high for 4 hours. Stir in the lime juice.

Meanwhile, in a small bowl, whisk together the sour cream, oil, and hot-pepper sauce. Cover and refrigerate until serving time.

Ladle the chili into bowls. Spoon 2 dollops of the sour cream mixture onto each serving.

cook's tip: For improved flavor and texture, cover and refrigerate the chili overnight in an airtight container, or for up to two days. Reheat in a large saucepan, covered, over medium heat for 10 minutes, or until heated through. Meanwhile, prepare the sour cream mixture. Top the chili as directed.

per serving

Calories 198	Cholesterol 5 mg	Dietary Exchanges
Total Fat 3.0 g	Sodium 342 mg	1½ starch, 2 vegetable,
Saturated Fat 0.5 g	Carbohydrates 34 g	½ lean meat
Trans Fat 0.0 g	Fiber 7 g	
Polyunsaturated Fat 0.5 g	Sugars 9 g	
Monounsaturated Fat 1.5 g	Protein 10 g	

chickpea and vegetable stew

serves 6
1⅓ cups stew and 1 tablespoon sauce per serving

slow cooker size/shape
3- to 4½-quart round or oval

slow cooking time
7 to 9 hours on low, **OR**
3½ to 4½ hours on high

- 1 cup dried chickpeas, sorted for stones and shriveled peas, rinsed, and drained
- 1 teaspoon olive oil
- 1 large onion, cut into 1-inch squares (about 1½ cups)
- 3 medium carrots, cut into 1-inch pieces (about 1½ cups)
- 4 medium garlic cloves, minced
- 1 tablespoon snipped fresh thyme and 1 tablespoon snipped fresh thyme, divided use
- 1½ teaspoons paprika and 1½ teaspoons paprika, divided use
- ¼ teaspoon salt and ¼ teaspoon salt, divided use
- ¼ teaspoon pepper and ¼ teaspoon pepper, divided use
- 8 ounces unpeeled small red potatoes, each cut into 4 wedges (6 wedges if large) (about 1½ cups)
- 8 ounces rutabaga, cut into 1-inch cubes (about 1½ cups)
- 1 large red bell pepper, cut into 1-inch squares

(continued)

It takes only a little smoky roasted red bell pepper sauce to add a lot of flavor to this satisfying stew of chickpeas and veggies. For extra creaminess, top each serving with a dollop of fat-free plain yogurt.

Fill a small saucepan with water. Bring to a boil over high heat. Stir in the chickpeas. Return to a boil. Reduce the heat and simmer for 15 minutes. Pour into a colander and rinse. Pour into the slow cooker. Set aside.

In a medium nonstick skillet, heat the oil over medium-high heat, swirling to coat the bottom. Cook the onion for 3 minutes, or until soft and lightly browned on the edges, stirring frequently. Stir in the carrots. Cook for 30 seconds, stirring constantly. Stir in the garlic. Cook for another 30 seconds, stirring constantly. Spoon over the chickpeas. Sprinkle with 1 tablespoon thyme, 1½ teaspoons paprika, ¼ teaspoon salt, and ¼ teaspoon pepper.

Top, in order, with one layer each of the potatoes, rutabaga, and bell pepper. Sprinkle with the remaining 1 tablespoon thyme, remaining 1½ teaspoons paprika, remaining ¼ teaspoon salt, and remaining ¼ teaspoon pepper. Pour the broth over all, making sure the chickpeas are covered. (Don't worry if the vegetables aren't covered.) Don't stir. Cook, covered, on low for 7 to 9 hours or on high for 3½ to 4½ hours, or until the chickpeas are tender but still slightly firm and the vegetables are tender.

Meanwhile, in a food processor or blender, process the roasted peppers, 2 tablespoons yogurt (if using), and the garlic until smooth. Transfer to a small bowl. If you make this mixture 2 hours or more before the stew is ready, cover and refrigerate it. If less than 2 hours, set it aside.

Using a slotted spoon, transfer the stew to bowls. Spoon enough cooking liquid over the stew to moisten it. Garnish with the sprigs of fresh thyme. Spoon the sauce over the stew. Spoon a dollop of the remaining ¼ cup plus 2 table-spoons of yogurt onto each serving.

3 cups fat-free, low-sodium vegetable broth, such as on page 33

■ ■ ■

½ cup roasted red bell peppers (about 4 ounces), drained if bottled

2 tablespoons fat-free plain yogurt (optional) and ¼ cup plus 2 tablespoons fat-free plain yogurt, divided use

½ medium garlic clove, minced

Sprigs of fresh thyme

per serving

Calories 220	Cholesterol 0 mg	Dietary Exchanges
Total Fat 3.0 g	Sodium 317 mg	2 starch, 2 vegetable
Saturated Fat 0.5 g	Carbohydrates 40 g	
Trans Fat 0.0 g	Fiber 10 g	
Polyunsaturated Fat 1.0 g	Sugars 12 g	
Monounsaturated Fat 1.0 g	Protein 10 g	

spicy vegetable curry

serves 8
1 cup curry and ½ cup rice per serving

slow cooker size/shape
4- to 6-quart round or oval

slow cooking time
9 to 10 hours on low, **OR**
4½ to 5 hours on high

1 tablespoon olive oil

3 tablespoons curry powder

1 teaspoon crushed red pepper flakes

1 cup chopped onion

2 cups fat-free, low-sodium vegetable broth, such as on page 33

2 medium potatoes, such as russet (about 8½ ounces each), peeled and cut into ½-inch cubes

2 15.5-ounce cans no-salt-added chickpeas, rinsed and drained

1 14.5-ounce can no-salt-added diced tomatoes, undrained

2 medium carrots, cut crosswise into ¼-inch slices (about 1 cup)

2 tablespoons uncooked instant, or quick-cooking, tapioca

3 medium garlic cloves, minced

½ teaspoon salt

½ teaspoon pepper

■ ■ ■

3 cups uncooked instant brown rice

2½ cups fat-free, low-sodium vegetable broth, such as on page 33

Protein-rich chickpeas and a variety of vegetables combine in this stew-like dish, which uses enough curry powder and crushed red pepper flakes to grab your attention!

In a small nonstick skillet, heat the oil over medium-high heat, swirling to coat the bottom. Cook the curry powder and red pepper flakes for 30 seconds, or until they start to brown and are aromatic, stirring constantly. Stir in the onion. Cook for 1 minute, stirring constantly. Transfer to the slow cooker.

Stir in 2 cups broth, the potatoes, chickpeas, tomatoes with liquid, carrots, tapioca, garlic, salt, and pepper. Cook, covered, on low for 9 to 10 hours or on high for 4½ to 5 hours, or until the potatoes and carrots are tender.

Just before serving time, prepare the rice using the package directions, omitting the salt and margarine and substituting the remaining 2½ cups broth for the water.

Serve the curry on the rice.

per serving

Calories 346	Cholesterol 0 mg	Dietary Exchanges
Total Fat 4.0 g	Sodium 231 mg	4 starch, 1 vegetable,
Saturated Fat 0.5 g	Carbohydrates 66 g	½ lean meat
Trans Fat 0.0 g	Fiber 9 g	
Polyunsaturated Fat 0.5 g	Sugars 5 g	
Monounsaturated Fat 2.0 g	Protein 11 g	

chickpea, cucumber, and tomato salad with feta

serves 4
1½ cups per serving

slow cooker size/shape
1½- to 2½-quart round or oval

slow cooking time
6 to 8 hours on low, **OR**
3 to 4 hours on high

■ ■ ■

1 cup dried chickpeas, sorted
for stones and shriveled peas,
rinsed, and drained

3 cups water

■ ■ ■

⅓ cup water

3 tablespoons red wine vinegar

2 tablespoons snipped fresh
dillweed

2 teaspoons olive oil (extra virgin
preferred)

1 teaspoon Dijon mustard

1 medium garlic clove

■ ■ ■

2 small tomatoes, chopped
(about 1¼ cups)

1 medium cucumber, diced
(about 1¼ cups)

½ cup sliced green onions (green
and white parts)

¼ cup low-fat feta cheese and
¼ cup low-fat feta cheese,
divided use

2 hard-cooked eggs, 1 yolk
discarded, chopped

Firm, filling, and full of fiber, chickpeas star in this salad, which is lightly dressed with a dill-infused vinaigrette.

Fill a small saucepan three-fourths full of water. Bring to a boil over high heat. Stir in the chickpeas. Return to a boil. Reduce the heat and simmer for 15 minutes. Pour into a colander and rinse. Pour into the slow cooker. Pour in 3 cups water. Cook, covered, on low for 6 to 8 hours or on high for 3 to 4 hours, or until the chickpeas are tender but still slightly firm. Drain in a colander. Rinse under cold running water to cool. Transfer to a large bowl.

While the chickpeas are cooking, in a food processor or blender, process the remaining ⅓ cup water, the vinegar, dillweed, oil, mustard, and garlic until smooth. If you make this dressing 2 hours or more before the chickpeas are ready, cover and refrigerate it. If less than 2 hours, set it aside.

Add the tomatoes, cucumber, green onions, and ¼ cup feta to the chickpeas, tossing gently to combine. Pour in ½ cup dressing, tossing to lightly coat. Discard the remaining dressing or save for another use. Spoon the salad onto plates. Sprinkle with the chopped egg whites and yolk and remaining ¼ cup feta.

per serving

Calories 267	Cholesterol 53 mg	Dietary Exchanges
Total Fat 8.5 g	Sodium 321 mg	2 starch, 1 vegetable,
Saturated Fat 2.5 g	Carbohydrates 34 g	1½ lean meat
Trans Fat 0.0 g	Fiber 9 g	
Polyunsaturated Fat 2.0 g	Sugars 8 g	
Monounsaturated Fat 3.0 g	Protein 16 g	

thai vegetable curry

serves 4
1½ cups per serving

slow cooker size/shape
3- to 4½-quart round or oval

slow cooking time
5 to 7 hours on low plus
10 minutes on high, **OR**
2½ to 3½ hours on high plus
10 minutes on high

1 teaspoon canola or corn oil

1 large onion, cut into 1-inch
squares (about 1½ cups)

4 medium garlic cloves, minced

2 teaspoons minced peeled
gingerroot

1 sweet potato (about 9 ounces),
peeled and cut into 1-inch
cubes

1½ cups 1-inch cauliflower florets

1 medium red bell pepper, cut
into 1-inch squares (about
1½ cups)

1 12.3-ounce package light extra-
firm tofu, drained, patted dry,
and cut into 1-inch cubes

1 13.5- to 13.75-ounce can lite
coconut milk

1 teaspoon soy sauce (lowest
sodium available)

½ teaspoon Thai green curry
paste, or to taste

(continued)

A creamy sauce of lite coconut milk spiked with green curry paste blankets brightly colored vegetables in this tofu-based curry. Feel free to vary the vegetables to take advantage of seasonal produce.

In a small skillet, heat the oil over medium heat, swirling to coat the bottom. Cook the onion for 3 minutes, or until beginning to soften, stirring frequently. Stir in the garlic and gingerroot. Cook for 1 minute, stirring constantly. Transfer to the slow cooker.

Top the onion mixture with one layer each, in order, of the sweet potato, cauliflower, bell pepper, and tofu. Don't stir.

In a small bowl, whisk together the coconut milk, soy sauce, and curry paste. Pour into the slow cooker. Don't stir. Cook, covered, on low for 5 to 7 hours or on high for 2½ to 3½ hours, or until the vegetables are tender.

If using the low setting, change it to high. Quickly add the broccoli (don't stir) and re-cover the slow cooker. Cook for 10 minutes, or until the broccoli is tender.

Meanwhile, put the cornstarch in a small bowl. Pour in the water, whisking to dissolve. Set aside.

Using a slotted spoon, transfer the vegetable mixture to a serving bowl, being careful to keep the tofu cubes intact.

Pour the cooking liquid into a medium saucepan. Bring to a boil over medium-high heat. Gradually whisk in about half the cornstarch mixture. Bring to a boil, still over medium-high heat, whisking constantly. Whisk in the remaining cornstarch mixture 1 teaspoon at a time until the desired consistency. Boil for 1 minute, whisking constantly. Pour the sauce over the tofu and vegetables. Serve sprinkled with the cilantro.

cook's tip: Thai green curry paste is a combination of chiles, herbs, and spices and is highly aromatic, flavorful, and very spicy. You probably can find it in the Asian section of your supermarket, or look in Asian grocery stores or online. If you like your curry hot, feel free to add more than the recipe calls for.

■ ■ ■

9 ounces frozen broccoli cuts, thawed

1½ tablespoons cornstarch

1½ tablespoons water

⅓ cup snipped fresh cilantro

per serving

Calories 244
Total Fat 8.0 g
 Saturated Fat 3.5 g
 Trans Fat 0.0 g
 Polyunsaturated Fat 1.0 g
 Monounsaturated Fat 1.5 g

Cholesterol 0 mg
Sodium 176 mg
Carbohydrates 33 g
 Fiber 7 g
 Sugars 10 g
Protein 12 g

Dietary Exchanges
 1 starch, 1 vegetable,
 1 lean meat, 1 fat

parmesan polenta with roasted vegetables

serves 4
1 cup vegetables and ½ cup polenta per serving

slow cooker size/shape
1½- to 2½-quart round

slow cooking time
1 to 1½ hours on high

Cooking spray

12 ounces canned fat-free evaporated milk

½ cup fat-free half-and-half

⅓ cup coarse polenta, coarse corn grits, or coarse cornmeal

1 tablespoon light tub margarine

¼ teaspoon salt

¼ teaspoon pepper

■ ■ ■

1 medium eggplant (about 1 pound)

1¾ cups sliced zucchini (about ¼ inch thick)

1 medium onion, cut into 8 wedges

3 medium Italian plum (Roma) tomatoes, quartered

¼ cup fat-free half-and-half

⅓ cup shredded or grated Parmesan cheese

An array of vegetables provides color and texture when spooned over creamy polenta. Keep in mind that it needs a quick stir every half-hour.

Lightly spray the slow cooker with cooking spray. Set aside.

In a small saucepan, whisk together the evaporated milk, ½ cup half-and-half, the polenta, margarine, salt, and pepper. Cook over medium-high heat for 4 minutes, or until the mixture comes to a boil, whisking constantly to prevent lumps from forming. Boil for 1 minute, whisking constantly.

Pour the polenta into the slow cooker. Cook, covered, on high for 1 to 1½ hours, quickly stirring and re-covering the slow cooker every 30 minutes. About 30 minutes before the polenta is ready, preheat the oven to 425°F.

Meanwhile, without peeling, cut the eggplant into 1-inch cubes. Place the eggplant, zucchini, and onion in a single layer on a baking sheet. Lightly spray them with cooking spray.

Roast the vegetables for 8 minutes. Stir. Roast for 5 minutes. Arrange the tomatoes on the baking sheet, keeping the vegetables in a single layer. Roast for 3 minutes, or until the vegetables are tender.

Just before serving, stir the remaining ¼ cup half-and-half and the Parmesan into the polenta. Spoon the polenta onto a deep serving platter. Spoon the vegetables on top.

per serving

Calories 243
Total Fat 4.0 g
  Saturated Fat 1.5 g
  Trans Fat 0.0 g
  Polyunsaturated Fat 0.5 g
  Monounsaturated Fat 1.5 g

Cholesterol 8 mg
Sodium 440 mg
Carbohydrates 40 g
  Fiber 7 g
  Sugars 21 g
Protein 16 g

Dietary Exchanges
½ starch, 1 fat-free milk, 3 vegetable, ½ lean meat

vegetable stew with cornmeal dumplings

serves 4
1 cup stew and 1 dumpling per serving

slow cooker size/shape
3- to 4½-quart round or oval

slow cooking time
7 to 8 hours on low plus 50 minutes on high, **OR**
3½ to 4 hours on high plus 50 minutes on high

3 cups chopped peeled butternut squash (about 1 pound)
6 ounces button mushrooms, sliced (about 2 cups)
1 14.5-ounce can no-salt-added diced tomatoes with basil, garlic, and oregano, undrained
1½ cups fat-free, low-sodium vegetable broth, such as on page 33
1 medium carrot, chopped
1 medium rib of celery, chopped
1 teaspoon dried minced onion
½ teaspoon dried oregano
½ teaspoon pepper
¼ teaspoon salt

■ ■ ■

½ cup all-purpose flour
⅓ cup yellow cornmeal
1 teaspoon baking powder
½ teaspoon dried Italian seasoning, crumbled
1 large egg
2 tablespoons fat-free milk
2 tablespoons olive oil
¼ cup snipped fresh parsley

Sweet butternut squash and cornbread-like dumplings make this stew so good that even the kids will enjoy eating their veggies.

In the slow cooker, stir together the squash, mushrooms, tomatoes with liquid, broth, carrot, celery, onion, oregano, pepper, and salt. Cook, covered, on low for 7 to 8 hours or on high for 3½ to 4 hours.

Just before the end of the cooking time, prepare the dumplings. In a medium bowl, stir together the flour, cornmeal, baking powder, and Italian seasoning.

In a small bowl, whisk together the egg, milk, and oil. Pour into the flour mixture, stirring with a fork just until combined but no flour is visible. Set aside.

When the stew is ready, quickly stir in the parsley. Drop four equal portions of the dumpling batter on top of the stew. Re-cover the slow cooker. If using the low setting, change it to high. Cook for 50 minutes, or until a wooden toothpick inserted in the centers of the dumplings comes out clean. (Don't remove the lid while cooking the dumplings.)

cook's tip: The dumpling batter will spread when you drop it on the stew, so you don't need to worry about making the portions a particular thickness.

per serving

Calories 280	Cholesterol 47 mg	Dietary Exchanges
Total Fat 8.5 g	Sodium 337 mg	2½ starch, 2 vegetable,
Saturated Fat 1.5 g	Carbohydrates 45 g	1 fat
Trans Fat 0.0 g	Fiber 6 g	
Polyunsaturated Fat 1.0 g	Sugars 7 g	
Monounsaturated Fat 5.5 g	Protein 8 g	

vegetables and side dishes

honey-roasted vegetables

serves 8
½ cup per serving

slow cooker size/shape
4- to 5-quart round or oval

slow cooking time
5 to 6 hours on low, **OR**
2½ to 3 hours on high

4 medium carrots, parsnips, or a
   combination (about 8 ounces
   total), cut crosswise into 1-inch
   pieces

8 whole boiling onions, or
   1 medium onion, cut into
   8 wedges

8 unpeeled red potatoes (about
   2 ounces each), halved

2 medium sweet potatoes (about
   8 ounces each), quartered

1 tablespoon snipped fresh
   thyme

½ teaspoon pepper

⅛ teaspoon salt

2 tablespoons water

■ ■ ■

1 tablespoon honey

2 teaspoons fresh lemon juice

A touch of honey and the subtle flavor of thyme accent this dish and bring out the natural flavors of the vegetables.

In the slow cooker, make one layer each, in order, of the carrots, onions, red potatoes, and sweet potatoes. Sprinkle with the thyme, pepper, and salt. Add the water. Don't stir. Cook, covered, on low for 5 to 6 hours or on high for 2½ to 3 hours.

Just before serving, in a small bowl, whisk together the honey and lemon juice. Drizzle over the vegetables.

cook's tip: So that all the veggies in this dish can slow cook together successfully, layer them, placing the carrots (and parsnips), which cook more slowly, on the bottom of the cooker, where they will get the most concentrated heat. The sweet potatoes slow cook more quickly than the other vegetables in this dish, so they go on top.

per serving

Calories 118	Cholesterol 0 mg	Dietary Exchanges
Total Fat 0.0 g	Sodium 104 mg	1½ starch, 1 vegetable
Saturated Fat 0.0 g	Carbohydrates 28 g	
Trans Fat 0.0 g	Fiber 4 g	
Polyunsaturated Fat 0.0 g	Sugars 8 g	
Monounsaturated Fat 0.0 g	Protein 3 g	

barley casserole

serves 10
½ cup per serving

slow cooker size/shape
3- to 4½-quart round or oval

slow cooking time
6 to 8 hours on low, **OR**
3½ to 4 hours on high

A terrific dish for a potluck, this casserole features often-overlooked barley, one of the world's oldest grains. Mixed-vegetable juice, Worcestershire sauce, and pepper bump up the flavor of this easy-as-can-be dish.

In the slow cooker, stir together all the ingredients except the almonds. Cook, covered, on low for 6 to 8 hours or on high for 3½ to 4 hours, or until the barley is tender. Sprinkle each serving with 1 teaspoon almonds.

8 ounces baby bella mushrooms,
sliced (2½ to 3 cups)

2 cups low-sodium spicy mixed-
vegetable juice

1 cup fat-free, low-sodium
vegetable broth, such as on
page 33

1 cup uncooked pearl barley (not
quick cooking or instant)

1 cup chopped onion

2 teaspoons Worcestershire
sauce (lowest sodium available)

3 medium garlic cloves, minced

1 teaspoon dried basil, crumbled

¼ teaspoon pepper

■ ■ ■

3 tablespoons plus 1 teaspoon
slivered almonds, dry-roasted
and coarsely chopped

---

per serving

Calories 108
Total Fat 1.5 g
  Saturated Fat 0.0 g
  Trans Fat 0.0 g
  Polyunsaturated Fat 0.5 g
  Monounsaturated Fat 0.5 g

Cholesterol 0 mg
Sodium 42 mg
Carbohydrates 21 g
  Fiber 4 g
  Sugars 3 g
Protein 4 g

Dietary Exchanges
1 starch, 1 vegetable

chipotle baked beans

serves 12
½ cup per serving

slow cooker size/shape
3- to 4½-quart round or oval

slow cooking time
8 hours on low
plus 2 to 4 hours on low

2 cups dried navy beans, sorted
for stones and shriveled beans,
rinsed, and drained

1 large Vidalia, Maui, Oso Sweet,
or other sweet onion, chopped

½ cup frozen orange juice
concentrate, thawed

½ cup molasses (dark preferred)

¼ cup no-salt-added tomato
paste

¼ cup water

2 large garlic cloves, minced

2 teaspoons chipotle pepper
canned in adobo sauce, or to
taste, finely chopped

2 teaspoons dry mustard

■ ■ ■

¼ teaspoon salt

¼ cup snipped fresh cilantro

These unorthodox baked beans will be the hit
of the next party or picnic. They pack a pleasing
punch, courtesy of heat from chipotle peppers
canned in adobo sauce.

Fill a large saucepan three-fourths full of water. Bring to a
boil over high heat. Stir in the beans. Return to a boil. Reduce
the heat and simmer for 15 minutes. Pour into a colander
and rinse. Pour into a large bowl.

Stir the onion, orange juice concentrate, molasses, tomato
paste, ¼ cup water, garlic, chipotle, and mustard into the
beans. Transfer to the slow cooker. Cook, covered, on low for
about 8 hours. Quickly check to see whether the beans look
like they're getting too dry. They aren't intended to be at all
soupy, but if you like a bit more liquid, stir in several tablespoons of water. Re-cover the slow cooker. Cook for 2 to
4 hours. When the beans are done, stir in the salt. Serve
garnished with the cilantro.

cook's tip: You can put the cooked beans directly into the slow cooker
instead of back in the bowl, but the inside of the slow cooker will get
less messy—and you can more easily combine all the ingredients—if you
use the bowl.

per serving

Calories 184
Total Fat 1.0 g
  Saturated Fat 0.0 g
  Trans Fat 0.0 g
  Polyunsaturated Fat 0.5 g
  Monounsaturated Fat 0.0 g

Cholesterol 0 mg
Sodium 71 mg
Carbohydrates 38 g
  Fiber 9 g
  Sugars 14 g
Protein 8 g

Dietary Exchanges
  2½ starch

balsamic-glazed beets with toasted walnuts

serves 4
½ cup per serving

slow cooker size/shape
1½- to 2½-quart round or oval

slow cooking time
3½ to 6 hours on low, **OR**
2 to 3 hours on high

1¼ **pounds beets (3 medium to large), peeled, halved, and cut into 1-inch wedges**

¼ **cup water**

⅓ **cup balsamic vinegar**

¼ **teaspoon firmly packed light or dark brown sugar**

¼ **cup chopped walnuts, dry-roasted**

As it reduces, balsamic vinegar thickens and becomes sweeter (though it does smell pungent), making it an addictively tasty, syrupy glaze for fresh beets. Serve the beets as a side dish or use a smaller amount on salads. *(See photo insert.)*

Put the beets in the slow cooker. Pour in the water. Cook, covered, on low for 3½ to 6 hours or on high for 2 to 3 hours, or until the beets are tender when pierced with a fork.

Meanwhile, in a small saucepan, stir together the vinegar and brown sugar. Bring to a boil over medium-high heat. Boil for 2 to 3 minutes, or until syrupy, stirring frequently (you will begin to see the bottom of the pan as you stir). Using a slotted spoon, transfer the beets to a serving bowl.

Drizzle the vinegar mixture over the beets. Sprinkle with the walnuts. Serve warm or at room temperature.

cook's tip on fresh beets: Peel the beets using a vegetable peeler and wear disposable gloves to avoid having your hands turn red as you peel.

per serving

Calories 108	Cholesterol 0 mg	Dietary Exchanges
Total Fat 5.0 g	Sodium 79 mg	2 vegetable, ½ other
Saturated Fat 0.5 g	Carbohydrates 15 g	carbohydrate, 1 fat
Trans Fat 0.0 g	Fiber 3 g	
Polyunsaturated Fat 3.5 g	Sugars 11 g	
Monounsaturated Fat 0.5 g	Protein 3 g	

braised broccoli rabe with cherry tomatoes

serves 4
½ cup per serving

slow cooker size/shape
3-quart round or oval

slow cooking time
3½ to 4 hours on low plus
30 minutes on high, **OR**
1½ to 2 hours on high plus
30 minutes on high

2 teaspoons olive oil

2 medium garlic cloves, thinly sliced

1 pound broccoli rabe, tough stems discarded, leaves and florets cut into 2-inch pieces (about 6 cups)

½ cup fat-free, low-sodium chicken broth, such as on page 31

⅛ teaspoon salt

⅛ teaspoon crushed red pepper flakes

■ ■ ■

1 cup cherry tomatoes

Cooking broccoli rabe until it is very tender softens its slightly bitter flavor, so the slow cooker is a good choice when preparing this staple of Italian cuisine.

In a small skillet, heat the oil over medium-high heat, swirling to coat the bottom. Cook the garlic for 2 minutes, or until lightly browned, stirring constantly. Transfer to the slow cooker.

Stir in the broccoli rabe, broth, salt, and red pepper flakes. Cook, covered, on low for 3½ to 4 hours or on high for 1½ to 2 hours, or until the broccoli rabe is tender.

If using the low setting, change it to high. Quickly stir in the tomatoes and re-cover the slow cooker. Cook for 30 minutes, or until the tomatoes are softened. Using a slotted spoon, transfer the mixture to plates.

cook's tip: This dish makes a delicious vegetarian meal for two when served over whole-grain pasta and sprinkled with a small amount of shredded or grated Parmesan cheese. (Be sure to use vegetable broth instead of chicken broth.) Unlike when you serve the broccoli rabe as a side dish, here you will want to spoon the cooking liquid over the pasta to add moisture and flavor.

per serving

Calories 69	Cholesterol 0 mg	Dietary Exchanges
Total Fat 2.5 g	Sodium 118 mg	2 vegetable, ½ fat
Saturated Fat 0.5 g	Carbohydrates 9 g	
Trans Fat 0.0 g	Fiber 1 g	
Polyunsaturated Fat 0.5 g	Sugars 3 g	
Monounsaturated Fat 1.5 g	Protein 5 g	

shredded brussels sprouts with almonds

serves 4
heaping ½ cup per serving

slow cooker size/shape
1½- to 2½-quart round or oval

slow cooking time
2 hours on high

2 teaspoons olive oil

1 small onion, thinly sliced

1 small carrot, diced

1 medium garlic clove, minced

10 ounces brussels sprouts, trimmed and shredded

½ cup fat-free, low-sodium vegetable broth, such as on page 33, or fat-free, low-sodium chicken broth, such as on page 31

¼ teaspoon salt

Pinch of pepper

■ ■ ■

2 tablespoons slivered almonds, dry-roasted

½ teaspoon red wine vinegar

A slow simmer makes these brussels sprouts tender and flavorful—but leaches out a lot of their color. We think you'll hardly notice that once you experience the flavor and crunch of this side dish, which is rich in vitamin C.

In a large nonstick skillet, heat the oil over medium-high heat, swirling to coat the bottom. Cook the onion and carrot, covered, for 6 minutes, or until tender, stirring occasionally. Stir in the garlic. Cook for 1 minute, stirring frequently. Transfer to the slow cooker.

Stir in the brussels sprouts, broth, salt, and pepper. Cook, covered, on high for 2 hours. Turn off the slow cooker. Just before serving, stir in the almonds and vinegar.

cook's tip: Use the coarse side of a box grater or the thin-slicing blade of a food processor to shred the brussels sprouts.

per serving

Calories 88	Cholesterol 0 mg	Dietary Exchanges
Total Fat 4.0 g	Sodium 180 mg	2 vegetable, 1 fat
Saturated Fat 0.5 g	Carbohydrates 11 g	
Trans Fat 0.0 g	Fiber 4 g	
Polyunsaturated Fat 1.0 g	Sugars 4 g	
Monounsaturated Fat 2.5 g	Protein 4 g	

sweet and tangy red cabbage

serves 8
½ cup per serving

slow cooker size/shape
3- to 4½-quart round or oval

slow cooking time
5 to 7 hours on low, **OR**
2½ to 3½ hours on high

1 **medium head red cabbage (about 1½ pounds), coarsely shredded (about 7 cups)**

1 **medium, tart apple, such as Honey Crisp, Granny Smith, or Cortland, cut into medium slices**

½ **cup diced onion**

3 **tablespoons cider vinegar**

2 **tablespoons dark brown sugar**

2 **tablespoons sweetened dried cranberries**

2 **tablespoons water**

¼ **teaspoon salt**

¼ **teaspoon pepper**

Sweetened dried cranberries temper the snap of cider vinegar in this jewel-toned side dish. Try it with lean pork roast or pork chops.

In the slow cooker, stir together all the ingredients. Cook, covered, on low for 5 to 7 hours or on high for 2½ to 3½ hours.

cook's tip on shredding cabbage: For quick and easy slicing, discard any tough outer cabbage leaves. Quarter the head and discard the core. Use the thin-slicing blade of a food processor, or cut the quarters crosswise into very thin strips.

per serving

Calories 63
Total Fat 0.0 g
  Saturated Fat 0.0 g
  Trans Fat 0.0 g
  Polyunsaturated Fat 0.0 g
  Monounsaturated Fat 0.0 g

Cholesterol 0 mg
Sodium 94 mg
Carbohydrates 15 g
  Fiber 3 g
  Sugars 11 g
Protein 1 g

Dietary Exchanges
½ fruit, 1 vegetable

pomegranate carrots

serves 6
scant ½ cup per serving

slow cooker size/shape
3- to 4½-quart round or oval

slow cooking time
4 to 4½ hours on high

1 pound baby carrots (halved
   lengthwise if extra large)

1 teaspoon olive oil

½ cup chopped onion

1 medium garlic clove, minced

¼ cup pomegranate juice

2 tablespoons Dijon mustard

2 tablespoons honey

2 teaspoons plain rice vinegar

1 teaspoon grated peeled
   gingerroot

■ ■ ■

1 tablespoon snipped fresh
   parsley

You'll be so taken with how the well-balanced combination of ingredients—pomegranate juice, Dijon mustard, rice vinegar, ginger, and honey—makes these carrots come alive with flavor that you probably won't mind their change in color.

Place the carrots in the slow cooker. Set aside.

In a small nonstick skillet, heat the oil over medium-high heat, swirling to coat the bottom. Cook the onion for 3 to 4 minutes, or until soft, stirring frequently. Stir in the garlic. Cook for 30 seconds, stirring constantly. Gently stir into the carrots.

In a small bowl, whisk together the remaining ingredients except the parsley. Pour into the slow cooker. Cook, covered, on high for 4 to 4½ hours, or until the carrots are tender-crisp. Just before serving, garnish with the parsley.

per serving

Calories 78
Total Fat 1.5 g
  Saturated Fat 0.0 g
  Trans Fat 0.0 g
  Polyunsaturated Fat 0.0 g
  Monounsaturated Fat 0.5 g

Cholesterol 0 mg
Sodium 157 mg
Carbohydrates 17 g
  Fiber 3 g
  Sugars 12 g
Protein 1 g

Dietary Exchanges
1 vegetable, ½ other
carbohydrate

crock-roasted carrots and parsnips with cumin-yogurt sauce

serves 6
½ cup vegetables and
1 tablespoon sauce per serving

slow cooker size/shape
1½- to 2½-quart round or
oval (preferred)

slow cooking time
5 to 7 hours on low, **OR**
2½ to 3½ hours on high

12 ounces medium carrots,
   each halved crosswise, then
   quartered lengthwise (cut into
   sixths if large) (strips should be
   ½ to ¾ inch thick)

12 ounces medium parsnips,
   each halved crosswise, then
   quartered lengthwise (cut into
   sixths if large) (strips should be
   ½ to ¾ inch thick)

¼ cup fat-free, low-sodium
   chicken broth, such as on
   page 31

■ ■ ■

⅓ cup fat-free plain yogurt

1 tablespoon fat-free milk

1 teaspoon ground cumin
   (dry-roasted preferred)

   Dash of pepper

1 tablespoon snipped fresh
   parsley

The key to success with this dish is to select carrots and parsnips of approximately equal size and cut them into pieces of similar size and shape so they will cook evenly at the same rate. Serve this dish with roasted meat or poultry.

In the slow cooker, make one layer of the carrots, then of the parsnips. Pour in the broth. Don't stir. Cook, covered, on low for 5 to 7 hours or on high for 2½ to 3½ hours, or until the vegetables are just tender and lightly browned on the edges that touch the sides of the crock.

Just before serving time, in a small bowl, whisk together the yogurt, milk, cumin, and pepper. Set aside.

Using tongs, transfer the vegetables to plates. Sprinkle with the parsley. Drizzle with the sauce.

cook's tip on dry-roasting ground spices: Many people dry-roast whole spices to intensify their flavor. It is common in Indian cooking to also dry-roast ground spices, as in this recipe.

per serving

Calories 76	Cholesterol 0 mg	Dietary Exchanges
Total Fat 0.5 g	Sodium 60 mg	1 starch, 1 vegetable
Saturated Fat 0.0 g	Carbohydrates 17 g	
Trans Fat 0.0 g	Fiber 4 g	
Polyunsaturated Fat 0.0 g	Sugars 7 g	
Monounsaturated Fat 0.0 g	Protein 2 g	

braised cauliflower with crisp garlic crumbs

serves 8
½ cup per serving

slow cooker size/shape
3- to 4½-quart round or oval

slow cooking time
2 hours on high

1 medium head of cauliflower (about 1½ pounds), cut into 1½-inch florets

½ cup fat-free, low-sodium vegetable broth, such as on page 33, or fat-free, low-sodium chicken broth, such as on page 31

■ ■ ■

2 slices whole-wheat bread (lowest sodium available), processed to crumbs, or 1½ cups plain whole-wheat panko (Japanese bread crumbs)

1 tablespoon olive oil

2 medium garlic cloves, minced

¼ teaspoon salt

⅛ teaspoon pepper

2 tablespoons snipped fresh parsley

Showering cauliflower with crunchy garlic-infused crumbs makes it irresistible!

In the slow cooker, cook the cauliflower and broth, covered, on high for 2 hours, or until the cauliflower is tender.

About 10 minutes before the cauliflower is ready, put the bread crumbs in a medium nonstick skillet. Drizzle with the oil. Using your fingers, combine until the crumbs are coated. Stir in the garlic, salt, and pepper. Cook over medium heat for 5 minutes, or until lightly browned, stirring frequently. Remove from the heat. Stir in the parsley. Set aside.

Using a slotted spoon, transfer the cauliflower to plates. Sprinkle with the crumb mixture.

per serving

Calories 42
Total Fat 2.0 g
  Saturated Fat 0.5 g
  Trans Fat 0.0 g
  Polyunsaturated Fat 0.0 g
  Monounsaturated Fat 1.5 g

Cholesterol 0 mg
Sodium 120 mg
Carbohydrates 5 g
  Fiber 1 g
  Sugars 1 g
Protein 2 g

Dietary Exchanges
1 vegetable, ½ fat

sicilian eggplant caponata

serves 10
½ cup per serving

slow cooker size/shape
3- to 4½-quart round or oval

slow cooking time
4 hours on low plus
3 to 4 hours on low, **OR**
2 hours on high plus
1 to 2 hours on high

Cooking spray

1½ **pounds Italian plum (Roma) tomatoes, seeded and chopped**

1 **1-pound eggplant, unpeeled, cut into ½-inch cubes**

1½ **cups chopped Vidalia, Maui, Oso Sweet, or other sweet onion**

2 **medium ribs of celery, cut crosswise into ¼-inch slices**

2 **medium garlic cloves, minced**

1 **tablespoon uncooked instant, or quick-cooking, tapioca**

2 **teaspoons sugar**

¼ **teaspoon salt**

¼ **cup no-salt-added tomato paste**

3 **tablespoons red wine vinegar**

■ ■ ■

5 **medium pimiento-stuffed green olives, finely chopped**

1 **tablespoon capers, drained, halved if large**

½ **cup snipped fresh parsley or chopped fresh basil (optional)**

You can enjoy this caponata in several ways: as a vegetable side dish, ladled over whole-grain pasta or polenta (see the Cook's Tip on Leftover Grits, page 202), as a vegetarian main dish for four, or spread lightly on thin pieces of toasted baguettes for bruschetta for 20. Add a sprinkling of Parmesan cheese when using the caponata as a main dish or bruschetta.

Lightly spray the slow cooker with cooking spray. Using half of each ingredient, make one layer each, in order, of the tomatoes, eggplant, onion, celery, and garlic in the slow cooker. Sprinkle with half each of the tapioca, sugar, and salt. Repeat. Don't stir.

In a small bowl, whisk together the tomato paste and vinegar. Pour into the slow cooker. Cook, covered, on low for 4 hours or on high for 2 hours. Quickly stir the vegetables and re-cover the slow cooker. Cook on low for 3 to 4 hours or on high for 1 to 2 hours, until the vegetables are tender.

Stir in the olives and capers. Change the setting to warm or turn off the slow cooker. For maximum flavor, let the caponata cool for about 30 minutes, or until room temperature. Just before serving, sprinkle with the parsley.

cook's tip: Refrigerate any leftovers in an airtight container for up to two days. Let them come to room temperature before serving.

per serving

Calories 50	Cholesterol 0 mg	Dietary Exchanges
Total Fat 0.5 g	Sodium 143 mg	2 vegetable
Saturated Fat 0.0 g	Carbohydrates 11 g	
Trans Fat 0.0 g	Fiber 3 g	
Polyunsaturated Fat 0.0 g	Sugars 6 g	
Monounsaturated Fat 0.0 g	Protein 2 g	

cheesy basil grits

serves 6
½ cup per serving

slow cooker size/shape
3- to 4½-quart round or oval

slow cooking time
4 hours on low, **OR**
2 hours on high

Cooking spray

3 cups water

1 cup uncooked grits (not instant or quick-cooking)

½ teaspoon garlic powder

■ ■ ■

⅛ teaspoon salt

¼ cup shredded or grated Parmesan cheese or finely shredded part-skim mozzarella

2 tablespoons chopped fresh basil

1 medium fresh jalapeño, seeds and ribs discarded, finely chopped

1 small tomato, seeded and diced

1 tablespoon olive oil (extra virgin preferred)

A little southern, a little Mediterranean, and a little south of the border, these grits qualify as comfort food wherever they're served. Keep in mind that you'll need to stir the grits several times as they cook to creamy goodness.

Lightly spray the slow cooker with cooking spray.

In the slow cooker, stir together the water, grits, and garlic powder. Cook, covered, on low for 4 hours or on high for 2 hours, or until the grits are creamy and tender, stirring every hour on low or every 30 minutes on high. Be sure to quickly stir and re-cover each time.

Spoon the grits into a shallow serving dish. Sprinkle in the order listed with the remaining ingredients except the oil. Drizzle with the oil.

cook's tip on leftover grits: Ever wonder what to do with leftover grits? The answer is simple—make polenta for a great side dish! Cover and refrigerate the cooked grits for up to two days, then cut into wedges. To microwave one serving, place a wedge on a microwaveable plate. Microwave, covered, on 100 percent power (high) for 20 to 30 seconds, or until heated through.

per serving

Calories 133	Cholesterol 2 mg	Dietary Exchanges
Total Fat 3.5 g	Sodium 110 mg	1½ starch, ½ fat
Saturated Fat 1.0 g	Carbohydrates 23 g	
Trans Fat 0.0 g	Fiber 2 g	
Polyunsaturated Fat 0.5 g	Sugars 1 g	
Monounsaturated Fat 2.0 g	Protein 4 g	

lentil and bell pepper salad with lemon-orange dressing

serves 8
½ cup per serving

slow cooker size/shape
1½- to 2½-quart round or oval

slow cooking time
2½ to 3½ hours on low, **OR**
1 hour 15 minutes to 1 hour
45 minutes on high

3 cups water

1 cup dried brown lentils (about 8 ounces), sorted for stones and shriveled lentils, rinsed, and drained

■ ■ ■

3 tablespoons frozen orange juice concentrate, thawed

1 teaspoon grated lemon zest

⅓ cup fresh lemon juice

1 teaspoon olive oil (extra virgin preferred)

½ teaspoon Dijon mustard

1 medium garlic clove, minced

⅛ teaspoon salt

⅛ teaspoon pepper

1 ounce baby spinach (about 1 cup), coarsely chopped

¾ cup diced yellow bell pepper

¾ cup diced orange bell pepper

⅔ cup cherry tomatoes, halved

¼ cup kalamata olives, halved

Lentils are nutritious and inexpensive but become visually appealing only when surrounded by colorful ingredients, such as the baby spinach, yellow and orange bell peppers, cherry tomatoes, and blackish-purple olives that brighten this salad. Adding the tangy citrus dressing to the lentils while they are still warm assures maximum flavor absorption.

In the slow cooker, stir together the water and lentils. Cook, covered, on low for 2½ to 3½ hours or on high for 1 hour 15 minutes to 1 hour 45 minutes, or until the lentils are just tender but still hold their shape.

Meanwhile, in a small bowl, whisk together the orange juice concentrate, lemon zest, lemon juice, oil, mustard, garlic, salt, and pepper. Set the dressing aside.

When the lentils are ready, drain well in a colander. Transfer to a large bowl. Pour ⅓ cup dressing over the lentils, lightly tossing to coat. Let stand for 15 minutes so the flavors blend.

Add the spinach, bell peppers, tomatoes, and olives to the lentils, tossing gently to combine, and adding 1 to 2 tablespoons of the extra dressing if the salad seems too dry.

per serving

Calories 132
Total Fat 2.0 g
  Saturated Fat 0.0 g
  Trans Fat 0.0 g
  Polyunsaturated Fat 0.5 g
  Monounsaturated Fat 1.5 g

Cholesterol 0 mg
Sodium 126 mg
Carbohydrates 23 g
  Fiber 4 g
  Sugars 6 g
  Protein 8 g

Dietary Exchanges
  1½ starch, ½ lean meat

roasted red potatoes with lemon and green onions

serves 4
4 potato halves per serving

slow cooker size/shape
3- to 4½-quart round or oval

slow cooking time
6 hours on low, **OR**
3 hours on high

Cooking spray

8 2-ounce red potatoes, halved crosswise

½ medium onion, thinly sliced

½ teaspoon garlic powder

½ teaspoon dried oregano, crumbled

1 tablespoon olive oil

■ ■ ■

2 medium green onions, finely chopped

2 tablespoons water

1 to 2 teaspoons grated lemon zest

1 tablespoon fresh lemon juice

⅛ teaspoon salt

1½ teaspoons olive oil (extra virgin preferred)

If you're looking for a versatile dish, you've found it. Ideal as a side dish, these flavorful potatoes also work well as an appetizer. They're easy to make and super easy to serve, and they're equally delicious warm or at room temperature.

Lightly spray the slow cooker with cooking spray. Put the potatoes, onion, garlic powder, oregano, and 1 tablespoon oil in the slow cooker, tossing to coat. (Be sure the potatoes are covered with the mixture.) Cook, covered, on low for 6 hours or on high for 3 hours, or until the potatoes are tender when pierced with a fork.

Turn off the slow cooker. Using a slotted spoon, transfer the potatoes to a shallow pan, such as a pie pan, leaving the drippings in the slow cooker. Stir the remaining ingredients into the drippings. Spoon over the potatoes, stirring gently to coat. Let stand for at least 10 minutes so the flavors blend and the potatoes are cool enough to eat.

per serving

Calories 138
Total Fat 5.0 g
  Saturated Fat 0.5 g
  Trans Fat 0.0 g
  Polyunsaturated Fat 0.5 g
  Monounsaturated Fat 3.5 g

Cholesterol 0 mg
Sodium 97 mg
Carbohydrates 21 g
  Fiber 3 g
  Sugars 3 g
Protein 2 g

Dietary Exchanges
1½ starch, 1 fat

maple-glazed quinoa

serves 8
½ cup per serving

slow cooker size/shape
1½- to 2½-quart round or oval

slow cooking time
2½ to 3½ hours on low, **OR**
1 hour 15 minutes to 1 hour
45 minutes on high

2 cups water

**1 cup uncooked quinoa, rinsed
well under cold running water
and drained**

1 medium carrot, diced

**2 tablespoons dark raisins or
sweetened dried cranberries**

1 tablespoon pure maple syrup

¼ teaspoon maple extract

By using maple extract to supplement pure maple syrup, you get more-intense flavor without added calories.

In the slow cooker, stir together all the ingredients. Cook, covered, on low for 2½ to 3½ hours or on high for 1 hour 15 minutes to 1 hour 45 minutes, or until the water is absorbed and the quinoa is tender. Fluff with a fork before serving.

cook's tip on quinoa: Quinoa (KEEN-wah), an ancient grain native to the Andes, contains complete protein, as well as contributing iron and calcium. Toss quinoa with dry-roasted pine nuts and fresh herbs, chill it to combine with fruit for a salad, or serve it as a breakfast cereal.

per serving

Calories 97	Cholesterol 0 mg	Dietary Exchanges
Total Fat 1.5 g	Sodium 10 mg	1 starch
Saturated Fat 0.0 g	Carbohydrates 18 g	
Trans Fat 0.0 g	Fiber 2 g	
Polyunsaturated Fat 0.5 g	Sugars 5 g	
Monounsaturated Fat 0.5 g	Protein 3 g	

pumpkin-sage risotto

serves 8
½ cup per serving

slow cooker size/shape
1½- to 2½-quart round or oval

slow cooking time
3½ to 4½ hours on low, **OR**
1 hour 45 minutes to 2 hours
15 minutes on high

1 teaspoon olive oil

⅓ cup minced shallots or onions

1 medium garlic clove, minced

2 tablespoons chopped fresh
sage

1 cup uncooked arborio rice

1 cup canned solid-pack pumpkin
(not pie filling)

3 cups fat-free, low-sodium
chicken broth, such as on
page 31

■ ■ ■

¼ cup fat-free half-and-half

¼ teaspoon salt

⅛ teaspoon pepper

Leaves or sprigs of fresh sage

Canned pumpkin adds a luscious reminder of fall to this risotto, which is made extra creamy with arborio rice and fat-free half-and-half.

In a small skillet, heat the oil over medium heat, swirling to coat the bottom. Cook the shallots for 2 minutes, or until beginning to soften, stirring constantly.

Stir in the garlic and chopped sage. Cook for 30 seconds, stirring constantly.

Stir in the rice. Cook for 2 minutes, stirring constantly. Transfer to the slow cooker.

Stir in the pumpkin. Pour in the broth, stirring until combined. Cook, covered, on low for 3½ to 4½ hours or on high for 1 hour 45 minutes to 2 hours 15 minutes, or until the rice is tender and creamy but with a slight bite and almost all the liquid is absorbed. Transfer to a large bowl.

Stir in the half-and-half, salt, and pepper. Serve the risotto garnished with the sage leaves or sprigs.

cook's tip on arborio rice: Make sure you cook arborio rice in oil for at least 2 minutes so the hull will begin to soften and the rice will stay creamy as it slow cooks. To preserve that creaminess, serve risotto as soon as possible after it has finished cooking. However, if your slow cooker has a warm setting, you can use it to let the risotto stand for up to 30 minutes.

per serving

Calories 110
Total Fat 0.5 g
  Saturated Fat 0.0 g
  Trans Fat 0.0 g
  Polyunsaturated Fat 0.0 g
  Monounsaturated Fat 0.5 g

Cholesterol 0 mg
Sodium 103 mg
Carbohydrates 23 g
  Fiber 2 g
  Sugars 2 g
Protein 4 g

Dietary Exchanges
1½ starch

wild rice with harvest vegetables

serves 12
½ cup per serving

slow cooker size/shape
3- to 4-quart round or oval

slow cooking time
5 to 6 hours on low

2½ **cups fat-free, low-sodium vegetable broth, such as on page 33, or fat-free, low-sodium chicken broth, such as on page 31**

1½ **cups chopped peeled butternut squash (about 8 ounces, already peeled and seeded)**

1 **cup uncooked wild rice, rinsed and drained**

1 **medium leek (white and light green parts), sliced crosswise (about 1 cup)**

1 **cup frozen whole-kernel corn, thawed**

½ **teaspoon dried summer savory, crumbled**

¼ **teaspoon salt**

¼ **teaspoon pepper**

■ ■ ■

¼ **cup snipped fresh parsley**

¼ **cup chopped pecans, dry-roasted**

Butternut squash, corn, and parsley provide a nice contrast to dark wild rice in this side that is elegant enough for a dinner party or a holiday family gathering.

In the slow cooker, stir together the broth, squash, rice, leek, corn, summer savory, salt, and pepper. Cook, covered, on low for 5 to 6 hours, or until the liquid is absorbed and the rice is tender.

Just before serving, stir in the parsley and pecans.

cook's tip on dry-roasting nuts on the stovetop: One way to dry-roast nuts is on the stovetop. Spread the nuts in a single layer in a skillet and dry-roast them over medium heat for 3 to 4 minutes, or until they're just fragrant, stirring frequently. Watch carefully so they don't burn. Remove them from the skillet immediately so they don't continue to cook. For how to dry-roast nuts in the oven, see the Cook's Tip on page 237.

cook's tip on dried savory: Milder than winter savory, summer savory has a thyme-like scent and a faint bitter, almost minty flavor. Summer savory can be used in side dishes, as in this recipe, as well as in meat dishes, bean dishes, stuffing, and soups. Both summer and winter savory are available in the spice aisle of grocery stores.

per serving

Calories 97	Cholesterol 0 mg	Dietary Exchanges
Total Fat 2.0 g	Sodium 64 mg	1 starch
Saturated Fat 0.0 g	Carbohydrates 18 g	
Trans Fat 0.0 g	Fiber 2 g	
Polyunsaturated Fat 0.5 g	Sugars 2 g	
Monounsaturated Fat 1.0 g	Protein 3 g	

vegetable and mixed-rice pilaf

QUICK PREP

serves 8
scant ⅔ cup per serving

slow cooker size/shape
3- to 4-quart round or oval

slow cooking time
5 to 6 hours on low, **OR**
3 to 3½ hours on high

This pilaf is filled with fresh vegetables, so you get two side dishes in one! Just add a simple grilled or roasted main course, and your meal is complete. *(See photo insert.)*

In the slow cooker, stir together the mushrooms, asparagus, carrots, and onion. Add the oil, stirring to coat.

Stir in the brown rice and wild rice. Stir in the broth, water, garlic, basil, thyme, seasoning blend, and salt. Cook, covered, on low for 5 to 6 hours or on high for 3 to 3½ hours.

Just before serving, sprinkle the pilaf with the parsley. Drizzle with the lemon juice. Using a fork, stir to combine the ingredients and fluff the rice.

3 to 4 ounces button mushrooms, sliced (about 1 cup)

6 ounces asparagus spears, trimmed and cut into 2-inch pieces (about 1 cup)

2 medium carrots, sliced

½ medium onion, chopped

1 teaspoon olive oil

½ cup uncooked brown rice (not instant)

½ cup uncooked wild rice, rinsed and drained

1¾ cups fat-free, low-sodium vegetable broth, such as on page 33

1 cup water

2 medium garlic cloves, minced

1 teaspoon dried basil, crumbled

½ teaspoon dried thyme, crumbled

½ teaspoon salt-free all-purpose seasoning blend

¼ teaspoon salt

cook's tip on wild rice: Wild rice is a marsh grass, not actually a type of rice, but nevertheless is considered a grain. Clean wild rice by rinsing it well. When the rice is cooked, it should be slightly chewy and will have a nutty flavor.

■ ■ ■

1 tablespoon snipped fresh Italian (flat-leaf) parsley

2 teaspoons fresh lemon juice

per serving

Calories 105	Cholesterol 0 mg	Dietary Exchanges
Total Fat 1.0 g	Sodium 102 mg	1 starch, 1 vegetable
Saturated Fat 0.0 g	Carbohydrates 21 g	
Trans Fat 0.0 g	Fiber 3 g	
Polyunsaturated Fat 0.5 g	Sugars 2 g	
Monounsaturated Fat 0.5 g	Protein 4 g	

acorn squash wedges with walnuts

serves 4
1 squash wedge and
2 tablespoons sauce
per serving

slow cooker size/shape
3- to 4-quart round or oval

slow cooking time
4 hours on low, **OR**
2 hours on high

Cooking spray

1 teaspoon canola or corn oil

1 medium onion, diced

¼ cup water

2 tablespoons chopped walnuts

¾ teaspoon ground cinnamon

¼ teaspoon ground nutmeg

1 large acorn squash (about 1¼ pounds), seeds and strings discarded, cut into 4 wedges

■ ■ ■

1 tablespoon plus 1 teaspoon firmly packed dark brown sugar

1 tablespoon light tub margarine

1 teaspoon vanilla extract

⅛ teaspoon salt

2 teaspoons canola or corn oil

Achieving an attractive browned finish to slow-cooked food usually isn't easy, but that isn't a problem here. The cut sides of acorn squash wedges lie on top of skillet-browned onions and brown as they slow cook; then the onions are incorporated into a brown-sugar-and-walnut sauce to top the squash. "Browning" never looked better.

Lightly spray the slow cooker with cooking spray. Set aside.

In a large nonstick skillet, heat 1 teaspoon oil over medium-high heat, swirling to coat the bottom. Cook the onion for 3 to 4 minutes, or until beginning to lightly brown, stirring frequently. Transfer to the slow cooker.

Stir in the water, walnuts, cinnamon, and nutmeg.

Arrange each squash wedge with a cut side down on top of the onion mixture, making sure that a cut side of each squash wedge touches the onion mixture. Cook, covered, on low for 4 hours or on high for 2 hours, or until the squash is tender when pierced with a fork.

Place the squash wedges on plates. Stir the remaining ingredients into the onion mixture. Spoon over the squash.

per serving

Calories 150
Total Fat 7.0 g
  Saturated Fat 0.5 g
  Trans Fat 0.0 g
  Polyunsaturated Fat 3.0 g
  Monounsaturated Fat 3.0 g

Cholesterol 0 mg
Sodium 102 mg
Carbohydrates 22 g
  Fiber 3 g
  Sugars 10 g
Protein 2 g

Dietary Exchanges
1½ starch, 1 fat

simple mashed sweet potatoes

serves 6
heaping ½ cup per serving
(plus 2 cups reserved for
Sweet Potato Bread Pudding,
page 243)

slow cooker size/shape
3- to 4½-quart round

slow cooking time
6 to 8 hours on low

3 **pounds sweet potatoes, peeled,
cut crosswise into ½-inch slices**

⅓ **cup firmly packed light brown
sugar**

¾ **teaspoon ground cinnamon**

¼ **teaspoon ground nutmeg**

⅓ **cup unsweetened apple juice**

This is one of the easiest ways to prepare mashed
sweet potatoes—no potato masher required!

In the slow cooker, make a layer of half the sweet potatoes.
Sprinkle with half each of the brown sugar, cinnamon, and
nutmeg. Repeat. Pour the apple juice over all. Don't stir.
Cook, covered, on low for 6 to 8 hours.

Just before serving, use the back of a large spoon to mash
the sweet potatoes against the side of the crock until the
desired consistency. Spoon 2 cups of the sweet potatoes into
an airtight container and refrigerate them to use later for
Sweet Potato Bread Pudding (page 243).

per serving

Calories 107
Total Fat 0.0 g
  Saturated Fat 0.0 g
  Trans Fat 0.0 g
  Polyunsaturated Fat 0.0 g
  Monounsaturated Fat 0.0 g

Cholesterol 0 mg
Sodium 51 mg
Carbohydrates 26 g
  Fiber 3 g
  Sugars 11 g
Protein 1 g

Dietary Exchanges
1½ starch

autumn apple-pear sauce

QUICK PREP

serves 6
½ cup per serving

slow cooker size/shape
3- to 4½-quart round or oval

slow cooking time
5 hours on low, **OR**
3 hours on high

4 large apples (about 1½ pounds total), peeled and cut into 1-inch chunks

4 large pears (about 1¾ pounds total), peeled and cut into 1-inch chunks

2 tablespoons sugar

1 tablespoon fresh lemon juice

⅛ teaspoon ground cinnamon

Pinch of ground nutmeg

When the produce stands are packed with the autumnal harvest of both apples and pears, you don't need to pick just one. Use your favorite variety of each in this wonderfully aromatic side dish, which teams well with entrées such as baked chicken breasts and roast beef. Even try this sauce as a complement to whole-wheat pancakes for breakfast on crisp fall mornings.

In the slow cooker, stir together all the ingredients. Cook, covered, on low for 5 hours or on high for 3 hours, or until the fruit is very tender. If you wish, mash the sauce to the desired consistency, keeping in mind that the sauce will thicken as it cools.

cook's tip: We used McIntosh apples and Anjou pears, but you can use any varieties you like for this recipe. You can even make the sauce using only apples or only pears if you prefer. Whatever you decide to use, you'll want 3 to 3½ pounds of fruit.

per serving ─────────────────────────────

Calories 134
Total Fat 0.5 g
  Saturated Fat 0.0 g
  Trans Fat 0.0 g
  Polyunsaturated Fat 0.0 g
  Monounsaturated Fat 0.0 g

Cholesterol 0 mg
Sodium 1 mg
Carbohydrates 36 g
  Fiber 5 g
  Sugars 26 g
  Protein 1 g

Dietary Exchanges
  2½ fruit

sauces and more

chunky tomato sauce with green olives

serves 4
½ cup per serving

slow cooker size/shape
1½ to 2½-quart round or oval

slow cooking time
6 hours on low, **OR**
3 hours on high

Cooking spray

1 teaspoon olive oil

1 medium green bell pepper, chopped

½ cup finely chopped onion

3 medium garlic cloves, minced

8 ounces Italian plum (Roma) tomatoes, halved lengthwise and cut crosswise into ¼-inch slices

8 ounces grape tomatoes

1 teaspoon sugar

⅛ teaspoon crushed red pepper flakes (optional)

■ ■ ■

8 small pimiento-stuffed green olives, finely chopped

2 to 3 tablespoons chopped fresh basil

1 tablespoon olive oil (extra virgin preferred)

You'll enjoy this sauce so much that you won't want to limit it to your favorite whole-grain pasta—try it over barley or quinoa for a change. Be sure to add the olives and basil just before serving for more pronounced flavors.

Lightly spray the slow cooker with cooking spray. Set aside.

In a large nonstick skillet, heat 1 teaspoon oil over medium-high heat, swirling to coat the bottom. Cook the bell pepper and onion for 3 minutes, or until the onion is soft, stirring frequently. Stir in the garlic. Cook for 30 seconds, stirring constantly. Transfer to the slow cooker.

Stir in the Italian plum and grape tomatoes, sugar, and red pepper flakes. Cook, covered, on low for 6 hours or on high for 3 hours, or until the onion is very soft.

Just before serving, stir in the olives, basil, and remaining 1 tablespoon oil.

cook's tip: This sauce is the perfect amount for a small household, but it doubles well. Use a 3- to 3½-quart slow cooker and the same timing.

per serving

Calories 92	Cholesterol 0 mg	Dietary Exchanges
Total Fat 6.0 g	Sodium 176 mg	2 vegetable, 1 fat
Saturated Fat 1.0 g	Carbohydrates 10 g	
Trans Fat 0.0 g	Fiber 2 g	
Polyunsaturated Fat 0.5 g	Sugars 6 g	
Monounsaturated Fat 4.0 g	Protein 2 g	

meaty mushroom pasta sauce

serves 12
⅔ cup per serving

slow cooker size/shape
4- to 6-quart round or oval

slow cooking time
8 to 10 hours on low, **OR**
4 to 6 hours on high

Cooking spray

2 teaspoons olive oil

1 pound ground skinless turkey breast

1 pound extra-lean ground beef

2 medium onions, chopped

4 medium garlic cloves, minced

8 ounces button mushrooms, thinly sliced

⅔ cup snipped fresh parsley

1 tablespoon dried Italian seasoning, crumbled

½ teaspoon pepper

¼ teaspoon salt

4 8-ounce cans no-salt-added tomato sauce

1 cup dry red wine (regular or nonalcoholic)

Once you smell the tantalizing aroma coming from the slow cooker, you're going to *know* that this sauce will taste great. Because the recipe makes about two quarts of sauce, you can either serve it to a group for a casual party or use some tonight on whole-grain pasta and freeze some for another meal, perhaps served over soft polenta.

Lightly spray the slow cooker and a large skillet with cooking spray. Set the slow cooker aside.

Heat the oil in the skillet over medium-high heat, swirling to coat the bottom. Cook the turkey for 3 minutes, or until it turns white, stirring occasionally.

Stir in the beef. Cook for 3 to 5 minutes, or until the turkey and beef are browned on the outside and no longer pink in the center, stirring occasionally to turn and break up the turkey and the beef.

Stir in the onions and garlic. Cook for 5 minutes, stirring occasionally. Transfer to the slow cooker.

Stir in the mushrooms, parsley, Italian seasoning, pepper, and salt. Stir in the tomato sauce and wine. Cook, covered, on low for 8 to 10 hours or on high for 4 to 6 hours.

cook's tip: Use a wide spatula, such as a pancake turner, in each hand to make turning and separating the ground turkey and ground beef into small pieces faster and easier.

per serving

Calories 161	Cholesterol 44 mg	Dietary Exchanges
Total Fat 3.0 g	Sodium 109 mg	2 vegetable, 2½ very
Saturated Fat 1.0 g	Carbohydrates 10 g	lean meat
Trans Fat 0.0 g	Fiber 2 g	
Polyunsaturated Fat 0.5 g	Sugars 6 g	
Monounsaturated Fat 1.5 g	Protein 19 g	

thick and rich root beer barbecue sauce

serves 6
¼ cup per serving

slow cooker size/shape
1½ to 2½-quart round or oval

slow cooking time
4½ to 5 hours on low, **OR**
2 hours 15 minutes to
2½ hours on high

Cooking spray
1 teaspoon canola or corn oil
1 large onion, finely chopped
1½ cups diet root beer
1 medium red bell pepper, diced
1 6-ounce can no-salt-added tomato paste
½ cup firmly packed dark brown sugar
¼ cup cider vinegar
1 tablespoon Worcestershire sauce (lowest sodium available)
1 teaspoon ground cumin
¼ teaspoon salt

■ ■ ■

¼ cup diet root beer or water, if needed
1 tablespoon grated peeled gingerroot

Root beer is a great "multitasking" ingredient in this sauce. It imparts sweetness and a deep, clovelike molasses flavor as well as adding a heady aroma during cooking. Use this version on grilled poultry and meats, just as you would an ordinary barbecue sauce.

Lightly spray the slow cooker with cooking spray. Set aside.

In a large nonstick skillet, heat the oil over medium-high heat, swirling to coat the bottom. Cook the onion for 3 minutes, or until soft, stirring frequently. Transfer to the slow cooker.

Pour 1½ cups root beer into the skillet. Bring to a boil, still over medium-high heat. Boil for 6 minutes, or until the root beer is reduced to ½ cup. Pour into the slow cooker.

Stir in the bell pepper, tomato paste, brown sugar, vinegar, Worcestershire sauce, cumin, and salt. Cook, covered, on low for 4½ to 5 hours or on high for 2 hours 15 minutes to 2½ hours, or until the sauce has thickened. For a thinner consistency, stir in the remaining ¼ cup root beer or water. Stir in the gingerroot.

per serving

Calories 112	Cholesterol 0 mg	Dietary Exchanges
Total Fat 1.0 g	Sodium 130 mg	1 vegetable, 1½ other
Saturated Fat 0.0 g	Carbohydrates 25 g	carbohydrate
Trans Fat 0.0 g	Fiber 1 g	
Polyunsaturated Fat 0.5 g	Sugars 22 g	
Monounsaturated Fat 0.5 g	Protein 1 g	

caramelized onions

serves 5
¼ cup per serving

slow cooker size/shape
1½- to 2½-quart round or oval

slow cooking time
5 to 8 hours on low, **OR**
2½ to 4 hours on high

**8 ounces onions, halved
lengthwise and cut crosswise
into ⅜-inch slices**

½ teaspoon olive oil

Pinch of sugar

Slow cooking onions until they're deep brown and caramelized gives them a deep, rich, slightly sweet flavor that complements many entrées and side dishes. Spoon them over chicken breasts, pork chops, steak, or turkey burgers, or skip the sausage and top your pizza with them. They also are very good when stirred into cooked brown rice or whole-wheat couscous or tossed with cooked vegetables, such as green beans, broccoli, or potatoes. Keep in mind that you'll need to do a quick stir every hour or so as the onions cook.

In a large bowl, toss together the onions, oil, and sugar to coat. Transfer to the slow cooker. Cook, covered, on low for 5 to 8 hours or on high for 2½ to 4 hours, or until the onions are golden brown, quickly stirring and re-covering every 1 to 2 hours to brown evenly. Unless you're making the Caramelized Onion-Mushroom Gravy (page 217), transfer the onions to an airtight container and refrigerate for up to one week or freeze in an airtight freezer container for up to three months.

per serving

Calories 22
Total Fat 0.5 g
  Saturated Fat 0.0 g
  Trans Fat 0.0 g
  Polyunsaturated Fat 0.0 g
  Monounsaturated Fat 0.5 g

Cholesterol 0 mg
Sodium 2 mg
Carbohydrates 4 g
  Fiber 1 g
  Sugars 2 g
Protein 1 g

Dietary Exchanges
1 vegetable

caramelized onion-mushroom gravy

serves 10
¼ cup per serving

slow cooker size/shape
1½- to 2½-quart round or oval

slow cooking time
3 to 4 hours on low plus
5 to 10 minutes on high, **OR**
1½ to 2 hours on high plus
5 to 10 minutes on high*

1 recipe hot Caramelized Onions (page 216)

■ ■ ■

2 cups fat-free, low-sodium chicken broth, such as on page 31

4 ounces sliced button mushrooms

1 teaspoon dried sage

⅛ teaspoon salt

⅛ teaspoon pepper

■ ■ ■

2 tablespoons cornstarch

2 tablespoons water

We've added fat-free, low-sodium chicken broth, sliced button mushrooms, and seasonings to the Caramelized Onions on page 216 to make a perfect gravy with no last-minute fuss; spoon it over dishes that you'd usually top with chicken gravy.

Have the caramelized onions ready in the slow cooker. Stir the broth, mushrooms, sage, salt, and pepper into the hot onions. Cook, covered, on low for 3 to 4 hours or on high for 1½ to 2 hours, or until the gravy comes to a full boil.

If using the low setting, change it to high. Put the cornstarch in a small bowl. Pour in the water, whisking to dissolve. Quickly stir about ¾ of the cornstarch mixture into the gravy and re-cover the slow cooker. Cook for 5 minutes. For a thicker gravy, stir in the remaining cornstarch mixture, re-cover the slow cooker, and cook for 5 minutes more, or until the desired consistency.

cook's tip: If you want to have plenty of onions for the gravy and other uses, double the recipe on page 216 and use a 2- to 3½-quart round or oval slow cooker. Cook for 3½ to 4½ hours on low or 1 hour 45 minutes to 2 hours 15 minutes on high.

per serving

Calories 22	Cholesterol 0 mg	Dietary Exchanges
Total Fat 0.5 g	Sodium 42 mg	1 vegetable
Saturated Fat 0.0 g	Carbohydrates 4 g	
Trans Fat 0.0 g	Fiber 1 g	
Polyunsaturated Fat 0.0 g	Sugars 1 g	
Monounsaturated Fat 0.0 g	Protein 1 g	

* These times don't include making the Caramelized Onions.

pickled beets

serves 6
⅓ cup per serving

slow cooker size/shape
1½- to 2½-quart round or oval

slow cooking time
6 to 7 hours on low, **OR**
3 to 3½ hours on high

1 cup water

½ cup cider vinegar

3 tablespoons honey

¼ teaspoon salt

¼ teaspoon black peppercorns

3 medium beets (about 1 pound total), trimmed, peeled, and cut into ⅛- to 3/16-inch slices

1 medium Vidalia, Maui, Oso Sweet, or other sweet onion, halved and thinly sliced

1 cinnamon stick (about 3 inches long)

1 medium dried bay leaf

Beets are anything but boring when they are pickled in a delightful combination of sweet and sour. Enjoy them hot or cold as a condiment to perk up entrées, and be sure to save some to use as a colorful addition to salads.

In a small bowl, stir together the water, vinegar, honey, salt, and peppercorns. Set aside.

In the slow cooker, make a layer of half the beets. Top with a layer of half the onion. Place the cinnamon stick and bay leaf on the onion. Repeat the layers of beets and onion.

Pour the vinegar mixture over the beet mixture. Don't stir. Cook, covered, on low for 6 to 7 hours or on high for 3 to 3½ hours, or until the beets are tender and the onion is soft.

Discard the cinnamon stick, bay leaf, and peppercorns. Serve the beets hot or transfer to a glass or other stainproof container and refrigerate, covered, for 6 to 8 hours to serve cold. The refrigerated beets will keep for up to one week.

cook's tip on slow cooking onions: For recipes using onions that aren't browned on the stovetop before being slow cooked, you may prefer sweet onions, such as Vidalia, Maui, or Oso Sweet, to white or yellow onions if you want milder flavor.

per serving

Calories 72
Total Fat 0.0 g
  Saturated Fat 0.0 g
  Trans Fat 0.0 g
  Polyunsaturated Fat 0.0 g
  Monounsaturated Fat 0.0 g

Cholesterol 0 mg
Sodium 152 mg
Carbohydrates 17 g
  Fiber 2 g
  Sugars 15 g
Protein 1 g

Dietary Exchanges
  2 vegetable, ½ other carbohydrate

pear and dried cherry chutney

serves 4
¼ cup per serving

slow cooker size/shape
3- to 4½-quart round or oval

slow cooking time
4 hours on low, **OR**
2 hours on high

Cooking spray

1 medium Anjou or Bartlett pear, chopped

¼ cup unsweetened dried cherries

2 tablespoons finely chopped red onion

1 tablespoon water

■ ■ ■

1 tablespoon sugar

1 tablespoon red wine vinegar

Take a break from salsas and sauces and serve a chutney instead. This tangy-sweet fruity creation is perfect served either hot or cold with grilled or roasted pork or poultry dishes.

Lightly spray a 2-cup heatproof glass measuring cup with cooking spray. Put the pear, cherries, onion, and water in the measuring cup (no stirring needed). Place in the slow cooker. Cook, covered, on low for 4 hours or on high for 2 hours, or until the onion is very soft.

Stir the sugar and vinegar into the pear mixture. Spread in a shallow pan, such as a pie pan, and let cool for about 20 minutes, or until thickened. Serve at room temperature or transfer to an airtight container and refrigerate for about 1 hour to serve chilled.

cook's tip: You might wonder why you need a medium-size slow cooker to make only one cup of chutney. It's because the handle of the measuring cup takes up too much space to fit into a smaller crock.

per serving

Calories 68	Cholesterol 0 mg	Dietary Exchanges
Total Fat 0.0 g	Sodium 1 mg	1 fruit
Saturated Fat 0.0 g	Carbohydrates 17 g	
Trans Fat 0.0 g	Fiber 2 g	
Polyunsaturated Fat 0.0 g	Sugars 12 g	
Monounsaturated Fat 0.0 g	Protein 1 g	

zesty tomato-apple chutney

QUICK PREP

serves 16
¼ cup per serving

slow cooker size/shape
3- to 4-quart round or oval

slow cooking time
6 to 7 hours on low, **OR**
3½ to 4 hours on high

Fruits and vegetables unite in this versatile chutney. Serve it as a relish to accompany curries or double the serving size (and the nutritionals) to serve eight as a side dish with roasted poultry or pork tenderloin. For an appetizer for 32 guests, spread room-temperature chutney on whole-grain, low-sodium crostini and garnish with a nibble of low-fat sharp Cheddar cheese.

Lightly spray the slow cooker with cooking spray. Put all the ingredients in the slow cooker, stirring to combine. Cook, covered, on low for 6 to 7 hours or on high for 3½ to 4 hours, quickly stirring once halfway through. Serve the chutney hot or transfer it to an airtight container and let it cool to room temperature, about 30 minutes. Refrigerate any leftovers in the container for up to two days.

cook's tip on fresh gingerroot: If you have a microplane, use it to make quick work of grating fresh peeled gingerroot.

Cooking spray

2½ cups Italian plum (Roma) tomatoes, seeded and finely chopped

2½ cups finely chopped semi-tart apples, such as Jonagold, Braeburn, or Gala

1 large red bell pepper, finely chopped

½ cup finely chopped Vidalia, Maui, Oso Sweet, or other sweet onion

¼ cup dried currants

1 medium fresh jalapeño, seeds and ribs discarded, minced

3 tablespoons cider vinegar

3 tablespoons honey

1 tablespoon plus 1 teaspoon uncooked instant, or quick-cooking, tapioca

2 teaspoons grated peeled gingerroot

¼ teaspoon salt

per serving

Calories 43	Cholesterol 0 mg	Dietary Exchanges
Total Fat 0.0 g	Sodium 39 mg	½ other carbohydrate
Saturated Fat 0.0 g	Carbohydrates 11 g	
Trans Fat 0.0 g	Fiber 1 g	
Polyunsaturated Fat 0.0 g	Sugars 8 g	
Monounsaturated Fat 0.0 g	Protein 1 g	

wine-spiked cranberry sauce

QUICK PREP

serves 10
¼ cup per serving

slow cooker size/shape
1½- to 2½-quart round or oval

slow cooking time
4 to 6 hours on low, **OR**
2 to 3 hours on high

12 ounces fresh or frozen
     cranberries, thawed if frozen

1 cup sugar

1½ teaspoons ground cinnamon

¼ teaspoon ground nutmeg

¼ teaspoon ground cardamom

⅛ teaspoon ground cloves

    Pinch of ground allspice

½ cup dry red wine (regular or
     nonalcoholic)

You'll think you're eating mulled wine transformed into a cranberry sauce when you experience this condiment alongside your holiday turkey or any other roasted meats.

In the slow cooker, stir together all the ingredients except the wine. Stir in the wine. Cook, covered, on low for 4 to 6 hours or on high for 2 to 3 hours, or until the cranberries have popped and are tender. To serve the day you make the sauce, pour it into a medium bowl and cover and refrigerate for at least 2 to 3 hours. To serve later, pour it into an airtight container and refrigerate until needed. The sauce is at its best if you make it within three days of serving, but it will stay fresh for up to one week.

per serving

Calories 105
Total Fat 0.0 g
    Saturated Fat 0.0 g
    Trans Fat 0.0 g
    Polyunsaturated Fat 0.0 g
    Monounsaturated Fat 0.0 g

Cholesterol 0 mg
Sodium 2 mg
Carbohydrates 25 g
    Fiber 2 g
    Sugars 22 g
    Protein 0 g

Dietary Exchanges
    1½ other carbohydrate

strawberry and dried fig spread

QUICK PREP

serves 5
¼ cup per serving

slow cooker size/shape
3- to 4½-quart round or oval

slow cooking time
4 hours on low plus
20 minutes on high, **OR**
2 hours on high plus
20 minutes on high

Cooking spray

2 cups fresh or frozen
unsweetened strawberries,
hulled if fresh, thawed if frozen
(about 8 ounces)

8 dried figs, chopped

3 tablespoons sugar

1 tablespoon water

½ teaspoon ground cinnamon

⅛ to ¼ teaspoon ground allspice

■ ■ ■

2 teaspoons cornstarch

1 tablespoon water

1 teaspoon vanilla extract

You already know that fruit spread is great on toast, so now go for the unexpected! Top a baked sweet potato for a refreshing side, spread some over fat-free cream cheese on low-fat whole-grain crackers for a snack, or spoon it over poached or baked fruit for a delicious dessert.

Lightly spray a 2-cup heatproof glass measuring cup with cooking spray. Put the strawberries, figs, sugar, 1 tablespoon water, the cinnamon, and allspice in the measuring cup (no stirring needed). Place in the slow cooker. Cook, covered, on low for 4 hours or on high for 2 hours, or until the figs are very soft.

Put the cornstarch in a small bowl. Add the remaining 1 tablespoon water and the vanilla, stirring to dissolve. Quickly stir into the strawberry mixture, breaking up any large pieces of fruit while stirring, and re-cover the slow cooker. If using the low setting, change it to high. Cook for 20 minutes, or until slightly thickened.

Carefully remove the measuring cup. Transfer the straw-berry mixture to a shallow pan, such as a pie pan. Cover and refrigerate for at least 1 hour to cool completely. Refrigerate leftovers in an airtight container for up to one month.

per serving

Calories 88	Cholesterol 0 mg	Dietary Exchanges
Total Fat 0.5 g	Sodium 2 mg	2 fruit
Saturated Fat 0.0 g	Carbohydrates 22 g	
Trans Fat 0.0 g	Fiber 3 g	
Polyunsaturated Fat 0.0 g	Sugars 17 g	
Monounsaturated Fat 0.0 g	Protein 1 g	

eggplant and basil mediterranean salsa

serves 6
¼ cup per serving

slow cooker size/shape
3- to 4½-quart round or oval

slow cooking time
4 hours on low, **OR**
2 hours on high

Cooking spray

1 teaspoon canola or corn oil

¼ medium eggplant (about
4 ounces), unpeeled, diced
(about 1 cup)

5 ounces grape tomatoes (about
1 cup)

1 medium banana pepper,
chopped, or ½ medium yellow
or red bell pepper, chopped

1 tablespoon water

½ teaspoon dried oregano,
crumbled

½ teaspoon garlic powder

¼ teaspoon fennel seeds, crushed
(optional)

■ ■ ■

2 tablespoons capers, drained,
halved if large

1 tablespoon chopped fresh basil

1 teaspoon red wine vinegar

Call it a cooked salsa, a caponata, or simply an eggplant topping, but whatever you call it, be sure to make this when you want compliments. It's delicious served with whole-grain pita wedges or on thin slices of lightly toasted whole-grain baguette.

Lightly spray a heatproof 2-cup glass measuring cup with cooking spray. Set aside.

In a large nonstick skillet, heat the oil over medium-high heat, swirling to coat the bottom. Cook the eggplant for 3 minutes, or until beginning to lightly brown, stirring frequently. Remove the skillet from the heat.

Stir in the tomatoes, banana pepper, water, oregano, garlic powder, and fennel seeds. Transfer the mixture to the measuring cup. Place in the slow cooker. Cook, covered, on low for 4 hours or on high for 2 hours, or until the eggplant is soft.

Carefully remove the cup from the slow cooker. Spoon the eggplant mixture into a shallow pan, such as a pie pan, and let stand for about 30 minutes, or until room temperature. Gently fold in the capers, basil, and vinegar, keeping the vegetables intact. Serve at room temperature for peak flavors.

per serving

Calories 21	Cholesterol 0 mg	Dietary Exchanges
Total Fat 1.0 g	Sodium 89 mg	Free
Saturated Fat 0.0 g	Carbohydrates 3 g	
Trans Fat 0.0 g	Fiber 1 g	
Polyunsaturated Fat 0.5 g	Sugars 1 g	
Monounsaturated Fat 0.5 g	Protein 1 g	

breads and breakfast dishes

spiced banana bread

serves 16
1 slice per serving

slow cooker size/shape
5- to 6-quart oval

slow cooking time
2½ hours on high

Cooking spray

1¾ cups white whole-wheat flour

⅓ cup firmly packed dark brown
sugar

⅓ cup sugar

2 teaspoons baking powder

½ teaspoon ground nutmeg

¼ teaspoon baking soda

⅛ teaspoon salt

1 cup very ripe mashed bananas
(about 2 medium)

4 large egg whites

⅓ cup low-fat buttermilk

¼ cup canola or corn oil

1 teaspoon vanilla, butter, and
nut flavoring or vanilla extract

¼ cup finely chopped pecans, dry-
roasted

Yes, you can use your slow cooker as a mini oven to bake tasty quick breads! The trick is to place the loaf pan on a rack or several balls of aluminum foil to raise it off the bottom of the slow cooker so your bread will "bake" evenly.

Lightly spray an 8½ x 4½ x 2½-inch loaf pan with cooking spray. Set aside.

In a large bowl, stir together the flour, sugars, baking powder, nutmeg, baking soda, and salt.

In a medium bowl, whisk together the remaining ingredients except the pecans. Add to the flour mixture, stirring until the flour mixture is just moistened, but no flour is visible. Don't overmix; the batter should be slightly lumpy. Spoon into the loaf pan, gently smoothing the top. Sprinkle with the pecans.

Place a metal rack with short legs, such as a pressure cooker rack, or three or four 12 x 6-inch sheets of aluminum foil crumpled into balls in the slow cooker. Put the loaf pan on top. Cook, covered, on high for 2½ hours, or until a wooden toothpick inserted in the center of the bread comes out clean.

Let the bread stand for 5 minutes. Using a metal spatula, loosen it from the pan. Turn out onto a cooling rack and let cool completely, about 1 hour. For the best results, wrap the bread in plastic wrap and let the flavors blend overnight.

per serving

Calories 141
Total Fat 5.0 g
  Saturated Fat 0.5 g
  Trans Fat 0.0 g
  Polyunsaturated Fat 1.5 g
  Monounsaturated Fat 3.0 g

Cholesterol 0 mg
Sodium 109 mg
Carbohydrates 21 g
  Fiber 2 g
  Sugars 11 g
Protein 3 g

Dietary Exchanges
  1½ other
  carbohydrate, 1 fat

steamed pumpkin bread

serves 16
1 slice per serving

slow cooker size/shape
7-quart oval

slow cooking time
2 to 2½ hours on high

Cooking spray

6 cups water

½ cup all-purpose flour

½ cup whole-wheat flour

½ cup cornmeal

1 teaspoon baking soda

1 teaspoon ground cinnamon

½ teaspoon ground allspice

¼ teaspoon salt

⅓ cup sweetened dried cranberries

⅓ cup chopped walnuts

¾ cup canned solid-pack pumpkin (not pie filling)

¾ cup low-fat buttermilk

2 large egg whites

¼ cup dark or light molasses

Pumpkin, dried cranberries, walnuts, and spices update a traditional steamed brown bread recipe. The result is moist and delicious.

Lightly spray a 9 x 5 x 3-inch ovenproof glass loaf pan with cooking spray. Place a metal rack with short legs, such as a pressure cooker rack, or three or four 12 x 6-inch sheets of aluminum foil crumpled into balls in the slow cooker.

In a large saucepan, bring the water to a boil over high heat.

Meanwhile, in a large bowl, stir together the flours, corn-meal, baking soda, cinnamon, allspice, and salt. Stir in the cranberries and walnuts. Make a well in the center.

In a medium bowl, whisk together the pumpkin, buttermilk, egg whites, and molasses. Pour into the well. Stir just until the flour mixture is moistened, but no flour is visible. Don't overmix. Pour into the loaf pan, gently smoothing the top. Cover tightly with aluminum foil. Secure with kitchen twine.

Place the pan on the rack or crumpled foil in the slow cooker. Pour the boiling water down the side of the crock until the water reaches midway up the side of the pan. Cook, covered, on high for 2 to 2½ hours, or until a wooden toothpick inserted in the center of the bread comes out clean. Carefully transfer the pan to a cooling rack. Discard the foil. Let the bread stand in the pan for 10 minutes. Turn out onto the cooling rack. Serve the bread warm.

per serving

Calories 92	Cholesterol 1 mg	Dietary Exchanges
Total Fat 2.0 g	Sodium 139 mg	1 starch
Saturated Fat 0.5 g	Carbohydrates 17 g	
Trans Fat 0.0 g	Fiber 2 g	
Polyunsaturated Fat 1.5 g	Sugars 6 g	
Monounsaturated Fat 0.5 g	Protein 3 g	

apricot-cinnamon granola

QUICK PREP

serves 14
½ cup per serving

slow cooker size/shape
3- to 4½-quart round or oval

slow cooking time
1½ hours on high plus
1 to 1½ hours on low

4 cups uncooked rolled oats (not instant)

1½ cups wheat bran cereal (not flakes)

½ cup ground flax seed

½ cup toasted wheat germ

½ cup raw shelled sunflower seeds

½ cup chopped walnuts

1 tablespoon ground cinnamon

½ teaspoon ground nutmeg

½ cup honey

3 tablespoons canola or corn oil

2 teaspoons vanilla extract

1 teaspoon almond extract

■ ■ ■

½ cup dried apricots, chopped

Making granola in the slow cooker produces an evenly browned, crisp cereal. This version is filled with good-for-you oats, flax seed, wheat germ, bran, and nuts. Be sure to make this recipe when you're going to be at home so you can stir the granola every 30 minutes.

In the slow cooker, stir together the oats, bran cereal, flax seed, wheat germ, sunflower seeds, walnuts, cinnamon, and nutmeg. Set aside.

In a medium glass measuring cup, whisk together the honey and oil. Microwave on 100 percent power (high) for 40 seconds to 1 minute, or until the honey is melted. Stir in the vanilla and almond extracts. Pour over the oat mixture, stirring until moistened.

Cook, with the lid slightly ajar, on high for 1½ hours, stirring every 30 minutes. Change the slow cooker setting to low. Cook, with the lid slightly ajar, for 1 to 1½ hours, or until the mixture is golden brown, stirring every 30 minutes. Watch carefully during the last 30 minutes to avoid overbrowning.

Stir in the apricots. Spread the granola on a large rimmed baking sheet. Let stand for 2 hours, or until completely cool. Store in an airtight container at room temperature for up to one month.

cook's tip: Cooking the granola on high at the beginning gets the browning started, and finishing on low with the lid partially open reduces the moisture.

per serving

Calories 262	Cholesterol 0 mg	Dietary Exchanges
Total Fat 11.5 g	Sodium 20 mg	2 starch, ½ fruit, 2 fat
Saturated Fat 1.0 g	Carbohydrates 38 g	
Trans Fat 0.0 g	Fiber 7 g	
Polyunsaturated Fat 5.5 g	Sugars 15 g	
Monounsaturated Fat 4.0 g	Protein 7 g	

nutty breakfast grits with pears

serves 6
⅔ cup grits and ¼ cup topping per serving

slow cooker size/shape
3- to 4½-quart round or oval

slow cooking time
3 hours on low, **OR**
1½ hours on high

Cooking spray

1 quart water

1 cup uncooked grits (not instant or quick-cooking)

¼ teaspoon salt

∎ ∎ ∎

¼ cup sugar

2 tablespoons light tub margarine

1½ teaspoons vanilla extract

½ teaspoon almond extract

1 medium pear, diced

¼ cup slivered almonds, dry-roasted and coarsely chopped

2 tablespoons sweetened dried cranberries, finely chopped

Think out of the box the next time you want hot cereal for breakfast: serve sweet grits prepared in a not-so-traditional way. Fresh pear combined with almonds and dried cranberries makes a crunchy topping that contrasts nicely with the creamy grits. The grits don't have to cook very long, but they will need to be stirred several times so they cook evenly and don't have lumps.

Lightly spray the slow cooker with cooking spray. Pour in the water. Stir in the grits and salt. Cook, covered, on low for 3 hours or on high for 1½ hours, or until the grits are creamy and tender, quickly stirring every hour if using the low setting or every 30 minutes if using the high setting. Re-cover the slow cooker after each stirring.

Add the sugar, margarine, and vanilla and almond extracts, stirring until the margarine has melted. Spoon into bowls.

In a small bowl, stir together the pear, almonds, and cranberries. Spoon over the grits.

cook's tip: If you have leftovers, refrigerate the grits and the topping in separate airtight containers for up to two days. For one serving, stir 3 to 4 tablespoons of fat-free milk into the grits. Reheat the grits in a small saucepan over medium heat for 3 to 4 minutes, or until heated through, stirring frequently. Top with the pear mixture.

per serving

Calories 196	Cholesterol 0 mg	Dietary Exchanges
Total Fat 4.0 g	Sodium 133 mg	2 starch, ½ fruit, ½ fat
Saturated Fat 0.0 g	Carbohydrates 38 g	
Trans Fat 0.0 g	Fiber 3 g	
Polyunsaturated Fat 1.0 g	Sugars 14 g	
Monounsaturated Fat 2.5 g	Protein 3 g	

cinnamon quinoa with peaches

QUICK PREP

serves 6
½ cup quinoa, ¼ cup peaches, ¼ cup half-and-half, and 1 tablespoon almonds per serving

slow cooker size/shape
3-quart round

slow cooking time
2 hours on low, **OR**
1 hour on high

Cooking spray

2½ cups water

1 cup uncooked quinoa, rinsed well under cold running water and drained

½ teaspoon ground cinnamon

■ ■ ■

1½ cups fat-free half-and-half

¼ cup sugar

1½ teaspoons vanilla extract

2 cups frozen unsweetened peach slices, thawed and sliced or diced

¼ cup plus 2 tablespoons chopped pecans, dry-roasted and coarsely chopped

A bowl of hot quinoa topped with sweetened fat-free half-and-half and peaches makes a nutritious, protein-rich breakfast. The quinoa doesn't need tending to while it cooks, allowing you to get yourself and the kids ready for the day while the slow cooker does the work. *(See photo insert.)*

Lightly spray the slow cooker with cooking spray. Pour in the water. Stir in the quinoa and cinnamon. Cook, covered, on low for 2 hours or on high for 1 hour, or until the water is absorbed and the quinoa is tender.

Just before the quinoa is ready, in a small bowl, stir together the half-and-half, sugar, and vanilla extract until the sugar has dissolved.

Spoon the quinoa into bowls. Top with the peaches. Pour in the half-and half mixture. Sprinkle with the pecans.

per serving

Calories 254	Cholesterol 0 mg	Dietary Exchanges
Total Fat 7.0 g	Sodium 65 mg	2 starch, 1 fruit, 1 lean
Saturated Fat 0.5 g	Carbohydrates 42 g	meat, ½ fat
Trans Fat 0.0 g	Fiber 4 g	
Polyunsaturated Fat 2.5 g	Sugars 17 g	
Monounsaturated Fat 3.5 g	Protein 10 g	

apple-maple oatmeal

QUICK PREP

serve 6
1 cup per serving

slow cooker size/shape
3- to 4½-quart round or oval

slow cooking time
6 to 7 hours on low

Cooking spray

4¾ cups water

1½ cups uncooked steel-cut oats

1 large tart apple (about 8 ounces), such as Granny Smith, peeled and chopped (about 1⅓ cups)

¼ cup pure maple syrup

1 teaspoon ground cinnamon

1 teaspoon vanilla extract

⅛ teaspoon salt

You can put these ingredients into your slow cooker in no time at all right before bed. Waking up to a hot, cinnamon-scented breakfast will definitely get your day off to a great start!

Lightly spray the slow cooker with cooking spray. Put all the ingredients in the slow cooker, stirring to combine. Cook, covered, on low for 6 to 7 hours, or until the oats are tender and the water is absorbed.

cook's tip: If you have leftovers, reheat in a small saucepan over medium-low heat, stirring occasionally and adding a small amount of water if the mixture seems too thick.

per serving

Calories 215	Cholesterol 0 mg	Dietary Exchanges
Total Fat 3.0 g	Sodium 56 mg	2 starch, 1 fruit
Saturated Fat 0.0 g	Carbohydrates 41 g	
Trans Fat 0.0 g	Fiber 9 g	
Polyunsaturated Fat 1.0 g	Sugars 12 g	
Monounsaturated Fat 1.0 g	Protein 6 g	

pb&o breakfast

serves 8
1 cup oatmeal and ½ banana
per serving

slow cooker size
4- to 5-quart round

slow cooking time
7½ to 8½ hours on low

Cooking spray

6 cups water

2 cups fat-free milk

2 cups uncooked steel-cut oats

½ cup firmly packed light brown
sugar

1 teaspoon ground cinnamon

1 teaspoon vanilla extract

■ ■ ■

¾ cup low-sodium smooth peanut
butter

4 medium bananas, sliced
crosswise

Ground cinnamon to taste

Having trouble getting the kids to eat a healthy
breakfast? Serve peanut butter and banana
oatmeal that has slow cooked overnight and watch
them chow down.

Lightly spray the slow cooker with cooking spray. Put the
water, milk, oats, brown sugar, 1 teaspoon cinnamon, and
the vanilla in the slow cooker, stirring to combine. Cook,
covered, on low for 7½ to 8½ hours.

At serving time, stir in the peanut butter until well blended.
Spoon into bowls. Top with the banana slices. Sprinkle the
cinnamon over all.

cook's tip: Cover and refrigerate leftover oatmeal for up to three days. To
reheat a single serving, spoon 1 cup oatmeal into a small microwaveable
bowl. Microwave, covered, on 100 percent power (high) for 1 to 2 minutes, or until heated through, stirring once halfway through, and adding
1 to 2 tablespoons fat-free milk as needed for the desired consistency.
(The oatmeal will have thickened in the refrigerator.)

cook's tip on steel-cut oats: Whenever a slow cooker recipe calls for
steel-cut oats, also known as Irish oats or pinhead oats, it is important to
use them, not rolled oats. Steel-cut oats can withstand the long cooking
time without getting mushy.

per serving

Calories 429	Cholesterol 1 mg	Dietary Exchanges
Total Fat 15.5 g	Sodium 40 mg	2 starch, 1 fruit,
Saturated Fat 2.5 g	Carbohydrates 62 g	1 other carbohydrate,
Trans Fat 0.0 g	Fiber 11 g	1 lean meat, 2 fat
Polyunsaturated Fat 4.5 g	Sugars 26 g	
Monounsaturated Fat 6.5 g	Protein 15 g	

breakfast hash brown casserole

serves 6
1 cup per serving

slow cooker size/shape
3- to 4½-quart round or oval

slow cooking time
4½ to 5 hours on low, **OR**
2 hours 15 minutes to
2½ hours on high

Cooking spray

1 teaspoon canola or corn oil and
1 tablespoon plus 2 teaspoons
canola or corn oil, divided use

1 3.5-ounce sweet Italian turkey
sausage, casing discarded

1 pound frozen fat-free diced
hash browns (lowest sodium
available), thawed

1 large onion, diced

1 large green or red bell pepper,
diced

1 cup egg substitute

¼ cup fat-free milk

½ teaspoon dried oregano,
crumbled

½ teaspoon pepper (coarsely
ground preferred)

⅛ teaspoon salt

⅛ teaspoon cayenne (optional)

■ ■ ■

⅛ teaspoon salt

½ cup shredded low-fat sharp
Cheddar cheese

Company coming for brunch? Rev up the slow cooker early, then relax with a cup of coffee and your morning paper until your guests arrive.

Lightly spray the slow cooker with cooking spray. Set aside.

In a medium nonstick skillet, heat 1 teaspoon oil over medium-high heat, swirling to coat the bottom. Cook the sausage for 1 to 2 minutes, or until browned, stirring frequently to break up the larger pieces. Set aside.

Put the hash browns, onion, and bell pepper in the slow cooker, stirring to combine and smoothing the top.

In a medium bowl, whisk together the egg substitute, milk, oregano, pepper, ⅛ teaspoon salt, the cayenne, and remaining 1 tablespoon plus 2 teaspoons oil. Pour over the hash brown mixture. Sprinkle the sausage on top.

Cook, covered, on low for 4½ to 5 hours or on high for 2 hours 15 minutes to 2½ hours, or until a knife inserted in the center of the casserole comes out clean. Turn off the slow cooker. Sprinkle the casserole with the remaining ⅛ teaspoon salt and the Cheddar. Let stand, uncovered, for 30 minutes for peak flavors and texture.

cook's tip: Don't skip the standing time; it's very important. The casserole will be a bit dry and the seasonings won't be blended in when you test it for doneness, but the liquid from the other ingredients will soak into the potatoes and create the desired texture during the standing time.

cook's tip: To quickly thaw the hash browns, place them in a large colander and run them under cold water for about 20 seconds (it will take a little longer if your colander is small). Shake off the excess water.

per serving

Calories 185	Cholesterol 16 mg	Dietary Exchanges
Total Fat 7.0 g	Sodium 378 mg	1 starch, 1 vegetable,
Saturated Fat 1.0 g	Carbohydrates 19 g	1 lean meat, ½ fat
Trans Fat 0.0 g	Fiber 2 g	
Polyunsaturated Fat 1.5 g	Sugars 4 g	
Monounsaturated Fat 4.0 g	Protein 11 g	

desserts

decadent chocolate pudding cake

serves 8
½ cup cake, ¼ banana,
2 tablespoons whipped
topping, and 1 teaspoon
pecans per serving

slow cooker size/shape
3- to 4½-quart round or oval

slow cooking time
2 hours on high

Indulge your sweet tooth and let your taste buds experience a little bit of paradise with every bite of this ooey, gooey chocolate creation. This recipe uses part whole-wheat flour, unsweetened dark cocoa powder, fat-free milk, and canola oil as substitutes for less-healthy ingredients.

Lightly spray the slow cooker with cooking spray. Set aside.

In a medium bowl, stir together the flours, sugar, 2 tablespoons cocoa powder, and the baking powder. Whisk in the milk, oil, and vanilla until smooth. Spoon the batter into the slow cooker, spreading to cover the bottom.

In a small bowl, stir together the brown sugar and remaining 3 tablespoons cocoa powder. Sprinkle over the batter.

Pour the boiling water over the batter. Don't stir. Cook, covered, on high for 2 hours, or until a wooden toothpick inserted in the center comes out almost clean. Let stand, uncovered, in the slow cooker for 30 minutes. Spoon into small bowls and top with the bananas, whipped topping, and pecans.

Cooking spray

½ **cup all-purpose flour**

½ **cup whole-wheat flour**

½ **cup sugar**

2 **tablespoons unsweetened
dark cocoa powder and 3
tablespoons unsweetened dark
cocoa powder, divided use**

1½ **teaspoons baking powder**

½ **cup fat-free milk**

1 **tablespoon canola or corn oil**

1½ **teaspoons vanilla extract**

½ **cup firmly packed light brown
sugar**

1½ **cups boiling water**

■ ■ ■

2 **medium bananas, each cut
crosswise into 16 slices**

1 **cup refrigerated fat-free
aerosol whipped topping**

3 **tablespoons chopped pecan
pieces, dry-roasted**

cook's tip: Spoon any leftover pudding cake (without the toppings) into an airtight container. Refrigerate for up to one day. To reheat an individual portion, spoon ½ cup of the pudding cake into a small microwaveable dish. Microwave on 100 percent power (high) for 20 to 25 seconds, or until warm. Top with the banana, whipped topping, and pecans.

per serving

Calories 240
Total Fat 4.5 g
  Saturated Fat 0.5 g
  Trans Fat 0.0 g
  Polyunsaturated Fat 1.0 g
  Monounsaturated Fat 2.5 g

Cholesterol 0 mg
Sodium 87 mg
Carbohydrates 49 g
  Fiber 3 g
  Sugars 32 g
Protein 4 g

Dietary Exchanges
  3 other carbohydrate,
  1 fat

carrot cake

serves 12
1 slice per serving

slow cooker size/shape
6-quart oval

slow cooker time
2½ to 3 hours on high

 Cooking spray
¾ **cup all-purpose flour**
¾ **cup sugar**
 1 **teaspoon pumpkin pie spice**
¾ **teaspoon baking soda**
¼ **teaspoon baking powder**
⅛ **teaspoon salt**
¾ **cup grated carrots**
⅓ **cup unsweetened applesauce**
 1 **large egg**
 1 **tablespoon fat-free milk**
¼ **cup chopped pecans, dry-roasted**

It's the combination of grated carrots, applesauce, and the slow cooking process itself that produces the moist goodness of this loaf cake.

Lightly spray an 8½ x 4½ x 2½-inch loaf pan with cooking spray. Cut parchment paper or wax paper to fit the bottom of the pan. Place the paper in the pan. Lightly spray the paper with cooking spray. Set aside.

In a large bowl, stir together the flour, sugar, pumpkin pie spice, baking soda, baking powder, and salt. Stir the carrots into the flour mixture until coated.

In a small bowl, whisk together the applesauce, egg, and milk. Stir into the flour mixture just until the batter is moistened but no flour is visible. Don't overmix. Stir in the pecans. Pour the batter into the pan, gently smoothing the top. Transfer the pan to the slow cooker. Cook, covered, on high for 2½ to 3 hours, or until a wooden toothpick inserted in the center comes out clean.

Carefully transfer the pan to a cooling rack. Let stand for 10 minutes. Invert the cake onto a plate. Let stand for 30 minutes, or until cooled completely.

cook's tip on using baking dishes in a slow cooker: Anytime a recipe calls for using a loaf pan or other baking dish in a slow cooker, be sure to check the fit before mixing your batter. Generally, oval slow cookers and loaf pans without protruding handles work best.

per serving

Calories 106	Cholesterol 16 mg	Dietary Exchanges
Total Fat 2.0 g	Sodium 123 mg	1½ other
Saturated Fat 0.5 g	Carbohydrates 21 g	carbohydrate, ½ fat
Trans Fat 0.0 g	Fiber 1 g	
Polyunsaturated Fat 0.5 g	Sugars 14 g	
Monounsaturated Fat 1.0 g	Protein 2 g	

strawberry, rhubarb, and peach crumble

serves 10
½ cup per serving

slow cooker size/shape
5- to 7-quart round or oval

slow cooking time
30 minutes on high plus
2 to 3 hours on low

Cooking spray

1 pound frozen unsweetened peach slices, set aside to partially thaw

1 pound fresh rhubarb, cut diagonally into ½-inch slices

1 quart fresh strawberries, hulled and halved, quartered if very large

⅓ to ½ cup sugar (depending on sweetness of strawberries and peaches)

2 tablespoons cornstarch

2 tablespoons uncooked instant, or quick-cooking, tapioca

1 tablespoon coarsely shredded or grated orange zest

■ ■ ■

½ cup uncooked quick-cooking oatmeal

¼ cup whole-wheat pastry flour or all-purpose flour

¼ cup chopped walnuts, dry-roasted

3 tablespoons firmly packed light brown sugar

3 tablespoons canola or corn oil

2 tablespoons unsweetened flaked coconut, toasted

1 tablespoon coarsely shredded orange zest

With its sweet-tart filling and crunchy topping, this crumble is a wonderful introduction to rhubarb for those unfamiliar with this springtime treat.

Lightly spray the slow cooker with cooking spray. Set aside.

In a very large bowl, gently but thoroughly stir together the peaches, rhubarb, strawberries, sugar, cornstarch, tapioca, and 1 tablespoon orange zest, separating any peach slices still frozen together. Transfer to the slow cooker. Cook, covered, on high for 30 minutes.

Meanwhile, put the remaining ingredients in a small bowl. Using a fork, stir together until crumbly. Set aside.

When the filling is cooked, quickly sprinkle with the topping. Re-cover the slow cooker, leaving the lid slightly ajar. Change the setting to low. Cook for 2 to 3 hours, or until the fruit is tender.

cook's tip: If you remove the peaches from the freezer and set them aside while you prep the rhubarb and strawberries, they will be partially thawed to just the right point.

cook's tip: You can dry-roast the walnuts and toast the coconut at the same time. Preheat the oven to 350°F. Spread the nuts and the coconut in a single layer in a shallow baking pan. Bake for 5 to 10 minutes, or until the nuts are fragrant and the coconut is golden brown, stirring several times. Transfer the mixture to a medium plate to stop the cooking. Let stand for about 10 minutes, or until cool.

per serving

Calories 202	Cholesterol 0 mg	Dietary Exchanges
Total Fat 7.5 g	Sodium 4 mg	2 other carbohydrate,
Saturated Fat 1.0 g	Carbohydrates 32 g	1½ fat
Trans Fat 0.0 g	Fiber 4 g	
Polyunsaturated Fat 3.0 g	Sugars 18 g	
Monounsaturated Fat 3.0 g	Protein 3 g	

apple jumble crumble

serves 6
½ cup per serving

slow cooker size/shape
3-quart round or oval

slow cooking time
3 hours 15 minutes to
3½ hours on low, **OR**
1½ hours to 1 hour 45 minutes
on high

Cooking spray

3 **medium apples, halved, then
cut lengthwise into ½-inch
slices**

1 **tablespoon fresh lemon juice**

1 **teaspoon vanilla, butter, and
nut flavoring or vanilla extract**

⅓ **cup firmly packed dark brown
sugar**

¼ **cup uncooked quick-cooking
oatmeal**

¼ **cup white whole-wheat flour**

¾ **teaspoon ground cinnamon**

¼ **teaspoon ground nutmeg**

½ **cup chopped pecans, dry-
roasted**

2 **tablespoons dark raisins**

3 **tablespoons light tub
margarine, melted**

When you just want a bowl of warm, sweet, delicious goodness, this jumble crumble will satisfy that craving. The dessert comes together quickly and needs absolutely no attention while it slow cooks. Talk about easy!

Lightly spray the slow cooker with cooking spray. Put the apples with a cut side down in the slow cooker. Sprinkle with the lemon juice and flavoring.

In a medium bowl, stir together the brown sugar, oatmeal, flour, cinnamon, and nutmeg. Sprinkle over the apples.

Sprinkle the pecans and raisins over the brown sugar mixture. Drizzle with the margarine.

Cook, covered, on low for 3 hours 15 minutes to 3½ hours or on high for 1½ hours to 1 hour 45 minutes, or until the apples are tender. Turn off the slow cooker. Let stand, uncovered, for 15 minutes for peak texture and flavor.

cook's tip on dry-roasting nuts in the oven: Dry-roasting nuts intensifies their flavor. Spread the nuts in a single layer in a baking pan or on a rimmed baking sheet. Roast at 350°F for 5 to 7 minutes, or until golden brown. Transfer the nuts to a plate so they don't burn. Let stand to cool. See the tip on page 207 if you would rather dry-roast nuts on the stovetop.

per serving —————————————————————

Calories 221	Cholesterol 0 mg	Dietary Exchanges
Total Fat 9.5 g	Sodium 50 mg	1 fruit, 1½ other
Saturated Fat 0.5 g	Carbohydrates 35 g	carbohydrate, 2 fat
Trans Fat 0.0 g	Fiber 4 g	
Polyunsaturated Fat 2.5 g	Sugars 24 g	
Monounsaturated Fat 5.0 g	Protein 2 g	

pears with raspberry-orange sauce

QUICK PREP

serves 4
1 pear and 1½ tablespoons sauce per serving

slow cooker size/shape
3- to 4½-quart round

slow cooking time
5 to 6 hours on low, **OR**
2½ to 3 hours on high

Cooking spray

4 medium, firm pears, peeled, stems left on

¼ cup dry white wine (regular or nonalcoholic)

2½ tablespoons sugar

■ ■ ■

½ cup raspberries

1 teaspoon vanilla extract

½ teaspoon grated orange zest

Fresh mint leaves (optional)

If you really want to impress, serve this dessert the next time you have dinner guests—or make it for your family tonight as a special surprise. Each person gets a whole cooked pear resting on ruby-red sauce. Serve this dessert in clear wine goblets or dessert bowls for dramatic effect. *(See photo insert.)*

Lightly spray the slow cooker with cooking spray. Put the pears with the stem end up in the slow cooker. Pour the wine over the pears. Sprinkle with the sugar. Cook, covered, on low for 5 to 6 hours or on high for 2½ to 3 hours, or until just tender when pierced with a fork.

Using a slotted spoon, carefully transfer the pears with the stem end up to a large plate, leaving the liquid in the crock. Set the pears aside.

Gently stir the raspberries, vanilla, and orange zest into the cooking liquid. Let stand, uncovered, for 1 hour, or until the sauce is slightly thickened. Spoon the sauce into bowls. Place the pears on the sauce. Garnish with the mint.

per serving

Calories 155	Cholesterol 0 mg	Dietary Exchanges
Total Fat 0.5 g	Sodium 3 mg	2½ fruit
Saturated Fat 0.0 g	Carbohydrates 38 g	
Trans Fat 0.0 g	Fiber 7 g	
Polyunsaturated Fat 0.0 g	Sugars 26 g	
Monounsaturated Fat 0.0 g	Protein 1 g	

apples with almond-apricot sauce

Cooking spray

2 tablespoons water

2 large apples (about 8 ounces
each), halved and cored

¼ cup chopped almonds

2 tablespoons chopped dried
apricots

2 tablespoons firmly packed dark
brown sugar

¼ teaspoon ground ginger or
ground allspice

½ teaspoon ground cinnamon

½ teaspoon vanilla extract

1 tablespoon plus 1 teaspoon
light tub margarine

Baked apples are always a treat, but coring whole apples can be a hassle. Just buy larger apples and cut them in half. Then all you have to do is scoop out the easily accessible core, add the sweet toppings, and let your slow cooker take it from there.

Lightly spray the slow cooker with cooking spray. Pour in the water. Add the apple halves with the cut side up.

In a small bowl, stir together the remaining ingredients except the margarine. Spoon onto each apple half. Top each with 1 teaspoon margarine. Cook, covered, on low for 2 to 2½ hours or on high for 1 hour to 1 hour 15 minutes, or until just tender. Be careful not to overcook; the apples will continue to cook while cooling.

Carefully transfer the apples to plates, leaving the sauce in the slow cooker. Stir the sauce. Spoon over the apples. Let cool completely, about 30 minutes. The sauce will thicken slightly while cooling.

cook's tip: If you let the apples overcook, they will become mushy.

per serving

Calories 149
Total Fat 5.0 g
  Saturated Fat 0.5 g
  Trans Fat 0.0 g
  Polyunsaturated Fat 1.0 g
  Monounsaturated Fat 3.0 g

Cholesterol 0 mg
Sodium 34 mg
Carbohydrates 27 g
  Fiber 4 g
  Sugars 21 g
Protein 2 g

Dietary Exchanges
  1 fruit, 1 other
  carbohydrate, 1 fat

sweet mango sticky rice

QUICK PREP

This variation of a popular Thai dessert is made with short-grain sweet rice, also known as Thai sweet rice or glutinous rice, cooked in mango juice and lite coconut milk. Coconut extract adds extra flavor and sweetness without additional calories or saturated fat.

serves 8
¼ cup plus 2 tablespoons rice and ¼ mango per serving

slow cooker size/shape
1- to 1½-quart round or oval

slow cooking time
3 to 4 hours on low, **OR**
1½ to 2 hours on high

1 cup uncooked sweet rice or jasmine rice

1⅓ cups mango juice or pineapple juice

1 cup lite coconut milk

2 tablespoons sugar

½ teaspoon coconut extract

⅔ cup lite coconut milk

2 medium mangoes, sliced

Put the rice in the slow cooker. Stir in the mango juice, 1 cup coconut milk, the sugar, and coconut extract. Cook, covered, on low for 3 to 4 hours or on high for 1½ to 2 hours, or until the rice is tender and slightly creamy and the liquid is absorbed. Transfer to a large bowl. Slowly and gently stir in the remaining ⅔ cup coconut milk. Let stand for 1 hour, or until room temperature. Spoon into bowls, making a small mound for each serving. Serve topped with the mango slices.

cook's tip on thai sweet rice: Look for Thai sweet rice in Asian markets and some supermarkets. If you prefer, you can substitute fragrant jasmine rice. It's a long-grain rice and will create a slightly different texture, but the results still will be excellent.

per serving

Calories 198
Total Fat 3.0 g
  Saturated Fat 2.0 g
  Trans Fat 0.0 g
  Polyunsaturated Fat 0.5 g
  Monounsaturated Fat 0.5 g

Cholesterol 0 mg
Sodium 20 mg
Carbohydrates 42 g
  Fiber 2 g
  Sugars 21 g
Protein 2 g

Dietary Exchanges
1½ starch, 1½ fruit,
½ fat

sugar plum pears

serves 8
½ cup per serving

slow cooker size/shape
3- to 4½-quart round

slow cooking time
3½ hours on low plus 15 minutes on high, **OR**
1 hour 45 minutes on high plus 15 minutes on high

Cooking spray

3 **medium, firm pears, cut lengthwise into ½-inch slices**

¼ **cup dry white wine (regular or nonalcoholic)**

3 **tablespoons sugar**

2 **tablespoons chopped crystallized ginger**

3 **small red plums or medium purple plums, cut lengthwise into ½-inch slices**

2 **teaspoons grated lemon zest**

1 **teaspoon vanilla extract**

Slow cooking firm pears for a while and later adding fresh plums lets the different fruits retain their distinct flavors and textures in this slightly syrupy dessert.

Lightly spray the slow cooker with cooking spray. Put the pears, wine, sugar, and ginger in the slow cooker, stirring to combine. Cook, covered, on low for 3½ hours or on high for 1 hour 45 minutes, or until the pears are just tender.

Quickly add the plums, lemon zest, and vanilla, gently stirring to coat, and re-cover the slow cooker. If using the low setting, change it to high. Cook, covered, for 15 minutes.

Transfer the pear mixture to a large pan, such as a 13 x 9 x 2-inch glass baking dish. Arrange the fruit in a single layer. Let cool completely, about 30 minutes. The plums will slightly cook and thicken the sauce as they cool.

per serving

Calories 87
Total Fat 0.0 g
  Saturated Fat 0.0 g
  Trans Fat 0.0 g
  Polyunsaturated Fat 0.0 g
  Monounsaturated Fat 0.0 g

Cholesterol 0 mg
Sodium 1 mg
Carbohydrates 21 g
  Fiber 3 g
  Sugars 15 g
Protein 1 g

Dietary Exchanges
1 fruit, ½ other carbohydrate

dried-fruit compote with pomegranate juice

serves 10
½ cup per serving

slow cooker size/shape
3- to 4½-quart round or oval

slow cooking time
5 hours on low, **OR**
3 hours on high

3 cups pomegranate juice

2 cups dried apricot halves (about 11 ounces)

1½ cups dried plums (about 8 ounces)

1 cup golden raisins (about 4¾ ounces)

⅓ cup firmly packed light brown sugar

1 cinnamon stick (about 3 inches long)

½ teaspoon whole allspice

¼ teaspoon whole cloves

■ ■ ■

1 teaspoon grated orange zest

Sweet and fragrant, this compote will stand on its own as a dessert, or you can stretch the number of servings by spooning it over fat-free vanilla ice cream. The compote is also excellent as an accompaniment to roasted pork or chicken. You can even top it with dollops of fat-free plain yogurt to break the breakfast routine.

In the slow cooker, stir together the juice, apricots, plums, raisins, brown sugar, and cinnamon stick.

Put the allspice and cloves in a tea ball or in the center of a 4-inch square piece of cheesecloth. If using the cheesecloth, bring the ends together to make a bag. Tie it securely with kitchen twine. Add to the slow cooker. Cook, covered, on low for 5 hours or on high for 3 hours, or until the fruit is soft and plump. Discard the spices and the cinnamon stick.

Stir in the orange zest. Serve the compote warm, let it cool for about 1 hour to serve at room temperature, or cover and refrigerate it for 3 to 4 hours to serve chilled.

cook's tip: If you prefer, substitute ¼ teaspoon ground cinnamon, ⅛ teaspoon ground allspice, and a pinch of ground cloves for the cinnamon stick, whole allspice, and whole cloves (no tea ball or cheesecloth bag needed).

per serving

Calories 224	Cholesterol 0 mg	Dietary Exchanges
Total Fat 0.0 g	Sodium 18 mg	4 fruit
Saturated Fat 0.0 g	Carbohydrates 58 g	
Trans Fat 0.0 g	Fiber 4 g	
Polyunsaturated Fat 0.0 g	Sugars 47 g	
Monounsaturated Fat 0.0 g	Protein 2 g	

sweet potato bread pudding

serves 16
one ½-inch slice per serving

slow cooker size/shape
6- to 7-quart oval (removable crock needed)

slow cooking time
3 to 4 hours on high

Cooking spray

2 cups cooked and mashed sweetened sweet potatoes with spices, such as from Simple Mashed Sweet Potatoes (page 210)

1½ cups unsweetened vanilla almond milk

3 large egg whites

¼ cup dark raisins

2 tablespoons lightly packed light or dark brown sugar

½ teaspoon ground cinnamon

⅛ teaspoon ground nutmeg

1 whole-wheat baguette (lowest sodium available), crust removed, cut into ¾-inch cubes to measure 6 cups, dried overnight (reserve any extra for another use)

5 to 6 cups boiling water

■ ■ ■

½ cup canned dulce de leche

1 teaspoon red hot-pepper sauce, or to taste

Using sweet potatoes ups the nutritional benefit of ever-popular bread pudding.

Lightly spray a 9 x 5 x 3-inch ovenproof glass loaf pan with cooking spray. Place a metal rack with short legs, such as a pressure cooker rack, or four 12 x 6-inch sheets of aluminum foil crumpled into balls in the slow cooker. Set aside.

In a large bowl, whisk together the sweet potatoes, milk, egg whites, raisins, brown sugar, cinnamon, and nutmeg. Add the bread cubes, folding until well coated. Spoon the mixture into the loaf pan. Cover tightly with aluminum foil, using kitchen twine to keep it secure. Place the loaf pan on the rack or crumpled foil in the slow cooker. The pan needs to be level and about ½ inch above the water. Pour the boiling water down the side of the crock until the water reaches midway up the side of the loaf pan.

Cook, covered, on high for 3 to 4 hours, or until the internal temperature registers at least 190°F on an instant-read thermometer and a knife inserted in the middle of the pudding comes out clean.

Carefully transfer the removable crock to a cooling rack. Let the bread pudding stand, still in the hot water, for 15 minutes.

Meanwhile, stir together the dulce de leche and hot-pepper sauce. Set aside.

Carefully remove the loaf pan from the crock. Cut the pudding into slices and transfer to plates. Drizzle the pudding with the sauce. Serve warm.

per serving

Calories 105	Cholesterol 3 mg	Dietary Exchanges
Total Fat 1.5 g	Sodium 113 mg	1 starch, ½ other
Saturated Fat 0.5 g	Carbohydrates 20 g	carbohydrate
Trans Fat 0.0 g	Fiber 1 g	
Polyunsaturated Fat 0.0 g	Sugars 12 g	
Monounsaturated Fat 0.0 g	Protein 3 g	

tapioca pudding with blueberries

serves 8
½ cup tapioca, ½ cup blueberries, and 2 tablespoons whipped topping per serving

slow cooker size/shape
2½- to 3-quart round

slow cooking time
1 hour to 1 hour 15 minutes on high plus 1 hour to 1 hour 15 minutes on high

2 cups fat-free milk

2 cups fat-free half-and-half

½ cup egg substitute

½ cup sugar

¼ cup plus 2 tablespoons uncooked instant, or quick-cooking, tapioca

2 teaspoons grated orange zest

2 teaspoons vanilla extract

¾ teaspoon ground cinnamon

■ ■ ■

4 cups blueberries

1 cup refrigerated fat-free aerosol whipped topping

Cooking homemade pudding on the stovetop can be tricky and tedious because the milk scorches easily and constant stirring is required. Fortunately, switching to a slow cooker solves both problems—and you don't need to feel guilty about enjoying this dessert, because it supplies a full serving of fruit for each diner.

In the slow cooker, whisk together the milk, half-and-half, egg substitute, sugar, tapioca, orange zest, vanilla, and cinnamon. Cook, covered, on high for 1 hour to 1 hour 15 minutes. Quickly stir the pudding and re-cover the slow cooker. Cook for 1 hour to 1 hour 15 minutes, or until the pudding is slightly thickened.

Carefully transfer the removable crock from the slow cooker to a cooling rack. Let stand, uncovered, for 20 to 30 minutes to cool. (If the slow cooker doesn't have a removable crock, spoon the tapioca into a large bowl for cooling.)

Spoon half the blueberries into 8 ramekins, custard cups, or wineglasses. Spoon the tapioca over the blueberries. Sprinkle with the remaining blueberries. If serving warm, top each serving with a dollop of whipped topping just before serving. To serve chilled, cover and refrigerate the tapioca for at least 2 hours. Just before serving, top with the whipped topping.

per serving

Calories 194
Total Fat 0.5 g
  Saturated Fat 0.0 g
  Trans Fat 0.0 g
  Polyunsaturated Fat 0.0 g
  Monounsaturated Fat 0.0 g

Cholesterol 1 mg
Sodium 118 mg
Carbohydrates 42 g
  Fiber 2 g
  Sugars 29 g
Protein 8 g

Dietary Exchanges
  1 fruit, 1 fat-free milk, 1 other carbohydrate

index